MICROSOFT® WINDOWS®
OPERATING SYSTEM

ESSENTIALS

MICROSOFT® WINDOWS® OPERATING SYSTEM
ESSENTIALS

Tom Carpenter

WILEY

John Wiley & Sons, Inc.

Senior Acquisitions Editor: Jeff Kellum
Development Editor: Jim Compton
Technical Editor: Rodney Fournier
Production Editor: Dassi Zeidel
Copy Editor: Liz Welch
Editorial Manager: Pete Gaughan
Production Manager: Tim Tate
Vice President and Executive Group Publisher: Richard Swadley
Vice President and Publisher: Neil Edde
Book Designer: Happenstance Type-O-Rama
Compositor: James D. Kramer, Happenstance Type-O-Rama
Proofreader: Amy J. Schneider
Indexer: Ted Laux
Project Coordinator, Cover: Katherine Crocker
Cover Designer: Ryan Sneed
Cover Image: © Jonny McCullagh / iStockPhoto

Dear Reader,

Thank you for choosing *Microsoft Windows Operating System Essentials*. This book is part of a family of premium-quality Sybex books, all of which are written by outstanding authors who combine practical experience with a gift for teaching.

Sybex was founded in 1976. More than 30 years later, we're still committed to producing consistently exceptional books. With each of our titles, we're working hard to set a new standard for the industry. From the paper we print on, to the authors we work with, our goal is to bring you the best books available.

I hope you see all that reflected in these pages. I'd be very interested to hear your comments and get your feedback on how we're doing. Feel free to let me know what you think about this or any other Sybex book by sending me an email at nedde@wiley.com. If you think you've found a technical error in this book, please visit http://sybex.custhelp.com. Customer feedback is critical to our efforts at Sybex.

Best regards,

NEIL EDDE
Vice President and Publisher
Sybex, an Imprint of Wiley

I dedicate this book to my wife and children.
You are the most important people in this world
to me. I cherish every moment with you
and love you more every day.

ACKNOWLEDGMENTS

I would like to acknowledge the great staff at Wiley. You always make a good book great. Specific thanks go out to the technical and copy editors who worked hard to make this a great book. Thanks to all of you. Additionally, I would like to thank my family, who tolerated me through yet one more book and this one in particular as the writing schedule was definitely one that consumed a lot of my time. You are all amazing. Finally, I want to thank God for giving me the strength to write this book and undertake every other endeavor in life. Thank you.

ABOUT THE AUTHOR

Tom Carpenter is a consultant and trainer based out of Marysville, OH. He is the founder and current Senior Consultant for The Systems Education and Consulting Company (SysEdCo). SysEdCo provides training on Microsoft technologies, wireless networking, security, and IT professional development. Tom is the author of several books on topics ranging from wireless network administration to SQL Server database administration and optimization. Tom holds several certifications, including MCITP: SQL Server 2008 Database Administrator, CWNA, CWSP, Project+, and several additional Microsoft certifications. He spends every spare moment he can with his amazing wife and children. You can reach the author by writing to carpenter@sysedco.com.

Contents at a Glance

CONTENTS

CHAPTER 5   Managing with the Control Panel   93

CHAPTER 6   Mobility and Remote Management   115

INTRODUCTION

Windows computers are important tools used on modern networks. They are used to send and receive emails, create documents, and use intensive business applications. Computer support administrators are in high demand and modern technologies such as virtual desktops and cloud computing have only increased the importance of the support professional's job.

The Microsoft Technology Associate Certification

The Microsoft Technology Associate (MTA) certification is a certification provided for entry-level professionals and those with long careers in the industry who have never acquired a certification credential. It includes three separate tracks: Information Technology (IT) Professional, Developer, and Database. The IT Professional track is for individuals pursuing work as administrators. The Developer track is for individuals pursuing work as programmers and software engineers. The Database track is for individuals pursuing work as database administrators and database developers.

The IT Professional series includes four certifications:

Windows Operating System (OS) Fundamentals This certification assumes no previous knowledge and allows you to start from the beginning to learn how to administer and support Windows 7 clients. The knowledge acquired through the Networking Fundamentals and Security Fundamentals certifications will be helpful as you study Windows OS fundamentals, but it is important to remember that the MTA certification exams have no prerequisites. The Windows OS Fundamentals exam and this book give you a solid foundation for working as a Windows Desktop administrator in a Microsoft technology environment. You earn this certification by taking and passing exam 98-349. This book covers the objectives for the 98-349 exam.

Windows Server Administration Fundamentals This certification assumes no previous knowledge and allows you to start from the beginning to learn how to administer Windows servers. The knowledge acquired through the Networking Fundamentals and Security Fundamentals certifications will be helpful as you study Windows Server administration fundamentals, but it is important to remember that the MTA certification exams have no prerequisites. The Windows Server Administration Fundamentals exam gives you a solid foundation for working as a server administrator in a Microsoft technology environment. You earn this certification by taking and passing exam 98-365. My book *Microsoft Windows Server Administration Essentials* (Sybex, 2011) covers the objectives for the 98-365 exam.

Networking Fundamentals   This is an important certification in the MTA IT Professional track. It lays a solid foundation of basic networking knowledge needed to administer modern networks and also helps you prepare for more advanced Microsoft Certified Technology Specialist (MCTS) and Microsoft Certified IT Professional (MCITP) tracks. You earn this certification by taking and passing exam 98-366. The book *Microsoft Windows Networking Essentials* by Darril Gibson (Sybex, 2011) covers the objectives for the 98-366 exam.

Security Fundamentals   Security Fundamentals is another important certification in the MTA IT Professional track. It complements the knowledge learned in the Networking Fundamentals certification and adds fundamental security knowledge needed by administrators. IT administrators in any environment need to be aware of the risks with IT systems. You earn this certification by taking and passing exam 98-367. The book *Microsoft Windows Security Essentials* by Darril Gibson (Sybex, 2011) covers the objectives for the 98-367 exam.

Each of these certifications can serve as a stepping-stone to Microsoft's next levels of certifications: Microsoft Certified Technology Specialist (MCTS) and Microsoft Certified IT Professional (MCITP).

Appendix B highlights the Microsoft certification program. The appendix also lists the exam objectives for Exam 98-349 and how they map to this book's content.

Who Should Read This Book

This book is for current or aspiring professionals seeking a quick grounding in the fundamentals of administration in a Microsoft Windows environment. The goal is to provide quick, focused coverage of fundamental skills.

If you want to start a career in Windows Desktop support or are already working in the field and want to fill in some gaps on fundamental topics, this book is for you. You can use the knowledge gained from this book as a foundation for more advanced studies. Additionally, this book will act as an excellent reference for the day-to-day tasks you must perform as a Windows Desktop administrator.

This book is focused on the objectives of the Microsoft Technology Associates (MTA) Windows OS Fundamentals certification. This is the first numbered certification in the MTA IT Professional series (with the exam number 98-349), but you can take the four IT Professional series exams in any order you desire. You can read more about the MTA certifications and MTA exam certification paths at www.microsoft.com/learning/en/us/certification/mta.aspx.

What You Will Learn

You will learn the essentials of Windows Desktop administration in a Microsoft environment. In addition, this book covers all the objectives of the Microsoft Technology Associates Windows Server Administration Fundamentals exam (exam 98-349).

What You Need

To perform the procedures provided throughout this book, you will need a Windows 7 Desktop to work with. This Desktop can be a virtual machine or a direct installation on computer hardware. The good news is that Windows 7 will run on practically any desktop computer that you can buy today. You can install the trial edition of Windows 7 and use it for up to 90 days. You can download the trial edition from http://technet.microsoft.com/en-us/evalcenter/cc442495.

If you want to run Windows 7 in a virtual machine on top of another Windows OS, you will need to have at least 4 GB of system memory in your computer and you will need to download the free VMware Player virtualization software. This software can run 64-bit and 32-bit operating systems, unlike Windows Virtual PC (which Microsoft provides for Windows 7). You can download the VMware Player from http://www.vmware.com/go/downloadplayer. Chapter 2, "Installing Windows," provides instructions for performing an installation of Windows 7.

What Is Covered in This Book

Microsoft Windows Operating System Essentials is organized to provide you with the knowledge needed to master the basics of administration in a Microsoft environment.

Chapter 1, "Windows Operating Systems Overview," provides an overview of the Windows operating system (OS) and the historical evolution of Windows. You also learn about the OS architecture and management interfaces.

Chapter 2, "Installing Windows," describes the options you have for Windows 7 installations and discusses the important considerations that you must take into account when upgrading. Virtualized installations are also explained.

Chapter 3, "Managing the Desktop," explains the Windows 7 Desktop and its features. Provides instructions for working with gadgets, display settings, shortcuts, and the Aero interface.

Chapter 4, "Using Native Applications," describes the applications included with Windows, such as Notepad, Paint, Calculator, Internet Explorer, and Windows Media Player. Also covers newer tools like the Snipping Tool.

Chapter 5, "Managing with the Control Panel," explains the Control Panel and its interfaces. Explores Administrative Tools available in Windows 7. Covers accessibility features and other important Control Panel applets.

Chapter 6, "Mobility and Remote Management," describes the mobility and remote management features of Windows 7, including SyncCenter, Windows Mobility Center, Remote Desktop, Remote Assistance, and Windows PowerShell remoting.

Chapter 7, "Managing Applications," provides instructions for planning and installing local and networked applications. Covers the use of Group Policy for application control and discusses important topics like application virtualization and the management of services.

Chapter 8, "Controlling Malware," explains what malware is and the different forms it takes. Describes options for malware protection and the specific Microsoft solutions available to secure your system from malware.

Chapter 9, "File Management," teaches the important aspects of filesystems and explains the differences among the available filesystems in Windows 7. Covers working with encryption and libraries as well.

Chapter 10, "Network Shares," explains file sharing and the process used to create shares. Addresses NTFS and share permissions. Defines the methods used to share printers and printer drivers.

Chapter 11, "Device Management," describes device drivers and how they interact with plug-and-play operations. Shows you how to use the Device Manager and connect and manage devices. Covers printers and system devices as well.

Chapter 12, "Storage Management," addresses the importance of understanding the various storage types available and selecting the right ones for your needs. Explains how to work with Disk Management and use online storage solutions.

Chapter 13, "Windows Troubleshooting," explains both the troubleshooting processes and the troubleshooting tools used to analyze problems in a Windows environment. Covers Disk Defragmenter, Disk Cleanup, and the Task Scheduler.

Chapter 14, "Backup and Recovery," describes the various backup planning actions and the backup options available in Windows 7. Provides instructions for using System Restore, system images, and Backup and Restore.

Chapter 15, "Windows Update," explains the planning and implementation of update procedures. Describes both Windows Update and Microsoft Update. Provides instructions for implementing a network-based update provisioning solution.

Appendix A, "Answers to Review Questions," includes all of the answers to the review questions found in "The Essentials and Beyond" section at the end of every chapter.

Appendix B, "Microsoft's Certification Program," maps the objectives in the MTA Windows Operating System Fundamentals (exam 98-349) to the specific chapters where each objective is covered.

In addition, we have created an online Glossary, as well as "Appendix C, Answers to Additional Exercises," which contains the suggested or recommended answers to the additional exercises we have included at the end of each chapter. You can download these at www.sybex.com/go/osessentials.

To Learn More or Contact Us

Sybex strives to keep you supplied with the latest tools and information you need for your work. Please check this book's web page at www.sybex.com/go/osessentials, where we'll post additional content and updates that supplement this book if the need arises. Enter **windows os administration essentials** in the Search box (or type the book's ISBN—**9781118195529**), and click Go to get to the book's update page.

As the author, I would be glad to help you in your learning process. If you ever have questions along the way, feel free to email me at carpenter@sysedco.com. Thanks for reading.

CHAPTER 1

Windows Operating Systems Overview

The Windows operating system (OS) has evolved over several decades of development. To fully understand the way Windows functions today, you should know the roots of the current system. In this chapter, you will learn the history of Windows.

To troubleshoot problems on Windows systems, you must be familiar with the basic architecture of the OS. For this reason, this chapter will also explore the Windows architecture. The architecture defines how the OS functions, and understanding it is essential to grasping many of the topics discussed in later chapters.

Finally, this chapter will describe the interfaces used by administrators and users of the Windows operating systems. This discussion includes exploratory overviews of the graphical user interface (GUI), the Command Prompt, and Windows PowerShell.

▶ **Discovering the history of Windows**

▶ **Understanding the OS architecture**

▶ **Identifying Windows interfaces**

Discovering the History of Windows

The modern Windows OS did not begin with the graphical capabilities it has today. The OS has its roots in text-based systems and simple graphical interfaces. In this section, I'll describe these earlier operating systems to help you understand where the current system came from and why it works as it does. You will also learn about the timeline of Windows development alongside the progressive development of personal computers (PCs). It all begins with the Disk Operating System, better known as DOS.

DOS—The Precursor

The first OS Microsoft sold was MS-DOS 1.0. The very name, Disk Operating System, was indicative of the time when it was released. In 1981, there were no document scanners, Universal Serial Bus (USB) microphones, game controllers, or digital cameras. The primary function of the OS was to allow for the loading of applications and the management of disks or storage. DOS was, and is, a text-based operating system. It had no built-in GUI, and it worked with basic typed commands. Many of these commands still exist in the most current Windows OS.

The DOS OS was popular from 1981 all the way to 1999. After 1999 and the release of Windows 2000, the GUI-based OSs became more popular in business settings.

DOS was originally developed by Microsoft for IBM. In fact, Microsoft licensed a product named QDOS/86 and used it as the starting point to develop MS-DOS. The first version of MS-DOS (version 1.0) was released in August 1981 and supported a maximum of 128 kilobytes of random access memory (RAM). It also supported the File Allocation Table (FAT) filesystem. Figure 1.1 shows the text-based interface for controlling and using DOS. This example is a screen capture from a DOS 6.22 installation showing the output of the CHKDSK command, which was used to view information about the contents of the disk and to analyze the disk for potential problems.

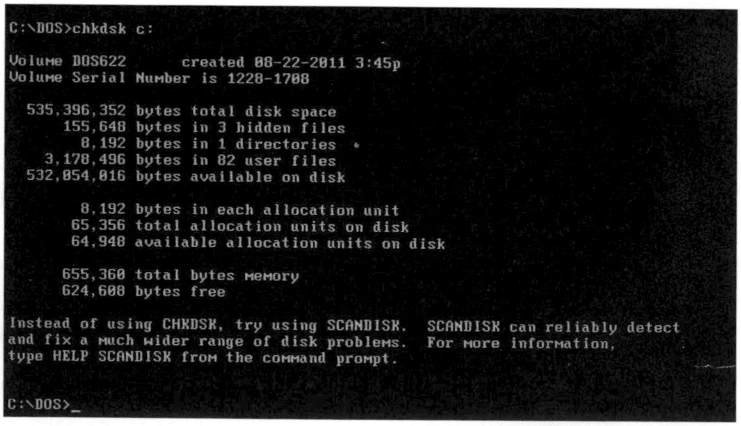

```
C:\DOS>chkdsk c:

Volume DOS622      created 08-22-2011 3:45p
Volume Serial Number is 1228-1708

  535,396,352 bytes total disk space
      155,648 bytes in 3 hidden files
        8,192 bytes in 1 directories  .
    3,178,496 bytes in 82 user files
  532,054,016 bytes available on disk

        8,192 bytes in each allocation unit
       65,356 total allocation units on disk
       64,948 available allocation units on disk

      655,360 total bytes memory
      624,608 bytes free

Instead of using CHKDSK, try using SCANDISK.  SCANDISK can reliably detect
and fix a much wider range of disk problems.  For more information,
type HELP SCANDISK from the command prompt.

C:\DOS>_
```

FIGURE 1.1 The DOS 6.22 text-based interface showing the output of the CHKDSK command

DOS applications could have a graphical interface, but the DOS system itself provided no greater graphical functions than a simple ASCII character–based interface. Figure 1.2 shows an example of a DOS ASCII-based application: the

ScanDisk application that shipped with DOS 6.22. ScanDisk checked the disk for errors and attempted to repair any that were discovered.

FIGURE 1.2 ScanDisk was an ASCII-based GUI application.

The DOS OS used four elements in the boot process. The first was the boot sector, or boot code. The boot code was stored on the boot drive and indicated that the IO.SYS file should be loaded to start the OS. The IO.SYS file called and loaded the MSDOS.SYS file. When the OS loaded, the command interpreter was loaded as the fourth and final part of the OS. The command interpreter was contained within the COMMAND.COM file. Most modern OSs still use the boot sector or boot code, but this code loads different files to start the OS. For example, in a Windows 7 system, the boot code loads the Windows Boot Manager (BOOTMGR.EXE) file to begin the OS load.

During the boot process, DOS systems used two primary configuration files to determine the drivers and settings for the machine. The first file loaded and processed was CONFIG.SYS. This text-based configuration file was used to set system parameters and load device drivers. The second file loaded was AUTOEXEC.BAT. This text-based configuration file could perform any function a standard batch file could perform. It was also used to load device drivers and initial applications on the machine.

Several versions of DOS were released from 1981 to the final release of version 6.22 in 1994. DOS was the underlying OS in all versions of Windows from Windows 1.0 to Windows ME, including the very popular Windows 95 and Windows 98 operating systems of the 1990s. The version of DOS used in Windows 95 through Windows 98 is often called DOS 7.0, and the version used in Windows ME is often called DOS 8.0. Many vendors released their own DOS distributions that could be used as an alternative to MS-DOS. These competing

The COMMAND.COM file contained DOS's internal commands, among them the DIR, CD, and CLS commands.

Batch files were used in DOS to group several commands together as a single unit for easy processing. They also provided scripting capabilities. Batch files are still used in Windows 7 today.

versions included Dr. DOS (with the latest release of Dr. DOS 8.1 in 2005), Novell DOS, IBM PC DOS, and PhysTechSoft's PTS-DOS.

Windows 3.1—The GUI

Although several companies, including Apple, Xerox, and Commodore, produced graphical interfaces, there can be no question as to which company has sold more licenses for its graphical interface—Windows GUI interfaces have outsold all the others combined many times over. This popularity is not an automatic testament to its superiority over other GUI interfaces, but it does mean that the typical computing professional is more likely to encounter it than any other interface today.

Windows shipped with several different GUIs from version 1.0 through version 3.0; however, the Windows 3.1 system became popular in the early to mid-1990s and set the path that modern Windows systems are still on today. Figure 1.3 shows the Windows 3.1 GUI, with the Program Manager in the background and the File Manager running in the foreground.

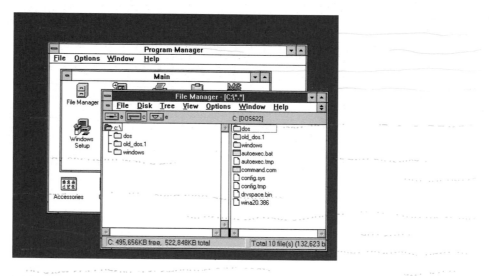

FIGURE 1.3 The Windows 3.1 GUI showing the Program Manager and the File Manager

The Windows 3.1 system included menus, windows that could be resized, and a launching system known as the Program Manager, which supported program groups and icon shortcuts. Many of the concepts used in the Windows 3.1 environment are still used in the modern Windows 7 GUI today.

The next version of Windows, which was based on the DOS and Windows 3.1 systems, was Windows 95. At the same time that the DOS and Windows 3.1 systems were being used, Microsoft provided another operating system, called Windows NT (New Technology). Windows NT was designed as a network operating system from the start, and it was a 32-bit operating system as well. NT used the same GUI as Windows 3.1. When Windows 95 was released, it drastically changed the launching environment to include a desktop with icons, a taskbar, and a Start menu, which took the place of the Program Manager and program groups. Figure 1.4 shows the Windows 95 interface.

Windows 95 was known as *Chicago* during beta stages. An application is placed in the beta stage for final testing before it is released to the public.

FIGURE 1.4 The Windows 95 Desktop and Start menu

When it released Windows 95, Microsoft implemented a new interface that has lasted for more than 15 years. Windows 7 still uses an interface very similar to the one offered by Windows 95—although we now have a Start menu button that is an orb with the Windows logo on it instead of the word Start, the basic concept remains the same.

In 1996, Microsoft released Windows NT 4.0, the first version of the NT-based OS to use the Windows 95–style interface. The Windows NT–based OSs were not based on DOS, as Windows 3.1 and Windows 95 were. Instead, these more robust OSs include their own boot loaders and kernels. Windows 7 is still based on this NT architecture.

The architecture of Windows 7 is explained in more detail later in this chapter, in the section "Understanding the OS Architecture."

The newest Windows graphical interface as of the release of Windows 7 is the Aero interface. It still provides a desktop and the Start menu and taskbar, but it adds graphically rich capabilities that are only possible with the proliferation of modern powerful graphics chipsets in today's computers. Figure 1.5 shows the Windows 7 interface.

FIGURE 1.5 The Windows 7 Aero interface offers enhanced capabilities compared to its predecessors.

How the Past Is Still in the Present

Many of the elements that we use every day in modern versions of Windows have their beginnings in the early days of personal computers. First, the Command Prompt, which is still very useful in Windows 7, is based on the functionality of the command interpreter, COMMAND.COM, that was part of MS-DOS. You can still use many of the same commands today that people used in the 1980s.

Second, the use of icons has been with us since the Xerox and Apple computers first introduced them and they are still the primary way that we launch files and applications. This is true for desktop and laptop computers as well as most handheld devices.

Third, from Windows 3.1 we still have the concept of the Control Panel in Windows 7. The Windows 3.1 Control Panel had a whopping 11 applets in it right after installing Windows. Needless to say, Windows 7 has many more applets in its Control Panel, but the Control Panel remains just the same.

To see an interesting video demonstrating the history of the Windows OS through sequential upgrades from one to the next, search for "Chain of Fools: Upgrading Through Every Version of Windows" at YouTube.com.

Windows Evolution

As you learned in the preceding section, the Windows OS did not just appear but has evolved over time. Initially, Windows was a graphical shell that ran on top of DOS. This functionality continued through the Windows 95 line of OSs until it ceased with Windows Millennium Edition (ME).

Starting in 1993, Microsoft sold an alternative OS named Windows NT that depended on an entirely different architecture. It used the same graphical interface, but it did not run on top of DOS. Windows NT 4.0 inherited the modern Desktop and Start menu concept from Windows 95, and this basic interface concept is still used in Windows 7 today. DOS no longer exists in Windows 7, but the Command Prompt interface provides a command line or text mode interface for interacting with the OS. The Command Prompt is very similar to DOS, and it is clearly based on its predecessor.

◄

For more information about the history of Microsoft Windows, visit http://windows .microsoft.com/ en-US/windows/ history.

Figure 1.6 shows a timeline that compares the evolution of PC hardware with the evolution of the Windows OS. As the image portrays, more powerful hardware has allowed for more features in the OS, so that we can use the graphically rich interfaces with animations and special effects that we use today. The memory amounts listed in Figure 1.6 do not represent the maximum supported memory of the named systems, but rather the common memory amounts used with them. (You'll notice that the timeline doesn't list every Windows operating system; its purpose is to display the "types" of operating systems. Windows for Workgroups 3.11, for example, was really just Windows 3.1 with networking built in. Windows 98 and ME are really just 95 with a few enhancements. Windows Vista, as discussed separately, never met with wide acceptance.)

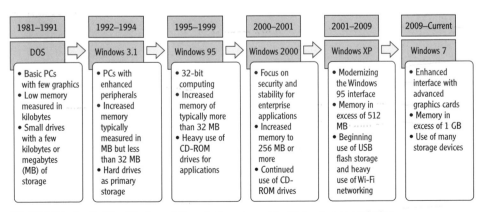

FIGURE 1.6 The Windows OS evolution alongside PC hardware evolution

WHAT ABOUT VISTA?

If you investigate Figure 1.6 closely, you will notice that Vista is not mentioned. This is not because it is an insignificant release of Windows—quite the opposite is true. Windows Vista was a revolutionary release of Windows that was a bit before its time. The hardware available at the time of its release was simply unable to take advantage of its full capabilities. For this reason, many users were frustrated with the performance of Vista on their computers and chose to run Windows XP instead. In addition, many applications and devices failed to work as needed on the Vista OS due to the lack of drivers required from hardware vendors.

Windows 7 resolved many of the problems with Vista by providing enhanced application compatibility solutions and improved hardware support. Additionally, with the passage of time, the hardware in common use at the time of Windows 7's release runs the newer OS very well. For this reason, Windows 7 has experienced an adoption rate on a scale unseen since the release of Windows 95 in the mid-1990s, with more than 240 million licenses sold in the first year of its release.

Understanding the OS Architecture

The architecture of an OS defines how it works instead of what it can do. The features define what it can do, but those features must work on top of an operational methodology. This methodology is the *architecture*. The current Windows OS architecture is based on the original architecture in the Windows NT OS first released in 1993. Windows 7, building on changes included in the less popular Windows Vista, introduces significant changes in several areas of the architecture, and they are addressed in this section. You will first explore the layers in Windows that make up its architecture and then compare it with other systems.

The Layers in Windows

The Windows OS is divided into layers, or modes of operation. The first is Kernel mode and the second is User mode, as depicted in Figure 1.7. Kernel mode is where the operating system kernel and other low-level processes operate. User mode is where your applications, such as Microsoft Word or Excel, and environment subsystems run.

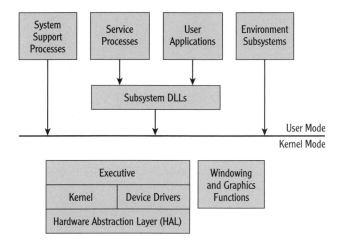

FIGURE 1.7 The basic Windows architecture components

Technically, Kernel mode operations take place in something called ring 0 of complex instruction set computing (CISC) processors. Most processors in use in computers today are CISC processors. The common x86 (32-bit) and x64 (64-bit) nomenclature refers to CISC processors based on their support for 32-bit and 64-bit computing. User mode operations take place in the processor's ring 3 (also known as nonprivileged mode). The different rings of operation simply define the level of access granted to the processes running in that ring. For example, ring 0 (also known as privileged mode) is like "God mode" in many games. In this mode, entered via cheat code, you can do anything you want without fear of dying or being injured within the game. In a similar way, ring 0 processes can do anything they want within the system. It is for this reason that only operating system functions, device drivers, and graphics capabilities reside here.

To simplify the way rings work in CISC processors, just remember that ring 3 processes can do only what ring 2 processes allow them to do. Ring 2 processes can do only what ring 1 processes allow them to do, and ring 1 processes can do only what ring 0 processes allow them to do. Because Windows uses only rings 0 and 3, we can simplify this and say that ring 3 processes can do only what ring 0 processes allow them to do.

Ring 3 processes are usually called user application processes. Because user applications must access hardware, which can only be done through Kernel mode, some method must exist to allow for this. Effectively, user applications switch from User mode processes to Kernel mode processes for short durations in order to accomplish Kernel mode tasks. However, even in such situations a Kernel mode process must authorize the switch, which brings us back to the

Rings 1 and 2 are not used in Windows systems. This decision was made when other processors were also supported that offered only two modes of operation within the processor.

Ring 0 is also known as privileged mode and ring 3 is known as nonprivileged mode.

When monitoring processor utilization on a Windows system, you will notice that most of the time is spent in Kernel mode because this mode has access to the hardware.

reality that User mode (ring 3) processes can do only what Kernel mode (ring 0) processes allow them to do.

In addition to Kernel mode and User mode, Figure 1.7 shows several components, described here:

System Support Processes   System support processes include system processes that do not run as services. These include processes like the logon process (WINLOGON.EXE) and the Session Manager subsystem (SMSS.EXE). The Session Manager is the first User mode process that starts when the OS loads. The Session Manager launches environment subsystems and the WINLOGON.EXE process.

Service Processes   Service processes are those system or application processes that do run as services. These include system services like the Task Scheduler and the Print Spooler, but they also include nonsystem services like SQL Server, which is a database server service. A service is an application or innate operating system component that provides services (capabilities) to the network, the local machine, or both.

User Applications   User applications are the actual applications that users execute. These include applications like Microsoft Excel and Adobe Photoshop. Five application types are supported in the Windows OS: Windows 32-bit and 64-bit applications, Windows 3.1 16-bit applications (on 32-bit editions of Windows 7), MS-DOS 16-bit applications (on 32-bit editions of Windows 7), and Portable Operating System Interface (POSIX) 32-bit applications through the use of the Subsystem for Unix-based Applications. 16-bit applications are not supported on the 64-bit editions of Windows.

> **Dynamic link libraries (DLLs) contain code that can be called upon by other processes so that programmers need not re-create the code for each application.**

Environment Subsystems   The environment subsystems and the subsystem dynamic link libraries (DLLs), which are defined next, work together to allow different application types to function on the system. For example, the Windows 32-bit environment subsystem allows 32-bit Windows applications to work on a 64-bit edition of Windows 7. This 32-bit environment subsystem will make calls to subsystem DLLs, and the subsystem DLLs may also communicate back with the environment subsystem if communication with the application is necessary.

Subsystem DLLs   The last User mode component is the subsystem DLLs. These translate application function calls into internal native system service calls. The subsystem DLLs communicate with the Kernel mode processes on behalf of the applications and may communicate with the applications through the environment subsystems as well.

Executive   The executive can be compared to an executive assistant. This component is responsible for process and thread management, memory management, security functions, input and output (I/O), networking, and communication between processes (interprocess communication). The executive consists of subcomponents responsible for specific tasks. For example, the Configuration Manager implements and manages the Registry, which stores settings for applications, users, and the OS. Additionally, the I/O Manager provides device-independent I/O and passes requests to the proper device drivers for actual processing on the hardware.

Windowing and Graphics Functions   A key feature of Windows is the graphical user interface, and these functions are implemented in Kernel mode. This is a major reason why unstable video drivers often cause the entire Windows OS to become unstable. The drawing of windows and user interface control objects (such as buttons, scroll bars, and title bars) is controlled here.

Kernel   While the executive is in charge of process and thread management, the kernel is in charge of thread scheduling. It decides which thread gets processor time and on which processor it gets time at any moment. It is also responsible for synchronization when multiple processors are used and for interrupt handling through the interrupt objects, which work in relation to the I/O Manager.

Device Drivers   Device drivers are Kernel mode components that provide a communication interface between the I/O Manager within the executive and the actual hardware for which they are written. Device drivers place calls to the Hardware Abstraction Layer, described next, to communicate with the hardware. Device drivers may be used to communicate with specific hardware or with filesystems, networks, and other protocols.

Hardware Abstraction Layer (HAL)   The HAL does exactly what its name implies—it abstracts or disconnects the OS from the core hardware, such as the processor architecture. Because of the HAL, Windows can run on systems that support 32-bit processing (x86) or 64-bit processing (x64). Additionally, with the x86 processors, it can run on either Advanced Configuration and Power Interface (ACPI) PCs or Advanced Programmable Interrupt Controller (APIC) PCs.

PCs that use the ACPI HAL are single-processor machines. PCs that use the APIC HAL are multiple-processor machines.

   Several files work together to provide the core functionality of the Windows OS. These files include the following:

`ADVAPI32.DLL`   One of the primary Windows subsystem DLLs providing access to APIs for Registry access, system shutdowns and restarts, and management of user accounts.

GDI32.DLL   One of the primary Windows subsystem DLLs providing graphics functions.

HAL.DLL   The Hardware Abstraction Layer (HAL) DLL that allows the Windows OS to run on different hardware platforms.

KERNEL32.DLL   One of the primary Windows subsystem DLLs providing kernel functions.

NTDLL.DLL   The DLL that exposes many of the Windows native API functions to User mode applications.

NTOSKRNL.EXE   The kernel image for the Windows OS; the kernel is responsible in part for process and memory management.

NTKRNLPA.EXE   The same as NTOSKRNL.EXE, but used on systems with Physical Address Extension (PAE) support.

USER32.DLL   One of the primary Windows subsystem DLLs providing access to the keyboard and mouse as well as window management (the actual application windows as opposed to the OS name).

WIN32K.SYS   The Kernel mode portion of the Windows subsystem.

> **PAE allows 32-bit or x86 processors to access memory in amounts greater than 4 GB. With PAE, it is possible for a system to support up to 64 GB.**

Windows 7 specifically modifies the architectural functionality of Windows in several ways. The following enhancements have been included in the Windows 7 architecture and design:

► The version number of the OS has changed to 6.1 from 6.0, which was the older version number in Windows Vista. Even though the version number seems to indicate that Windows 7 is a minor release (6.1) and Windows Vista was a major release (6.0), Microsoft considers Windows 7 a major release.

► More than 400 footprint reductions were implemented across all Windows 7 components, resulting in a smaller memory footprint than Windows Vista.

► The Desktop Window Manager (DWM), which provides the Aero window interface capabilities, has a 50 percent reduced memory footprint.

► Microsoft added power management efficiency tests to assist users in increasing battery life. The POWERCFG.EXE command can be used to generate a report on power issues.

► The Windows 7 OS is prepared for BitLocker immediately after installation because a 100 MB volume is created for BitLocker use during installation.

> ► BitLocker also supports encryption of USB flash drives through BitLocker to Go.

> ► Microsoft added the ability to boot the system from a virtual hard disk (VHD). A VHD is used to provide hard disks to virtual machines in virtualization systems like Windows Virtual PC and Hyper-V. Booting from a VHD allows for simpler dual-booting and testing. Windows 7 systems can boot from USB flash drives, VHD files, hard drives, CD/DVD drives, and other USB-type drives.

For more information on the architectural changes in Windows 7, view the following page at the Microsoft Developers Network (MSDN) website: `http://msdn.microsoft.com/en-us/library/dd371741(v=VS.85).aspx`.

Windows Compared to Other Systems

The architecture of Windows is very similar to other operating systems, including Linux and Mac OS X. A key difference is in the area of graphics processing. Windows includes graphics capabilities in the Kernel mode of the operating system, which can potentially improve graphics performance. Linux does not include the graphics functions in the kernel, which removes those functions from the core OS and can potentially improve stability.

The Mac OS X operating system is now based on BSD Unix. This flavor of Unix has been around for more than 30 years. However, the hardware on which you run it today is not 30 years old, and therefore, the length of development time does not automatically result in improved stability. For example, Windows has been developed since the official Microsoft announcement in 1983. Therefore, the length of development history is really no different when comparing Windows with any other OS.

Apple provides an open-source version of its core OS known as Darwin. Darwin is the OS used for Mac OS X, but the GUI is provided through Quartz and Aqua, which are not available in the open-source version. Quartz is the drawing engine and Aqua is the theme. The most widely used open-source version of Darwin is PureDarwin, which is available at `www.PureDarwin.org`.

Visit the following websites to learn more about differences between Windows OSs and other operating systems:

> ► `www.microsoft.com/canada/windowsserver/compare/default.mspx`

> ► `windows.microsoft.com/en-US/windows7/products/compare/pc-vs-mac`

> ► `www.michaelhorowitz.com/Linux.vs.Windows.html`

> ► `www.cio.com/article/41140/Windows_vs._Linux_vs._OS_X`

◄

The stability versus performance issue is hotly debated in the industry. For more information on the differences between Linux and Windows, see `http://en.wikipedia.org/wiki/Comparison_of_Windows_and_Linux`.

Identifying Windows Interfaces

The Windows OS has three primary interfaces for working with applications and performing administrative tasks. Most users will spend the majority of their time in the GUI, but administrators can benefit greatly from the Command Prompt and Windows PowerShell interfaces. This section includes explanations and examples of all three interfaces in the Windows 7 OS.

Using the GUI Interface

The Windows GUI is composed of windows, buttons, text boxes, and other navigation elements. To support Windows systems effectively, you must understand the basics of these elements. Figure 1.8 shows the Start menu and taskbar elements included in the Windows 7 GUI.

FIGURE 1.8 The Windows 7 GUI interface with the Start menu expanded

> You can quickly access the Start menu by pressing the Windows key on a keyboard or by pressing Ctrl+Esc if the keyboard lacks a Windows key.

The first element is the Start menu. As you can see in Figure 1.8, the Start menu is similar to earlier versions of Windows, but it includes new capabilities. First, a graphical orb icon (first introduced in Windows Vista) is still the button used to bring up the Start menu in Windows 7. The Start menu includes the ability to pin icons so that they are always displayed on the menu, and it features a listing of the recent applications launched for quick access.

To customize the Start menu, simply right-click the Start menu button (the orb) and select Properties to access the Taskbar And Start Menu Properties dialog, shown in Figure 1.9. You can use the Customize button to change how the Start menu looks and behaves. You can also configure the Start menu's Power button to do any of the following tasks: shut down, switch user, log off, lock, restart, or sleep. Finally, you can configure Privacy settings according to your needs.

FIGURE 1.9 The Taskbar And Start Menu Properties dialog

Using the Taskbar And Start Menu Properties dialog, you can also configure the taskbar. On the Taskbar tab you have several options, including the ability to lock the taskbar, auto-hide the taskbar, and use small icons so that the taskbar can contain more icons at lower screen resolutions. You can also define the taskbar location on the screen and the way the taskbar buttons should be displayed. For example, you can display the taskbar buttons in groups so that they stack on top of each other for multiple instances of the same application, or you can display them as completely separate buttons. Finally, you can customize the Notification Area. This area is, by default, in the lower-right corner of the Desktop and is displayed as part of the taskbar. It displays icons that allow you to interact with the system and applications, such as the volume control icon and alert icons that display important information related to your system. You can control which icons should be displayed in the Notification Area and which should not.

The next major portion of the Windows OS GUI is the Desktop. The Desktop is shown in Figure 1.8 with the Windows logo in view and the Recycle Bin icon

The screen resolution defines the number of pixels used horizontally and vertically to draw the screen. Common resolutions are 1024×768 and 1280×1024.

displayed. The Desktop can contain system icons and custom icons. It can also display gadgets such as weather and system resource gadgets for quick display of potentially important information. To add gadgets to the Desktop, right-click the Desktop and select Gadgets. To customize the system icons on the Desktop, right-click the Desktop and select Personalize; then choose Change Desktop Icons on the Personalization screen. From here, you can add any of the following icon items to the Desktop and change the icon used to represent the item:

▶ Computer

▶ User's Files

▶ Network

▶ Recycle Bin

▶ Control Panel

Applications are not forced to use the standard application window. Many applications run in full-screen mode. Games are a perfect example of this behavior.

Figure 1.10 shows the next important component in the Windows GUI: a standard application window. In this case, I've chosen the Notepad application as an example because it represents the most basic interface elements used by Windows GUI applications. The primary elements are the title bar, menus, application control buttons, and the application workspace. The title bar typically displays the application name and any open document name. Programmers can display anything they want in the title bar, but the common practice is to display this information.

FIGURE 1.10 Notepad is an example of a typical application window.

The menus are a collection of one or more groupings of commands. For example, the File menu typically provides file management functions such as opening or closing files and saving files. Each application has its own distinct set of menus, but the File, Edit, View, and Help menus are common across applications.

The application control buttons are located in the upper-right corner of the application window. The first button, shown on the left in Figure 1.10, is used to minimize the application to the taskbar. The second button is used to maximize the application. The final button, depicted with an X, is used to close the application. The following keyboard shortcuts apply to these buttons in Windows 7:

- ► Maximize: Windows Key+Up Arrow
- ► Minimize: Windows Key+Down Arrow
- ► Close: Alt+F4

You will use the graphical interface for most of the instructions provided throughout the rest of this book; however, it is important to understand the text-mode interfaces as well, and the following two sections explain them. Chapter 3, "Managing the Desktop," provides detailed information about desktop management in the Windows GUI.

Using the Command Prompt Interface

The Command Prompt is based on the oldest interface Microsoft has provided: the command interpreter in DOS. In Windows 7, the Command Prompt is either a 32-bit or 64-bit command-line interface to the operating system. It is not DOS, but it has many similarities to it.

On 32-bit editions of Windows 7, the Command Prompt is a 32-bit application. On 64-bit editions, the Command Prompt is 64-bit by default; however, a 32-bit version of the Command Prompt is located in the %WinDir%\SysWOW64 folder as CMD.EXE. To access the 32-bit version of the Command Prompt on the 64-bit edition of Windows 7, follow these steps:

1. Click Start.

2. In the Start menu search field, enter *%windir%*\syswow64\cmd.exe.

3. Press Enter.

The Command Prompt interface is shown in Figure 1.11. You can access the this prompt using several methods. To access it from the Start menu, click Start ➤ All Programs ➤ Accessories ➤ Command Prompt. To access it from the search field, click Start and then enter **cmd.exe** in the search field and press Enter.

Throughout this book, the variable %WinDir% is a reference to the location where Windows is installed, which is typically C:\Windows. This is also a variable for the same location within the OS.

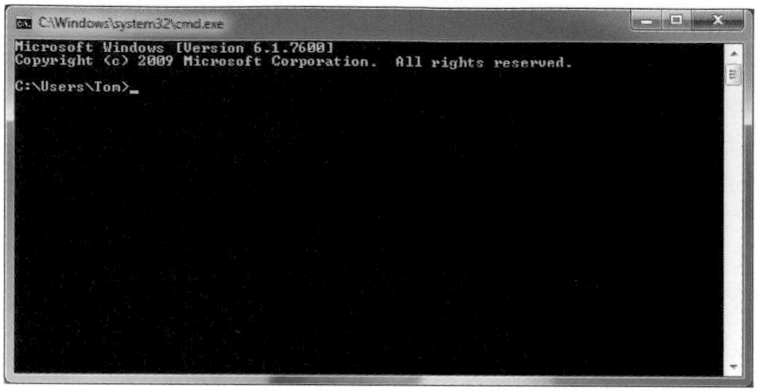

FIGURE 1.11 The Windows Command Prompt interface

You can configure several items in the Command Prompt Properties dialog. To access this dialog, with the Command Prompt open click the icon in the upper-left corner of the application window and select Properties. From here you can configure the Options, Font, Layout, and Colors settings. Many people enjoy creating a custom color scheme for the Command Prompt. One of the most important settings to configure from the Properties dialog is Screen Buffer Size. You will usually want to set the Height value to something much greater than 300, which is the default. Higher values allow you to scroll back through more information. On modern computers with plenty of RAM, it is acceptable to set the Height value to 9,999, which is the highest possible value.

For more detailed information on the various commands available at the Command Prompt, visit www.WindowsCommandLine.com. At this free website, I've documented each command with examples, and video demonstrations are planned for the future.

Using Windows PowerShell

Windows PowerShell is the new command-line interface Microsoft first released as an add-on to earlier versions of Windows. PowerShell 2.0 comes with Windows 7 out of the box and it is Microsoft's preferred environment for developing administrative tools in the future. In fact, many Microsoft technologies now come with a complete set of *cmdlets* (the name for commands in the PowerShell interface) for administration purposes and the graphical interfaces call the PowerShell cmdlets to do their work. For example, Exchange Server 2010 comes with a complete set of administration cmdlets and the GUI management tool for Exchange Server 2010 calls these cmdlets to perform administrative actions.

Figure 1.12 shows the Windows PowerShell interface running on Windows 7. Like the Command Prompt, PowerShell has a Properties dialog where you can modify several properties. Many of the same settings available for the Command Prompt are available for Windows PowerShell, and you will use Windows PowerShell in several examples throughout this book. It plays a significant role in Windows OS administration now and will continue to do so for the foreseeable future.

FIGURE 1.12 The Windows PowerShell interface

Among the primary benefits of Windows PowerShell are its scripting and automation interfaces. Using the built-in support for variables and logical functions, you can accomplish much more with PowerShell than you could with a batch file at the Command Prompt. Additionally, you can use PowerShell to execute commands against remote computers using the built-in support for the Windows Remote Management (WinRM) service.

For more detailed information about using Windows PowerShell and the available cmdlets for various purposes, visit www.MasterWindowsPowerShell.com. At this free website, I've documented the PowerShell interface, and video demonstrations are also available.

THE ESSENTIALS AND BEYOND

In this chapter, you were introduced to the Windows OS. First, you explored the history of Windows, which began in MS-DOS, worked its way through Windows 3.1, and ended up where we are today in Windows 7. Next, you explored the architecture of Windows 7, which is based on the original Windows NT architecture from the 1990s. The architecture

(Continues)

THE ESSENTIALS AND BEYOND *(Continued)*

employs a layering scheme with user applications running primarily in User mode and the OS and device drivers running in Kernel mode. Finally, you learned about the three basic interfaces available for Windows OS interaction: the GUI interface based on windows, icons, and graphics; the Command Prompt, which is the earliest text-mode interface to the Windows OS; and Windows PowerShell, the newest interface to the Windows systems that provides exceptional power in scripting and automation.

ADDITIONAL EXERCISES

▶ Research the differences between Windows and other OSs online.

▶ Use the `Import-Module` cmdlet to add a Windows PowerShell module that is not included in the Windows PowerShell interface by default.

▶ Review the history of Microsoft Windows at the Microsoft website to learn how it has evolved to become the operating system it is today.

To compare your answers to the author's, please visit www.sybex.com/go/osessentials.

REVIEW QUESTIONS

1. What OS preceded Windows and was the foundation for Windows 3.1 and Windows 95?

    A. OS/2   **C.** DOS

    B. Mac OS X   **D.** Linux

2. True or false. Batch files that are commonly used in Windows 7 today were also used in DOS.

3. Which one of the following components that existed in Windows 3.1 is still in Windows 7 today?

    A. Program Manager   **C.** Action Center

    B. Calendar   **D.** Control Panel

4. What Windows OS operational mode includes device drivers and the window and graphics management code?

5. What new Windows 7 command can be used to generate a power management report?

    A. POWERCFG.EXE   **C.** TASKLIST.EXE

    B. SC.EXE   **D.** NET.EXE

(Continues)

THE ESSENTIALS AND BEYOND (Continued)

6. Define Windows PowerShell.

7. Define a process.

8. In what directory or folder is the 32-bit version of the Command Prompt located on 64-bit systems?

   A. `C:\Windows\DOS32`   **C.** `C:\Program Files(x86)`

   B. `C:\Windows\System32`   **D.** `C:\Windows\SysWOW64`

9. What is the command used to launch the Windows command prompt in Windows 7?

   A. `CMD.EXE`   **C.** `COMMAND.COM`

   B. PowerShell   **D.** Prompt

10. True or false. You can add the Control Panel to the Desktop in Windows 7.

CHAPTER 2

Installing Windows

Over the years, the installation process for Windows has become simpler; however, this does not mean that you can just start installing it without any forethought. You must plan the installation effectively, which means choosing the proper edition, ensuring that OS requirements are met, selecting between a clean installation and an upgrade, performing a media-based installation or an automated network installation, and finally determining whether virtualized installations should be used. Clearly, many decisions must be made, and this chapter will help you make these decisions as you explore the following topics:

▶ **Exploring OS editions**

▶ **Planning clean installs vs. upgrades**

▶ **Understanding installation types**

▶ **Using virtualized installations**

Exploring OS Editions

Windows 7 comes in different editions, and the installer must choose the best edition for her needs. Most organizations standardize on a specific edition and use it for all computers in order to make the selection process easier and to make the environment more consistent and stable, as well as easier to troubleshoot. In this section, you will learn about the various editions of Windows, the system requirements for those editions, and the PC Upgrade Advisor, a tool that can be used to report on the readiness of a machine for Windows 7.

Comparing Windows Editions

Microsoft bundles features and capabilities into distributions of Windows that it calls *editions*. The editions start with the fewest features and capabilities and go to the highest-level editions with all available features and capabilities. As an installation technician, you must be aware of the different editions and the features they offer. The following editions are available for Windows 7:

Starter   Windows 7 Starter edition is available on new computers that run low-end processors. It is mostly used on netbook-scale laptops and not on full-scale laptops or desktops. A maximum of one physical processor is supported.

Home Basic   This edition is available in emerging markets only. It does not include support for the Aero interface. Like Starter edition, this edition supports a maximum of one physical processor.

Home Premium   This is the lowest edition available for purchase in retail stores and shipping with computers in existing markets. The full Aero interface is supported in Home Premium. It is important to know that this edition cannot be joined to a domain. Up to two physical processors may be used with this edition.

Professional   The Professional edition is the lowest level that has the ability to join a domain. When a Windows machine is part of a domain, the machine can be used to access resources within the domain and the administrators can better manage and restrict the machine. Like Home Premium, this edition supports up to two physical processors. Professional is very similar to Home Premium except for the added ability to join a domain.

Ultimate and Enterprise   The Ultimate and Enterprise editions are effectively the same. Enterprise edition is available only to volume licensing customers. Ultimate edition is available to anyone. Both editions can join a domain and add enhanced features such as BitLocker and AppLocker. Like Professional edition, these editions support a maximum of two physical processors.

In addition to the general descriptions of the editions, you should understand the features and capabilities available in each edition. Table 2.1 compares the editions by available features.

TABLE 2.1 Windows 7 editions comparison

Feature	Starter	Home Premium	Professional	Ultimate/ Enterprise
Bluetooth support	Yes	Yes	Yes	Yes
Join a homegroup	Yes	Yes	Yes	Yes

(Continues)

The Aero interface provides the transparent window elements and the ability to use enhanced graphics features like 3D Flip and the taskbar thumbnails.

A Windows *domain* is a special network that is implemented using a Windows server running the Active Directory Domain Services. For more information, see my book *Microsoft Windows Server Administration Essentials* (Sybex, 2011) in this same series.

TABLE 2.1 *(Continued)*

Feature	Starter	Home Premium	Professional	Ultimate/ Enterprise
Join a domain	No	No	Yes	Yes
Create and play DVDs	No	Yes	Yes	Yes
Action Center	Yes	Yes	Yes	Yes
64-bit support	No	Yes	Yes	Yes
Aero support	No	Yes	Yes	Yes
Windows XP Mode support	No	No	Yes	Yes
AppLocker support	No	No	No	Yes
BitLocker support	No	No	No	Yes
BranchCache support	No	No	No	Yes
Direct boot from VHD	No	No	No	Yes
DirectAccess	No	No	No	Yes

You can upgrade from one edition to another according to certain limitations. This is called a Windows Anytime Upgrade. The following constraints apply to Windows Anytime Upgrade:

▶ You can upgrade to a more advanced or higher-level edition, but you cannot downgrade.

▶ You can upgrade only within the same bit level. For example, you cannot upgrade from Windows 7 Home Premium 32-bit to Windows 7 Ultimate 64-bit.

▶ You cannot use Windows Anytime Upgrade to upgrade from a previous version of Windows, such as Windows Vista, to Windows 7.

Defining System Requirements

The system requirements for a given software program or OS are provided by the vendor. Microsoft specifies the following minimum hardware requirements for Windows 7 Starter and Home Basic:

- ▶ 512 MB of RAM

- ▶ 1 GHz processor (either 32-bit or 64-bit for Home Basic)

- ▶ 16 GB hard disk drive for Starter or 20 GB hard disk drive for Home Basic with 15 GB free for either

- ▶ A graphics card that supports DirectX 9 with at least 32 MB of graphics memory

The following minimum requirements are specified for Windows 7 Home Premium, Professional, Ultimate, and Enterprise:

- ▶ 1 GB of RAM for 32-bit installations and 2 GB of RAM for 64-bit installations

- ▶ 1 GHz processor (either 32-bit or 64-bit for Home Basic)

- ▶ 40 GB hard disk drive with 15 GB free

- ▶ A graphics card that supports DirectX 9 with at least 128 MB of graphics memory and a Windows Display Driver Model (WDDM) driver with Pixel Shader 2.0 hardware

It is important that a Windows 7 support professional understand the difference between minimum requirements and the system specifications required for a specific scenario. A user running high-end CAD software will require a more powerful computer than a user running simple email and web browsing applications. To determine the actual system specification required for a scenario, considering the following questions:

- ▶ What applications will the user run?

- ▶ How many applications will the user run concurrently?

- ▶ What background processes will run on the machine?

After gathering this information, you can determine the specific needs for a given scenario. It is common for organizations to stipulate a baseline computer and then add extra memory, CPU power, graphics capabilities, and hard

Although it is less common today, some users still share data on the network using their desktop computers. This is an example of a background process.

▶

disk space from there depending on the needs of the users. For example, the following is a common baseline specification set for organizations running Windows 7:

- ► 2 GB of RAM

- ► 2 GHz total processing power (*total processing power* is a reference to the potential for multiple processors or processors with multiple cores)

- ► 512 MB of graphics memory

- ► 80 GB hard disk

Creating a baseline specification like this can ensure that all users have acceptable performance.

Using the PC Upgrade Advisor

The PC Upgrade Advisor, also known as the Windows 7 Upgrade Advisor, can be used to test a PC for compatibility with Windows 7. You can download the software from http://windows.microsoft.com/upgradeadvisor. Once it is downloaded, you will need to install and run it on your current operating system. Figure 2.1 shows the Windows 7 Upgrade Advisor running the compatibility check.

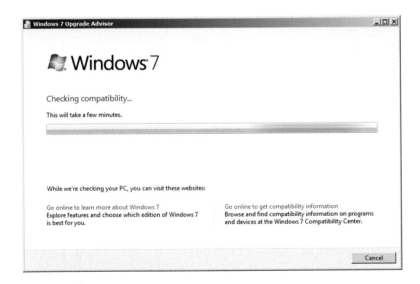

FIGURE 2.1 Running the compatibility check in the Windows 7 Upgrade Advisor

When the Upgrade Advisor completes the check, you can view report information similar to that in Figure 2.2. Notice that the advisor indicates that the "Most complete Windows 7 is installed." This simply means that the advisor was executed on a machine already running either Windows 7 Enterprise or Ultimate edition. But it also demonstrates that the tool can be used on older OSs to determine whether the hardware is ready for Windows 7. It can also be used on existing Windows 7 installations to determine whether the machine can use Windows Anytime Upgrade to install a more complete edition of Windows 7.

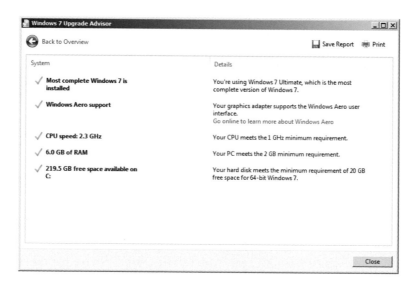

FIGURE 2.2 Viewing the reports in the Windows 7 Upgrade Advisor

Planning Clean Installs vs. Upgrades

Windows systems have always supported upgrading from previous versions. An upgrade attempts to maintain existing applications and settings while installing the new version of the OS. Although the option of upgrading an older OS to the newer version may seem like the best choice at first glance, with further investigation problems can appear. In this section, you will learn about the pros and cons of a "clean install" compared to an upgrade. You will also explore application compatibility issues and learn about the solutions Microsoft provides for these issues. Finally, you will examine the important steps required to perform either an upgrade or a clean install of Windows 7.

Understanding Upgrade Paths

Upgrading is the process of installing a new OS and maintaining application and operating system settings. Additional data stored on the hard disk is maintained as well. You cannot upgrade from all versions of Windows to Windows 7. In fact, you can only truly upgrade from Windows Vista if it is running at least Service Pack 1 (SP1) installed directly to Windows 7. Figure 2.3 shows the methods available for moving from earlier versions of Windows up to Windows 7.

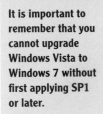

It is important to remember that you cannot upgrade Windows Vista to Windows 7 without first applying SP1 or later.

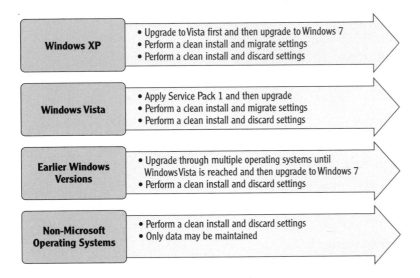

FIGURE 2.3 Upgrade paths from earlier versions of Windows and other operating systems

Several facts are important to remember based on the information provided in Figure 2.3:

▶ You cannot upgrade from any version of Windows to Windows 7 except Windows Vista.

▶ Windows XP can be migrated to Windows 7 by installing a clean installation of Windows 7 and then transferring user settings and data over to the new machine.

▶ Earlier versions of Windows can be upgraded to Windows 7 only if you first go through a series of upgrades from one OS version to another along the path to the newest version.

▶ A non-Microsoft OS cannot be upgraded or migrated, but you can copy the data from it to a Windows 7 computer (assuming an application exists for Windows 7 that can open the data).

A migration occurs when the new OS is installed as a clean installation and then the data and settings (both user and system) are copied over to the new installation.

Considering Application Compatibility

The most common problem that occurs after installing a new version of an OS is application failures. An important task for the installation technician is the testing of applications for compatibility with the new OS. The good news is that Microsoft provides several tools to assist you in this process. These tools are bundled together in a download called the Application Compatibility Toolkit (ACT). Microsoft releases a new version of ACT periodically and you should always use the newest version that is compatible with your existing and target OSs. Version 5.6 can be downloaded here: www.microsoft.com/download/en/details.aspx?id=7352.

ACT includes the following important components:

Application Compatibility Manager (ACM)   ACM is the hub for your actions in the ACT solution. This tool is used to create the modules that are distributed to client computers to inventory the software and hardware in your environment. It is also used to analyze the collected information and track your findings and actions related to software compatibility.

Standard User Analyzer (SUA)   The SUA tool is used to locate the breakpoints in applications. It will help you locate items that should be corrected to make the applications work. Some applications simply cannot be made to work, but those that can are best tested with this tool to locate the proper fixes.

Compatibility Administrator   The fixes that are discovered with SUA are collected together into what is called a *shim*, a collection of fixes intended to make an application work on Windows 7. The shims are stored in shim databases, which can be imported into a system in order to repair application compatibility issues. The Compatibility Administrator is the tool you use to view the system shims and create custom shim databases.

ACT 5.6 requires a Microsoft SQL Server, but it can use the free version of SQL Server called SQL Server Express. The basic process of using ACT is as follows:

1. Install SQL Server (remember, this can be the free version).

2. Install ACT 5.6.

3. Use the configuration wizard to create the ACT database and install the log processing service (this wizard runs automatically the first time you run the ACM).

4. Create and deploy data collection packages (DCPs) with the ACP.

5. Analyze the results.

When considering upgrades and migrations, the existing OS is the one you run today. The target OS is the one to which you are moving.

If you create a shim database, you can import it into Windows 7 systems using the Command Prompt SDBINST .EXE command. This command is built into Windows 7 systems by default.

WHY APPLICATIONS BREAK AFTER UPGRADES

Applications break when moving from one OS version to another for several reasons. For example, an application may not work because it was designed for a bit level that is no longer supported by your version of Windows 7. If you use the 64-bit edition of Windows 7, you can no longer run 16-bit Windows 3.1 applications; however, they may work fine on the 32-bit version of Windows 7.

Additionally, Microsoft sometimes removes features from a new version of Windows. If your application depends on one of these features, it may not work properly in the new version. These features are typically deprecated at least two versions before they are removed, but it is not uncommon to continue using an application for more than a decade, and this means that such an older application is more likely to have problems on Windows 7.

Finally, an application may break because of new features. For example, some applications simply will not work if User Account Control is enabled in Windows 7. Microsoft recommends never disabling User Account Control, but you may encounter scenarios where you cannot upgrade the application and you must run Windows 7. In such scenarios, you may have to either disable User Account Control or implement Windows XP Mode or another virtualization solution to resolve the problem.

The following Wikipedia article will be helpful in locating features that were in Windows Vista but are no longer in Windows 7:

▶ `http://en.wikipedia.org/wiki/List_of_features`
  `_removed_in_Windows_7`

The following Wikipedia article will be helpful if you are moving directly from Windows XP to Windows 7 because it lists the items that were removed from Vista:

▶ `http://en.wikipedia.org/wiki/List_of_features`
  `_removed_in_Windows_Vista`

For the latter, you will need to know the features removed from Vista as well as Windows 7 to determine if any features on which your applications depend have been removed.

Planning for Upgrades

If you choose to implement an upgrade instead of a clean install, you will want to answer the following questions in your upgrade planning process:

- ▶ What version of Windows am I currently running?
  - ▶ If XP, how will I migrate the data?
  - ▶ If Vista, am I currently running SP1?
- ▶ Does my hardware meet the minimum requirements for Windows 7?
- ▶ Will I deploy 32-bit or 64-bit editions of Windows 7?
  - ▶ If I deploy 64-bit editions, will my applications work?
  - ▶ Do I require 64-bit editions for any new applications?
- ▶ What edition will I deploy? (Professional or Enterprise in most cases)
- ▶ Are all my applications compatible with Windows 7?
  - ▶ For those that are not, how will I resolve the problems?

Planning for Clean Installs

If you choose to implement clean installs instead of upgrades, you will want to answer the following questions in your upgrade planning process:

- ▶ Does my hardware meet the minimum requirements for Windows 7?
- ▶ Will I deploy 32-bit or 64-bit editions of Windows 7?
  - ▶ If I deploy 64-bit editions, will my applications work?
  - ▶ Do I require 64-bit editions for any new applications?
- ▶ What edition will I deploy? (Professional or Enterprise in most cases)
- ▶ Are my applications compatible with Windows 7?
  - ▶ For those that are not, how will I resolve the problems?

You may have noticed that the list of questions for clean installs is very similar to the list for upgrades. The only real differences are the fact that you no longer have to factor in the current version of Windows and the way you will migrate the data and settings over to the new installation.

Understanding Installation Types

Windows can be installed using several methods. All methods use a technology known as imaging, but you can pull the image for a given computer from several sources, such as removable media or network locations. This section introduces you to these various installation types and the important task of managing product identification keys.

Installing from Removable Media

The first installation method and the most commonly used in smaller organizations is via removable media. This includes DVDs and USB media. To install from USB, you must create a bootable USB flash drive with the Windows 7 installation source files on it. Do so using the following steps:

1. Connect the USB flash drive to a computer that already has Windows 7 installed.

2. Open a Command Prompt as an administrator and run diskpart.

3. Use the list disk command to determine the disk number for the USB flash drive.

4. Use the select disk X command to select the USB flash drive as the current disk, where X is the USB flash drive number determined in step 3.

5. Execute the clean command.

6. Execute the create partition primary command.

7. Execute the format fs-fat32 quick command.

8. Execute the active command.

9. Type exit to close the diskpart utility.

10. Type exit to exit the Command Prompt.

11. Copy all the files from the Windows 7 DVD to the USB flash drive and then use the resulting flash drive to boot a computer and begin the installation of Windows 7.

To install from DVD, simply insert the Windows 7 disc into the computer's DVD drive and power on the machine. Ensure that the BIOS is configured to boot from

> You can install Windows 7 in a virtual machine (VM). The following steps will be the same regardless of whether you install to a physical computer or a virtual machine.

DVD first or select the boot time option for your computer that allows you to select to boot from the DVD. The Windows 7 installation will start automatically. Take the following steps to install Windows 7 from a DVD:

You can download a free trial copy of Windows 7 to install for use with this book. It includes a built-in product ID and will work for 90 days without interruption.

1. Insert the Windows 7 DVD into the DVD drive and power on the computer or VM.

2. Select the option to boot from the DVD.

3. On the Install Windows screen, choose the regional settings according to your needs, as shown in Figure 2.4, and click Next.

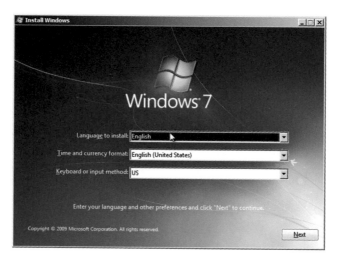

FIGURE 2.4 Windows 7 installation regional settings screen

4. Click Install Now to begin the installation.

5. When the license agreement appears, read it; then select I Accept The License Terms and click Next.

6. On the next screen, choose Custom to perform a clean installation. Note that you can choose Upgrade on this screen to upgrade an existing version of Windows that is acceptable as an upgrade source.

7. On the next screen, you can create a custom disk partition configuration or simply click Next to let the installation engine partition your disk for you automatically. To customize it, choose the option Drive Options (Advanced), as shown in Figure 2.5; otherwise, click Next.

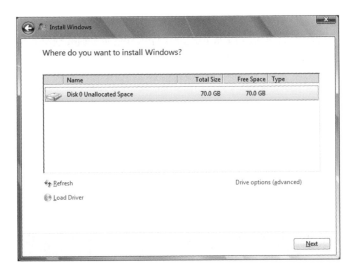

FIGURE 2.5 Windows 7 installation disk partition screen

8. The file copy and extraction process will now begin. This process can take from a few minutes to more than an hour depending on the speed of your computer. When the installation process completes, the machine will reboot automatically.

9. After the reboot, you will be asked to enter a username and computer name. This user will also be an administrator on the local machine, which means the user will be a member of the local Administrators group on the machine. The computer name should be unique on the network for management purposes. After entering the two elements (the username and computer name), click Next.

10. On the next screen, you should enter a password and retype the password for verification. In most business settings, you will leave the hint blank or provide contact information for the support desk in your organization. In home and small business installations, it is not uncommon to enter a hint to assist the user in remembering the password. Enter the password information and click Next.

11. The next screen (Figure 2.6) asks for the settings you desire to use with Windows Update. In a lab environment, you will likely choose Ask Me Later to prevent network congestion from unnecessary updates. In a production environment, you should choose the setting specified by

Chapter 15, "Windows Update," provides more information about Windows Update and the available settings.

your network administrator. Many organizations will configure this setting through Group Policy. Choose the setting you desire, and the wizard will automatically move to the next stage.

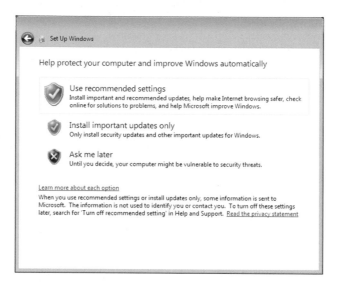

FIGURE 2.6 The Windows Update settings screen

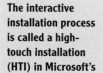

You will learn more about networking features in Windows 7 in Chapter 10, "Network Shares."

12. The next screen provides an interface for selecting the current date and time and choosing your time zone. Select the appropriate settings and click Next.

13. Finally, assuming the installation detected a compatible network adapter, you'll be asked to choose the network type to which you are connected. For now, choose the Work Network.

14. The installation is now complete, and you are taken to the Windows 7 Desktop to begin using the OS.

The interactive installation process is called a high-touch installation (HTI) in Microsoft's documentation.

In addition to the interactive installation process outlined in the preceding set of instructions, you can automate the installation of Windows 7 using answer files. An answer file is an Extensible Markup Language (XML) file that provides answers to the questions asked during installation. Through the use of such a file you can perform two installation types:

Lite Touch Installation (LTI)   LTI requires interaction at the beginning of the installation, but it does not require any more interactions from the installation technician. The primary task is booting the computer and starting the installation. The answer file provides the answers to all remaining questions.

Zero Touch Installation (ZTI)   ZTI requires no interaction at all; however, it requires the purchase and implementation of System Center Configuration Manager (SCCM). SCCM provides the network service for image selection and deployment to machines.

For more information about LTI and ZTI deployments, see "Choosing a Deployment Strategy" at http://technet.microsoft.com/en-us/library/dd919185(WS.10).aspx.

Performing Network-Based Installations

Network-based installations are performed from network shares or special installation servers like the Windows Deployment Services (WDS) server role, which is available on Windows Server 2008 and Windows Server 2008 R2.

When performing the installation from a network share, you must install the Microsoft Deployment Toolkit (MDT) 2010, which is a free download available from Microsoft. MDT includes the software needed to create the shares, import and customize images, and create the automated installation answer files. The Windows System Image Manager (WinSIM) is used to create the answer files. MDT 2010 can run on a Windows client computer or a Windows server. It creates a custom Windows Preinstallation Environment (PE) boot disc that can be used to boot a computer and install the OS from the network.

When using WDS, you will create custom images of the OS and then import them into the WDS server. The clients can either boot from discs or use PXE-compliant network adapters. With a PXE-compliant adapter, no boot disc is needed and the installation can be mostly automated. To fully automate the installation, SCCM will still be required.

Managing Product Identification Keys

Microsoft uses product identification (PI) keys to validate Windows 7 installations and attempt to reduce piracy. Several PI key types exist, including the following:

Multiple Activation Key (MAK)   This key type can be used to activate multiple installations. The activation takes place across the Internet and new installations can be activated until the key pool is exhausted.

Retail Product Key   This key may allow for multiple activations; it is provided with boxed purchases of the OS or through the Microsoft website.

OS virtual memory is a reference to the use of hard drive space for temporary storage of data to allow your system to use more memory than is available in physical RAM.

There's another important consideration related to virtual memory. If the OS virtual machine uses excessive virtual memory stored on the VHD files, just as an operating system running on a physical machine uses virtual memory, it can degrade the disk performance significantly. It is usually even more important to reduce the use of OS virtual memory within VMs than it is in physical machines.

Virtual Networks   VMs can access the network just like physical machines. In fact, VMs appear just like physical machines when you connect to them across the network. Microsoft Hyper-V supports three different virtual network types. The first is the External network, which binds to the physical network adapter card and allows communications on the real network to which the host is connected. The second is the Internal network, which allows communications only between the VMs and the parent partition (host OS) on the host server. The third is the Private network, which allows communications only between the VMs; the parent partition is not accessible.

In addition to these three common network types, you can configure a dedicated network. In this case, you assign a single network adapter to a single guest VM. No other VM can use that adapter. If you have several adapters in the server, this method can be used to improve server performance.

Recoverability   Recoverability can be achieved in simple Hyper-V deployments using snapshots and saved states. A snapshot is a point-in-time capture of a VM. You can create a snapshot and then revert to it later if a new driver or configuration setting causes problems within the VM.

Saved states are different from snapshots. You can shut off a VM and indicate that you want to save its state. This is similar to placing a laptop in the hibernation state. When you power the VM back on at a later time, it will restore the saved state rather than going through the normal boot process.

Using Third-Party Virtualization Software

Several virtualization technologies exist. Microsoft provides virtualization solutions, but other vendors provide solutions as well. These third-party virtualization solutions include the following:

▶ VMware ESX

▶ VMware Workstation, Fusion, and Player

▶ Parallels (Mac-only virtualization software)

▶ VirtualBox

To learn more about the VMware solutions, visit www.vmware.com. To learn more about Parallels for the Mac, visit www.parallels.com. More information about VirtualBox can be found at www.virtualbox.org.

Understanding Windows XP Mode

The final installation task you may be required to perform is the installation of Windows XP Mode. Windows XP Mode is a special installation of Windows Virtual PC and the Windows XP OS as a virtual machine. No license is required for Windows XP to use Windows XP Mode; however, it is supported only on Windows 7 Professional, Enterprise, or Ultimate editions.

Windows XP Mode is used to allow applications that will not run on Windows 7 natively to run in a VM on your Windows 7 computer. When an application runs in Windows XP Mode, you see the application windows on your local Windows 7 Desktop as if it were running locally, but it is actually running in a background Windows XP VM.

While you could run Windows XP Mode on a computer with as little as 1 GB of RAM, I recommend that you have at least 2 GB of RAM to use this feature.

To learn more about Windows XP Mode and take a tour of its offerings, visit www.microsoft.com/windows/virtual-pc/get-started.aspx.

◄

VirtualBox is an excellent open-source virtualization solution. It runs on Windows, Linux, and Mac computers and supports running guest operating systems, including multiple Windows and Linux versions.

THE ESSENTIALS AND BEYOND

In this chapter, you learned about the system requirements for Windows 7 and the various editions available. You learned the difference between clean installations and upgrades and the important questions you should ask when planning each type. You also learned the specific steps required to perform an interactive installation and about the different automated installation techniques available. Finally, you explored virtualization and how it might be used to run Windows 7 or to provide support for older applications on Windows 7 through Windows XP Mode.

ADDITIONAL EXERCISES

▶ Tour the features and capabilities of Windows XP mode for Windows 7.

▶ Perform an installation of Windows 7 on a computer.

▶ Install and configure Windows XP Mode on a Windows 7 computer.

To compare your answers to the author's, please visit www.sybex.com/go/osessentials.

(Continues)

THE ESSENTIALS AND BEYOND *(Continued)*

REVIEW QUESTIONS

1. You currently run Windows 7 Professional edition and you want to upgrade it to the Enterprise edition. What solution should you use?

   A. Windows Edition Overhaul   **C.** Windows Anytime Upgrade

   B. Windows Overtime Upgrade   **D.** Windows Clean Install

2. True or false. Windows 7 Enterprise requires a minimum processor speed of 2 GHz.

3. What utility is used at the Command Prompt to prepare a USB flash drive for use as a bootable device for Windows 7 installations?

   A. FDISK   **C.** Format

   B. Diskpart   **D.** Deltree

4. What Microsoft virtualization solution runs on Windows Server 2008 R2 and could be used to provide virtual desktop interfaces?

5. What solution allows for remote access and control of a desktop and requires licensing?

   A. Remote Desktop   **C.** Remote Desktop Services

   B. Remote Assistance   **D.** VNC

6. Define the term *requirements*.

7. Define a shim.

8. What kind of installation requires interaction to start the installation but the remaining steps are automated?

   A. High Touch   **C.** Zero Touch

   B. Lite Touch   **D.** Out of Touch

9. What application is used to view the ACT 5.6 inventory of software and hardware after it is collected using a data collection package (DCP)?

   A. SUA   **C.** Compatibility Administrator

   B. ACM   **D.** Deployment Workbench

10. True or false. ACT 5.6 comes with a tool that can reveal the cause of application failures on Windows 7.

CHAPTER 3

Managing the Desktop

The Windows Desktop is the primary user interface providing access to applications and operating system utilities. In Windows 7, this interface was enhanced based on significant changes first made in Windows Vista. This chapter introduces the Desktop—its features and the various methods used to interact with it. Topics include:

▶ **Understanding Desktop features**

▶ **Working with gadgets**

▶ **Changing display settings**

▶ **Creating shortcuts**

▶ **Configuring the Aero interface**

Understanding Desktop Features

The Windows Desktop has evolved from the original Program Manager in Windows 3.*x* to the modern Desktop with a Start menu, Desktop icons, shortcuts, and specialized components called *gadgets*. In this section, you will explore the Desktop interface and learn about the various Desktop configuration interfaces available. You will also learn about the information user profiles store that is related to each user's Desktop and Start menu settings.

Exploring the Desktop

The Windows Desktop is actually part of the Explorer application, so it is fitting that we explore this Desktop interface. In the process, you will learn about the features provided by the Explorer Desktop. Figure 3.1 shows the Desktop with each feature or component labeled.

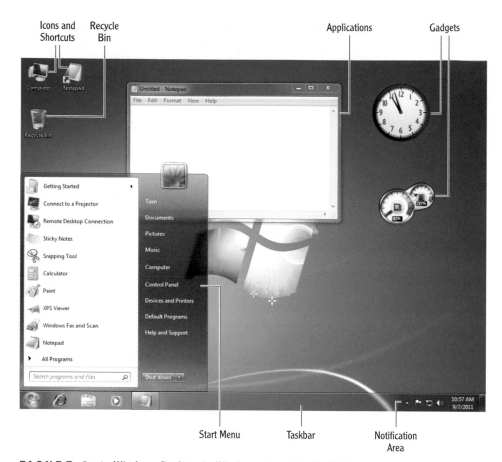

FIGURE 3.1 Windows Desktop in Windows 7 provided by Explorer

Here's a look at each Desktop component:

Start Menu   The Start menu is the primary interface used to launch applications and administrative or configuration utilities. In Figure 3.1, the white area of the Start menu represents recently used applications as well as pinned items that may be placed permanently on the Start menu. The blue area is for specialized links to important areas of the computer system, including Control Panel, Devices and Printers, and special storage areas for user data. The All Programs link is used to access all installed Windows applications through a branching menu structure.

Taskbar   The taskbar is used to both launch applications and manage them once running in the newer versions of Windows. Starting with Windows XP, you had the ability to add icons to what was called the Quick Launch bar located on the taskbar. Today, in Windows 7 you have a built-in capability for pinning applications to the taskbar. In Figure 3.1, Internet Explorer, Windows Explorer (the system file management interface), and Windows Media Player are all pinned to the taskbar. The Notepad icon is displayed on the taskbar because the Notepad application is currently running.

Notification Area   The Notification Area is on the left side of the taskbar when the taskbar is located at the bottom (the default location) or top of the Desktop. When the taskbar is located at the left or right of the Desktop, the Notification Area will be at the bottom of the taskbar. The Notification Area displays system information, such as the time and network connectivity, as well as notifications related to Windows Updates, Windows Firewall, and other security issues. Third-party applications may also add icons to the notification area. For example, it is common for antivirus software to place an icon in the Notification Area so that the user is aware that the software is running and the system is protected.

In earlier versions of Windows, the Notification Area was known as the Task tray.

Icons and Shortcuts   The Windows Desktop can contain both icons and shortcuts. The icons link to system components such as Computer, the Control Panel, or the Recycle Bin. The shortcuts link to applications, folders, or documents the user wishes to access quickly. Many application installation processes will ask your permission to place a shortcut on the Desktop for the application being installed. The shortcuts are noticeably different from system icons because they have a blue arrow in the lower-left corner.

Gadgets   Gadgets were introduced in Windows Vista. At first, the gadgets were linked to a sidebar and could not be placed in any other location on the Desktop. Windows 7 introduced floating gadgets, allowing them to be placed anywhere on the Desktop. The gadgets are still loaded and managed by an application named Sidebar, but the sidebar component that was in Windows Vista is no longer visible in Windows 7. Several gadgets are included with the OS and many more are available online. See the section "Working with Gadgets" later in this chapter to learn more about Windows gadgets.

Recycle Bin   The Windows Recycle Bin is not really part of the Desktop; however, unless you customize the installation process with an answer file, the Recycle Bin is the only icon on the Desktop after installation completes. The Recycle Bin exists on each internal hard drive within a Windows computer. It is a hidden folder into which files are copied when they are deleted. The copy of the files may be restored at a later time. When space is need on the hard drive, the files that have been in the Recycle Bin for the longest time are deleted first to make room for new data. You can empty the Recycle Bin by right-clicking it and selecting Empty Recycle Bin.

The default taskbar settings keep it in view when maximizing applications. The taskbar can be configured to automatically hide so that applications can use the full screen space.

Applications   Standard applications run on the Windows Desktop and may be in one of three states: maximized, minimized, or normal. In the maximized state, the Desktop is completely covered and only the taskbar remains in view. In the minimized state, the application is no longer visible on the Desktop but you can access it quickly by clicking the application's icon on the taskbar. In the normal state, the application window is constrained to a size that does not cover the entire Desktop, as shown with Notepad in Figure 3.1.

Nonstandard applications may consume the entire screen and completely hide the Desktop and taskbar regardless of taskbar settings. An example of such an application is a full-screen game, like Crysis 2 or StarCraft II. Such games are among the most popular Windows applications for the consumer market. These full-screen applications are less common in business settings; however, some multimedia applications, such as e-learning applications, may still consume the entire screen.

Desktop Workspace   The final component of the Desktop, though not directly labeled in Figure 3.1, is the Desktop workspace. This is the area on which you can place icons, shortcuts, and gadgets. It is also the area you can customize using wallpaper or a nondefault Desktop color. You will learn how to customize the Desktop, Start menu, and taskbar in the next section.

Consistent Desktop settings may reduce support costs by allowing Desktop support staff to locate items more easily and use the system during repairs and troubleshooting.

With an understanding of these various components, you are ready to explore the interfaces used to customize them. Remember that it is usually best to have a standard interface in a business setting, but each organization will have to decide for itself what is best for its users and support staff.

Using the Desktop Configuration Interfaces

Configuring a Windows 7 Desktop involves the Start menu, the taskbar, the Notification Area, and the Desktop itself. In this section, you will learn to configure the Start menu, taskbar, and Notification Area. In later sections, you will learn to configure gadgets, display settings, shortcuts, and the Windows Aero interface (which provides the 3D capabilities for the Desktop and the transparent Window effects).

Start Menu Settings

You can access Start menu settings by right-clicking the Start button and selecting Properties. Figure 3.2 shows the Start Menu tab of the Taskbar And Start Menu Properties dialog.

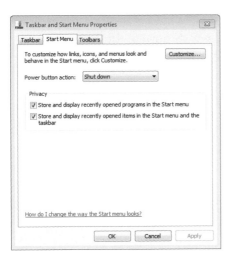

FIGURE 3.2 The Start Menu tab for configuring Start menu settings in Windows 7

The topmost item on the Start Menu tab allows you to customize links, icons, and menus. When you click the Customize button, the Customize Start Menu dialog shown in Figure 3.3 opens. Use this dialog to specify the icons as well as the number of recent programs you want to display on the Start menu. You can also specify the number of recent items you want to display in jump lists. (*Jump lists* are used by the Start menu and taskbar. The Jump Lists setting in the Customize Start Menu dialog applies to the taskbar too.) Recent programs are simply the programs (applications) you've accessed most recently. Recent items are documents you've accessed within those applications. For example, if you use Microsoft Word as a word processor and you've opened seven different documents in the application, those documents will be displayed in a menu when you hover over the Microsoft Word application on the Start menu. This is how recent-item jump lists work.

The next item on the Start Menu tab is the Power Button Action configuration. This setting is configured using a drop-down combo box and can be set to one of the following settings:

- ▶ Switch User
- ▶ Log Off
- ▶ Lock
- ▶ Restart
- ▶ Sleep
- ▶ Shut Down
- ▶ Hibernate

Some systems do not support the Hibernate option. On these systems, the option will simply not be displayed.

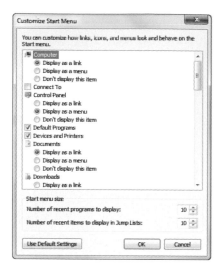

FIGURE 3.3 Using the Customize
Start Menu dialog

If you choose to enable the power button with the Shut Down option, which
is the default, the remaining five items will be available from a *callout* or *expansion*
menu, displayed by clicking the arrow to the right of the power button, as
shown in Figure 3.4.

FIGURE 3.4 Using the expansion menu on
the power button

The final two settings on the Start Menu tab are related to privacy. Some
users do not want their recently opened programs or items (documents) displayed
on the Start menu. By deselecting both check boxes in the Privacy section,
you can turn off this recent history.

Taskbar Settings

In the same Taskbar And Start Menu Properties dialog that is used to configure
the Start menu settings are the taskbar settings. (In fact, you'll also use this

dialog to configure Notification Area settings.) Figure 3.5 shows the Taskbar tab of the dialog. Two sections of the tab are dedicated to the taskbar itself: Taskbar Appearance and Preview Desktop With Aero Peek.

FIGURE 3.5 The Taskbar tab of the Taskbar And Start Menu Properties dialog

In the Taskbar Appearance section, you can configure the following options:

Lock The Taskbar   When taskbar locking is enabled, the taskbar cannot be resized or moved. When it is disabled, the taskbar can be moved to the top, left, right, or bottom of the screen. It can also be resized by moving the mouse to the edge of the taskbar and then clicking and dragging. Resizing the taskbar provides more room for additional icons for pinning and running applications. When the taskbar is locked, it prevents accidental moving or resizing of the taskbar itself. You can also lock or unlock the taskbar by right-clicking it directly and selecting or deselecting the Lock The Taskbar pop-up menu item.

Auto-Hide The Taskbar   When the auto-hide feature is enabled, the taskbar will slide off the screen when it is not in use. You will then move the mouse cursor to the edge of the screen where the taskbar is usually displayed to make it reappear. This feature can be useful if you must run a lower screen resolution for devices like netbook laptop computers.

Use Small Icons   The use of small icons conserves space on the taskbar and also reduces the space it requires on the Desktop. Figure 3.6 shows the difference between using small icons and using standard icons with the option deselected (which is the default).

Small Icons Enabled

Standard Icons Enabled

FIGURE 3.6 Comparing small icons to standard icons on the taskbar

> The taskbar should be located at the bottom of the screen in default business installations. This is because Windows users are most familiar with that location.

Taskbar Location On Screen   In addition to dragging the taskbar to one of the four sides of the screen, you can directly position it using the Taskbar tab. You must unlock the taskbar before you can drag it to a different side of the screen than its current location. However, using the Taskbar tab, you can move it without first unlocking it.

Taskbar Buttons   The taskbar buttons are the buttons displayed on the taskbar when applications run. If the application has a pinned icon on the taskbar, the pinned icon can be the icon for all instances of the application, or a separate icon can be used for each instance of the application. Additionally, the taskbar can be configured to automatically combine icons into a single icon should the taskbar become full. When one icon represents multiple instances of an application, each instance can be displayed by hovering over the icon, as shown in Figure 3.7. The default setting is to always combine icons and hide the text labels that describe the application or folder; it is called Always Combine, Hide Labels in the drop-down combo box. The two alternative settings are called Combine When Taskbar Is Full and Never Combine.

FIGURE 3.7 Displaying multiple application instances with the Always Combine, Hide Labels option enabled

Notification Area Settings

To access the Notification Area settings, you must first access the Taskbar tab of the Taskbar And Start Menu Settings dialog. On this tab, you click the Customize button in the Notification Area section of the tab. Here, you can determine how you will be notified by various system icons (such as Action Center, Network, and Volume) and whether all icons and notifications should be shown. You can also restore icons to their default behaviors, as shown in Figure 3.8.

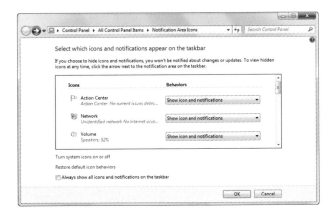

FIGURE 3.8 Configuring Notification Area icon settings

The Start menu, taskbar, and Notification Area settings may also be configured using Group Policy. This approach allows for centralized administration of the Start menu settings. For an explanation of Group Policy, see the sidebar "Group Policy Centralization" later in this chapter. The Group Policy settings for these interfaces are available in the User Configuration ➢ Administrative Templates ➢ Start Menu And Taskbar location of a Group Policy Object (GPO). More than 70 Group Policy settings are available for configuring the Start menu and taskbar. The Group Policy location is shown in Figure 3.9. To access this GPO location, follow these steps:

1. Click Start.

2. Enter gpedit.msc in the search field and press Enter.

3. Expand User Configuration ➢ Administrative Templates ➢ Start Menu And Taskbar. You'll see the settings listed in Figure 3.9.

FIGURE 3.9 The Start Menu And Taskbar location in the Local Computer Policy (local GPO)

GROUP POLICY CENTRALIZATION

When Microsoft introduced Windows 95 in August 1995, they provided a feature called System Policies, which allowed administrators to configure Windows 95 and Windows NT 4.0 computers in various ways from a central server. Eventually, System Policies evolved into what we call Group Policy today.

Group Policy is a solution that allows you to configure, restrict, and enable OS settings, applications, and functionality in Windows clients and servers. The best part about Group Policy is that it can be centralized. You can configure Group Policy Objects (GPOs) on the network that will be downloaded and applied to the computers that participate on the network. To use centralized GPOs, you must have an Active Directory domain, which requires at least one Windows server running Windows 2000 or later. Windows 2000 is no longer supported by Microsoft and organizations should consider using newer versions of Windows Server to implement Group Policy. Group Policy settings can also be applied on the local computer in nondomain environments.

Throughout this book, when appropriate, you will be provided with the location of settings in GPOs that apply to the current topic. This will allow you to configure the settings through the direct management interfaces or through Group Policy, whichever works better for your situation.

Understanding User Profiles and Desktop Relationships

Now that you've explored the features of the Windows Desktop and the configuration interfaces provided for the taskbar and Start menu, you are ready to learn where all the things that you place on the Start menu or the Desktop are actually stored. They are stored in a location called the *user profile*. User profiles contain the Desktop, Start menu, and document folders that are unique to a user. What is displayed on the Windows Desktop and Start menu is a combination of the user's unique profile and the Public profile, which contains universal icons and items that should be available to all users.

Windows 7 includes three specific profile types on the local machine:

Public Profile   The Public profile is the new name for the All Users profile that existed in earlier versions of Windows. When you add shortcuts or files to this profile, they will be available to all user profiles—both newly created profiles and existing profiles. When you install an application and it asks if you would like to install it for all users on the computer or only the current user, it is asking whether you want to place the shortcuts and application settings in the Public profile (applying to all users) or the user profile (applying only to the current user).

Default Profile   The Default profile is the profile you use when initially creating user profiles. If you want all users to start with default settings (but do not necessarily require that they stay at the default settings), you can make the changes to the Default profile. For example, if you add a shortcut to the Desktop folder in the Default profile folder, that shortcut will be on the Desktop for all users when their profiles are initially created; however, they could delete the shortcut to remove it.

User Profiles   The user profiles are specific to a user. When a user logs onto the computer for the first time, the Default profile is copied to a directory for the user and becomes the user's profile. When the user changes settings, such as the color scheme, wallpaper, Desktop icons, and so on, the changes are saved to that user's profile. It is very important to know that documents placed on the Desktop are actually stored in the user profile and should be backed up like any other documents.

In Windows Vista and Windows 7, the user profiles are stored in the Users folder on the root of the system drive, which is typically the C drive. Within the Users folder will be a single folder for each user profile, named after the user, and two additional folders—one for the Public profile and one for the Default profile.

By default, you will be unable to see the Default profile when you access the Users folder. You will see the Public and the user profile folders. To view hidden folders, follow this procedure:

1. Click the Windows Explorer button on the taskbar to open a Windows Explorer instance.

2. Click the Organize button in the upper left and select Folder And Search Options.

3. On the View tab, select the option Show Hidden Files, Folders, Or Drives.

4. Click OK.

After performing these steps, you can navigate to the C:\Users folder and view the Default profile folder as well as the user and Public folders.

You can display the menus that were in older Windows versions of Windows Explorer. Tap the Alt key while in the Windows Explorer window.

Working with Gadgets

Gadgets were first introduced to the Desktop with Windows Vista. Windows 7 provides the additional enhancement of floating gadgets that no longer require attachment to the sidebar. Gadgets provide Desktop-based interfaces for information and application purposes. For example, a gadget can display the weather, and another gadget can be used to search the company intranet. In this section, you are introduced to the processes used to add gadgets to the Desktop, configure gadgets, and install and remove them.

Adding Gadgets to the Desktop

Windows 7 comes with the following gadgets, as shown in Figure 3.10:

► Calendar

► Clock

► CPU Meter

► Currency

► Feed Headlines

► Picture Puzzle

► Slide Show

▶ Weather

▶ Windows Media Center

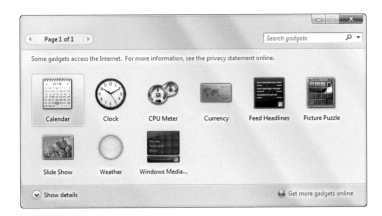

FIGURE 3.10 Adding gadgets from the list of installed gadgets

Adding an installed gadget to the Desktop is a simple process:

1. Right-click an open area of the Desktop and select Gadgets.

2. In the displayed window, shown in Figure 3.10, either double-click the gadget you wish to add or click-and-drag the gadget to the Desktop.

After you have added gadgets to the Desktop, you can position them by dragging them to the location you desire. When you move a gadget to the edge of the screen, it will automatically snap to that edge.

Configuring Gadgets

Most gadgets offer some configurable parameters. You can access the configuration settings in one of two ways. First, you can right-click the gadget and select Options. If the Options menu item is not available, it indicates that the gadget has no configurable parameters. For example, the built-in CPU Meter gadget has no configurable parameters. However, even it can be sized and have universal gadget settings configured, such as whether it is always on top and the opacity (transparency) of the gadget.

The second method used to access the configurable parameters is to move the mouse cursor over the gadget and click the Options button, which looks like a wrench. Figure 3.11 shows the available options for the built-in Clock gadget.

FIGURE 3.11 The options dialog for the Clock gadget

Installing and Removing Gadgets

You can install and remove additional gadgets using the Microsoft Desktop Gadgets website, located at `http://windows.microsoft.com/en-US/windows/downloads/personalize/gadgets`. You can access the site through the Gadget Add and Remove screens built into Windows 7. To install new gadgets, follow this procedure:

1. Right-click an open area of the Desktop and select Gadgets.

2. Click the link in the lower-right corner that reads Get More Gadgets Online.

3. Browse through the gadgets to locate the one you wish to add to your installation of Windows 7.

4. When the desired gadget is located, click the Download button.

5. If necessary, click Install to start the installation.

6. In the Windows Internet Explorer pop-up windows, click Open.

7. If the Desktop Gadgets—Security Warning dialog is displayed, read it and then click Install if you still wish to install the gadget.

▶

Some gadgets are submitted without verification, and you may be prompted to verify that you wish to install the gadget in such cases.

After you've done this, you will see the newly installed gadget in the Gadget Add And Remove screen, but you must still add it to the Desktop using the instructions in the preceding section.

If you later decide to remove the gadget, or any other gadget, you can do so using these steps:

1. Right-click an open area of the Desktop and select Gadgets.

2. Right-click the gadget you wish to remove and select Uninstall.

3. In the notification dialog, click Uninstall to complete the removal.

Changing Display Settings

The ability to change display settings is important for the users of any operating system. For those who desire more screen space, a higher resolution is needed. For those who desire larger icons and fonts, either a lower resolution or screen magnification is required. In addition, modern systems often support multiple display devices. In this section, you will learn how to configure the screen resolution, screen magnification, and support for multiple display devices.

Configuring the Screen Resolution

Screen *resolution* refers to the number of pixels used to display information on the screen. Higher resolutions use more pixels and lower resolutions use fewer pixels. In most cases, screen resolutions are represented by the number of pixels wide by the number of pixels tall. For example, 1024×768 indicates 1024 pixels wide by 768 pixels tall.

Users may need to change the screen resolution for several reasons:

► An application requires a higher resolution than the current setting.

► An application requires a lower resolution than the current setting.

► The current user is unable to view the fonts and screen information well at the current resolution.

► The computer has been connected to a device that works best at higher or lower resolutions.

► A new video card has been installed, and new resolutions are not supported.

Whatever the reason, changing the screen resolution is a simple task in Windows 7. To change the resolution, follow these steps:

1. Right-click the Desktop and select Screen Resolution.

2. In the Screen Resolution dialog, shown in Figure 3.12, change the Resolution drop-down box to the desired setting.

3. Click Apply.

4. If you like the resulting change, click Keep Changes in the pop-up; if not, click Revert.

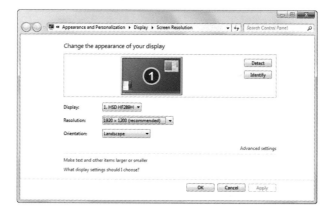

FIGURE 3.12 Adjusting the screen resolution

Configuring Screen Magnification

Sometimes you want to change the size of text and other items on the screen. To do so, you can use screen magnification, which can be set to the default of Smaller (100%) or Medium (125%) or Larger (150%). To change the screen magnification setting:

> In addition to configuring screen magnification, you can use the Magnifier tool to zoom into extreme levels.
>
> ▶

1. Right-click the Desktop and select Personalize.

2. Click the Display link in the lower-left corner of the Personalization dialog.

3. Choose the magnification setting you prefer.

Using Multiple Display Devices

Windows 7 supports using multiple display devices concurrently. You can connect a laptop to a projector and still use the internal screen. You can connect a Desktop computer to several displays at the same time. When multiple display devices are detected and connected, the Screen Resolution dialog will show the different displays, and you can configure each one with a different resolution, if you want.

You can also configure your multiple display settings easily by pressing the Windows key+P to bring up the Presentation Settings dialog. Figure 3.13 shows the Presentation Settings dialog used to configure the output for various displays.

FIGURE 3.13 Using the Windows key+P shortcut dialog

Creating Shortcuts

Shortcuts have existed in Windows since its very early versions. A shortcut points to an executable file, a document, or a folder. As the name implies, shortcuts are used to provide a faster way to access these items. Without shortcuts, you would have to browse through all the files on the hard drive each time to locate the one file desired. In this section, you learn to create shortcuts, modify shortcut settings, and add system icons to the Desktop.

Creating a New Desktop Shortcut

Creating a shortcut requires several pieces of information depending on its purpose, but two parameters are required for all shortcuts:

- ► The location of the item for which you would like to create a shortcut. This would be the folder and filename for the shortcut. For example, it could be C:\Program Files\TheApplication\Application.exe.

- ► The name you wish to give the shortcut. This name is simply any textual information you want to use to define the shortcut, such as My Application.

Optional parameters include:

▶ The shortcut key to use for shortcut launching, such as Ctrl+Shift+G, or some other keystroke combination

▶ The state of the window, such as normal, minimized, or maximized

▶ A comment to describe the shortcut

▶ A custom icon for the shortcut

▶ Permissions for the shortcut

SHORTCUT PERMISSIONS

You can create a shortcut that is available for display to all users but that can be used only by assigned users. NTFS permissions allow for this. The benefit is that you can create a shortcut in a folder other than the Desktop that provides easy access to resources for administrators; however, if a user happens to see it, he will not be able to use it to access the same resources.

To create a shortcut on the Desktop, follow these steps:

1. Right-click an open area of the Desktop and select New ➢ Shortcut.

2. In answer to the prompt "What Item Would You Like To Create A Shortcut For?" enter the location or browse for it with the Browse button and then click Next.

3. In answer to the prompt "What Would You Like To Name The Shortcut?" enter the desired shortcut name. This name will be displayed below the icon for the shortcut.

4. Click Finish to create the shortcut.

In addition to standard shortcuts, you can create special shortcuts to folders that reference globally unique identifiers (GUIDs), which are internal to the Windows 7 system. For example, you can create a folder that points to a listing of all Control Panel functions and then create a shortcut to that folder. To do this, follow this procedure:

1. Open Windows Explorer.

2. Navigate to the C drive.

3. Right-click the root of the C drive and select New ➢ Folder.

4. Enter the following folder name: **Super List.**
{ED7BA470-8E54-465E-825C-99712043E01C}

5. Press Enter to create the folder.

The period and GUID after Super List are the most important elements. You can replace the Super List text with any other name you desire in this example.

Once you perform this procedure, you will see a new folder with a special icon. Double-click the folder and you will see a listing of all Control Panel functions organized by functional categories. You can create a shortcut to this newly created folder and place the shortcut on your Desktop or your Start menu for quick and easy access.

In addition to creating Desktop shortcuts, you can create Start menu shortcuts. To create a shortcut on the Start menu, follow the same procedure used to create a Desktop shortcut, but first click Start and then right-click All Programs and select Open All Users. In the resulting Windows Explorer windows, create the shortcut you desire or browse to the specific Start menu folder and then create the shortcut.

WHAT IS THE START MENU, REALLY?

The Start menu has existed in Windows since the release of Windows 95 in August 1995. Since that time, little has changed in the basic structure of the Start menu. It is really nothing more than a collection of folders on the hard drive with shortcuts in them.

If you want a new folder on the Start menu, you simply create it in the `Start Menu\Programs` folder on the hard drive. In Windows 7, the full default path to the Start menu for all users is `C:\ProgramData\Microsoft\Windows\Start Menu`. The Start menu for a specific user is in that user's profile directory. The path is now different than in previous versions of Windows as it is buried deeply in the following path: `C:\Users\`*UserName*`\AppData\Roaming\Microsoft\Windows\Start Menu`, where *UserName* is the actual user profile name you wish to modify.

In the end, the Start menu always has been and still is a collection of folders and shortcuts displayed as a menu structure for easy access.

Modifying a Shortcut

After a shortcut is created, you can modify it by right-clicking it and selecting Properties. In the window that appears, you can change the optional settings listed in the preceding section. For example, you may wish to customize the icon so that it stands out when compared to other shortcuts in the same location. When you click the Change Icon button on the Shortcut tab, only those icons embedded in the shortcut target will be displayed. However, you can browse and select other executable files (EXEs) or dynamic link libraries (DLLs) that may contain icons. For example, if you browse to C:\Windows\Shell32.dll, it contains dozens of icons you can use for your shortcuts.

Another important action you can perform when modifying shortcuts is assigning administrator requirements to the shortcut. If an application requires administrator permissions to run, click the Advanced button on the Shortcut tab and select Run As Administrator.

Adding System Icons to the Desktop

The final type of shortcut that you can add to the Desktop is the system icon. A system icon is not a traditional shortcut and is easily identified because it does not have the blue arrow in the lower-left corner by default. System icons include the following:

> ▶ Computer

> ▶ User's Files

> ▶ Network

> ▶ Recycle Bin

> ▶ Control Panel

The blue arrow can be removed and it cannot be the sole identifier of shortcuts. Right-click and select Properties to see if an icon is a shortcut.

To add a system icon to the Desktop:

1. Right-click an open area of the Desktop and select Properties.

2. Click the Change Desktop Icons link in the left panel.

3. Select the icons you want displayed on the Desktop and click OK.

After adding the icons to the Desktop, you can quickly access them to browse files, manage the Recycle Bin, or access Control Panel. You can also use them as quick methods to access administrative interfaces. For example, you can right-click the Computer icon on the Desktop and select Properties to view the Control Panel System page.

Configuring the Aero Interface

The Aero interface was first introduced in Windows Vista. While the traditional Start menu and Desktop from Windows XP and earlier are still included in the systems using the Aero interface, this new interface allows for many enhanced features. In this section, you will learn about the features, themes, and settings of the Aero interface that allow you to get the most out of Windows Vista or Windows 7 and to best configure it for business users.

Understanding the Aero Features

The Aero interface introduces several useful features for window management in Windows 7. These features include:

Aero Snap   Aero Snap allows you to quickly place application windows. If you click the title bar of a window and drag to the edge of the screen, Windows 7 will display an outline showing where the window will be placed. Additionally, you can cause a normal state window to fill the full height of the screen without changing the window width. To do this, simply move your mouse cursor to the top edge of the window, then click and drag to the top of the screen and release.

Aero Shake   If you have several windows open, you can click the title bar of one window and then jiggle the mouse back and forth to minimize all other windows. Perform the action again, and the other windows return to their previous states.

Aero Peek   Aero Peek allows you to make all windows temporarily transparent so that you can see the Desktop. This is accomplished in one of two ways. You can hover over the Desktop button at the far end of the taskbar, or you can press the Windows key+spacebar.

Translucent Windows Glass   Inherent to the Aero themes is the use of translucent (or partially transparent) window frames. This allows you to see through the title bars to the application windows and objects behind them. It is also the feature that allows Aero Peek to function.

Flip 3D   The Flip 3D feature allows you to switch between windows with a large 3D image of the active windows in view. The windows display animations even during flipping. For example, a video application will continue to play the video while in Flip 3D mode. To use Flip 3D, use the Windows key+Tab shortcut.

◀

To use Aero Snap and all other Aero features, you must have an Aero-capable computer and use an Aero theme.

Taskbar Previews   The icons on the Windows 7 taskbar provide large thumbnail previews of running applications. When you hover over the icons, the thumbnails for all running instances display in a pop-up window. You can also hover over the thumbnails to bring the actual application window temporarily into view.

Improved Task Switcher   Also known simply as Windows Flip, the task switcher includes large thumbnails of the active applications and provides active content like Flip 3D. The traditional Alt+Tab shortcut is used to access Windows Flip.

To use the Aero features, your system must meet the hardware requirements, which are as follows:

▶ 64 MB of graphics memory for up to 1280×1024 resolutions (technically, a resolution with fewer than 1,310,720 pixels)

▶ 128 MB of graphics memory for more than 1280×1024 resolutions and up to 1600×1200 resolutions (technically, a resolution with between 1,310,720 and 2,304,000 pixels)

▶ 256 MB of graphics memory for more than 1600×1200 resolutions (technically, a resolution with greater than 2,304,000 pixels)

In addition to these requirements, you must use an Aero theme and you must have the Aero settings enabled that allow the features to work. The next two sections explain both topics.

Using Aero Themes

Aero themes are Windows 7 themes that include support for Aero features, such as translucency. Two primary theme types are available in Windows 7: Aero themes and basic themes. Basic themes do not provide the Aero features, and Aero themes do. If you are working with a Windows 7 computer and it does not support Aero features like Flip 3D, Snap, and Shake, check to ensure that an Aero theme is in use.

Aero themes may be displayed in one of two locations in the Personalization dialog. First, the system Aero themes will show up in the Aero Themes section. Aero themes may also be displayed in the My Themes section. The simplest way to determine if a theme is an Aero theme or a basic theme is to apply it and then check for the existence of Aero features. For example, you could quickly press Windows key+Tab and check for the Flip 3D functionality. If the functionality was there before but is missing after applying a theme, that means it is a basic theme.

To select a theme, follow these steps:

1. Right-click an open area of the Desktop and select Personalize.

2. Choose a theme from the list by clicking the desired theme.

3. Close the Personalization dialog using the close button (the X) in the upper-right corner.

You will then see a transformation of the Windows interface. New colors may be used for the application windows, and the Desktop wallpaper is likely to change as well. Microsoft provides dozens of additional themes at their website.

Configuring Aero Settings

Several settings impact the functionality of the Windows Aero interface. First, you can determine whether window transparency will be supported using these steps:

1. Right-click an open area of the Desktop and select Personalize.

2. Click the Window Color button at the bottom of the Personalization dialog.

3. Select or deselect Enable Transparency according to your needs.

You can also enable or disable dozens of features related to performance and the Windows Desktop. Using the Performance Options dialog shown in Figure 3.14 you can enable or disable transparency, but you can also control many other Aero visual effects that impact performance. To access the Performance Options dialog, follow this procedure:

1. Click Start and then right-click Computer and select Properties.

2. Click the Advanced System Settings option in the left panel of the System dialog.

3. On the Advanced tab of the System Properties dialog, click the Settings button in the Performance section.

4. Choose the Visual Effects tab.

For more information on how you can improve your system's performance by adjusting Aero settings and other system settings, see the following article at Microsoft's website: http://windows.microsoft.com/en-US/windows7/ Ways-to-improve-your-computers-performance.

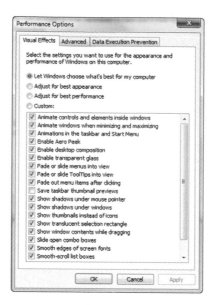

FIGURE 3.14 Configuring performance settings

In addition to manually enabling or disabling each feature, you can select to do one of the following:

► Let Windows Choose What's Best For My Computer

► Adjust For Best Appearance

► Adjust For Best Performance

The default setting is to let Windows choose what's best for the computer. The chosen features will depend on the performance of your machine. If you choose to adjust for best appearance, all features will be enabled. If you choose to adjust for best performance, all features will be disabled. When you select custom, you can pick just the features you desire.

THE ESSENTIALS AND BEYOND

In this chapter, you learned how to manage the Windows Desktop. You began by learning about the basic features of the Desktop and how to configure the Start menu, taskbar, and Notification Area. Then you explored the use, installation, and removal of gadgets. Next you learned to create shortcuts and place system icons on the Desktop. Finally, you saw how to work with the Windows Aero features and themes.

(Continues)

THE ESSENTIALS AND BEYOND (Continued)

ADDITIONAL EXERCISES

▶ Configure Control Panel, on the Start menu, so that it displays as a menu.

▶ Create a shortcut on the Desktop to the Notepad application.

▶ Adjust the Aero performance settings so that you achieve the best performance.

To compare your answers to the author's, please visit www.sybex.com/go/osessentials.

REVIEW QUESTIONS

1. You want to use a resolution of 1920×1200. What minimum amount of graphics memory will be required to allow Aero features to function at this resolution?

    A. 32 MB   **C.** 128 MB

    B. 64 MB   **D.** 256 MB

2. True or false. The Aero Peek functionality allows you to see the Command Prompt automatically without closing other windows.

3. Which profile contains settings for all users and applies changes to existing users as well as new users?

    A. Performance   **C.** Default

    B. User Profile   **D.** Public

4. What Windows 7 feature is used to show recently launched programs and recently opened documents?

5. What item exists on the Windows Desktop by default and is used to recover previously deleted files and folders?

    A. Recovery Basket   **C.** Recycle Basket

    B. Recovery Bin   **D.** Recycle Bin

6. Define a Desktop shortcut.

7. Define a gadget.

8. In what directory or folder is the user's Start menu located by default?

    A. `C:\Users\UserName\Start Menu`

    B. `C:\Users\UserName\AppData\Roaming\Microsoft\Windows\Start Menu`

    C. `C:\ProgramData\Microsoft\Windows\Start Menu`

    D. It is not in a folder, but it is in the system Registry.

(Continues)

THE ESSENTIALS AND BEYOND *(Continued)*

9. What kind of theme will provide the best performance?

   A. Basic

   B. Aero

10. True or false. Optimizing Windows Aero for best appearance enables all visual effects features.

CHAPTER 4

Using Native Applications

As you work with Windows operating systems over the years, you will notice that some applications continue on from version to version whereas others seem to fall out of use. In this chapter, you will learn about the native applications within the Windows OS. The most popular applications from the traditional text and image editors to the tools that allow you to view system configuration settings will be reviewed in this chapter. The following topics are addressed:

▶ **Using the traditional tools**

▶ **Working with Internet Explorer**

▶ **Creating screenshots**

▶ **Using media applications**

▶ **Viewing configuration settings**

Using the Traditional Tools

Many tools have existed in Windows since the earliest versions, and several still exist in Windows 7 today that were in Windows 3.1 in the early 1990s. Among these are text editors, image editors, and the Calculator. In this section, you will review these tools and the features they offer.

Editing Text

When it comes to text editors, Windows 7 offers two primary tools. For editing simple text files, the Notepad application is provided. For editing more complex documents, Windows 7 provides the WordPad application (formerly known as Write in Windows 3.1). Administrators can use these text editors to modify configuration files on servers and clients. Of course, they can also use them for the same purposes that end users do: to edit text documents.

The most frequently used text editor in Windows is Notepad. Notepad has existed in Windows for several versions and is a simple tool used to create and edit text files, such as batch files, script files, and standard text documents. Text files are documents that contain only text. No graphics are supported, and no special formatting is used for words or characters. The Notepad application, shown in Figure 4.1, includes the following features:

The encoding format defines how the textual characters are stored in the file.

▶ Support for editing text documents in four encoding formats: ANSI, Unicode, Unicode Big-Endian, and UTF-8. See the following Microsoft TechNet article (which though written for Windows XP still applies to Notepad in Windows 7) to learn more about these formats: www.microsoft.com/resources/documentation/windows/xp/all/proddocs/en-us/win_notepad_whatis_intro.mspx?mfr=true

▶ Support for custom page margins when printing

▶ Support for headers and footers

▶ Full copy-and-paste capabilities

▶ Search functions and find/replace capabilities

▶ Automatic insertion of the current time and date with the F5 shortcut key

▶ Word Wrap for easy viewing of text data with long lines stored in the file

▶ The use of custom font types and sizes for display purposes

When you configure a custom font, it is not retained in the text file. It is simply used for the display of all text files.

▶ Optional display of a status bar that shows the current line number and column number

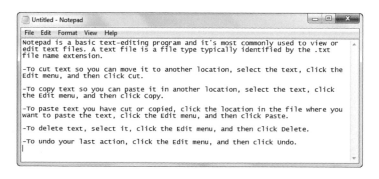

FIGURE 4.1 The Notepad application

When using text editors like Notepad, it is important to understand how they encode information. If you understand that, you will be better equipped to deal with scenarios where a text file does not appear in Notepad (or another text editor) as you expect. Particularly, different editors and operating systems encode the Enter key in various ways. When you are typing a text document in the editor and press the Enter key, you will see a movement to the next line in the file; however, behind the scenes the actual Enter key keystroke may be encoded differently. The follow hexadecimal (hex) values are used by the named operating systems:

► Windows: 0d 0a

► Linux and Mac OS X: 0a

► Mac OS 9 and earlier: 0d

It is important to understand this difference between the operating systems in how you use the Enter key. When a text file is created on Linux or Mac OS X, it is common for the text file to lose all line breaks when you open it in Notepad on Windows. This is because the file contains only a 0a for the line break and Windows is expecting a 0d 0a character set. You can use a quick trick, in most cases, to solve this problem:

1. Select all the text in Notepad and cut and paste it into WordPad.

2. Select all the text in WordPad and cut and paste it into Notepad.

3. Note that the line breaks have been restored.

Because WordPad is a more advanced text editor with formatting capabilities, it treats the line feed as a line break. When you copy and paste back into Notepad, the text is regenerated with the 0d 0a (carriage return and line feed combination).

When you know that hex numbers use a base-16 system, you can convert between hex and decimal. You can also use the Windows Calculator to perform the conversion. For example, 0d is equal to 13 in decimal and 0a is equal to 10 in decimal. Because text editors are really creating American Standard Code for Information Interchange (ASCII) text, you can use the ASCII table to discover that decimal 13 is equal to a carriage return and decimal 10 is equal to a line feed. Table 4.1 shows the standard ASCII codes.

TABLE 4.1 Standard ASCII codes

Decimal	Hex	Character	Decimal	Hex	Character
0	00	NUL	64	40	@
1	01	SOH	65	41	A

(Continues)

TABLE 4.1 *(Continued)*

Decimal	Hex	Character	Decimal	Hex	Character
2	02	STX	66	42	B
3	03	ETX	67	43	C
4	04	EOT	68	44	D
5	05	ENQ	69	45	E
6	06	ACK	70	46	F
7	07	BEL	71	47	G
8	08	Backspace	72	48	H
9	09	HTAB	73	49	I
10	0a	Line feed	74	4a	J
11	0b	VTAB	75	4b	K
12	0c	Form feed	76	4c	L
13	0d	Carriage return	77	4d	M
14	0e	SO	78	4e	N
15	0f	SI	79	4f	O
16	10	DLE	80	50	P
17	11	DC1	81	51	Q
18	12	DC2	82	52	R
19	13	DC3	83	53	S
20	14	DC4	84	54	T
21	15	NAK	85	55	U
22	16	SYN	86	56	V
23	17	ETB	87	57	W

Decimal	Hex	Character	Decimal	Hex	Character
24	18	Cancel	88	58	X
25	19	EM	89	59	Y
26	1a	SUB	90	5a	Z
27	1b	Escape	91	5b	[
28	1c	FS	92	5c	\
29	1d	GS	93	5d	]
30	1e	RS	94	5e	^
31	1f	US	95	5f	_
32	20	Space	96	60	`
33	21	!	97	61	a
34	22	"	98	62	b
35	23	#	99	63	c
36	24	$	100	64	d
37	25	%	101	65	e
38	26	&	102	66	f
39	27	'	103	67	g
40	28	(	104	68	h
41	29	)	105	69	i
42	2a	*	106	6a	j
43	2b	+	107	6b	k
44	2c	,	108	6c	l
45	2d	-	109	6d	m
46	2e	.	110	6e	n

(Continues)

TABLE 4.1 *(Continued)*

Decimal	Hex	Character	Decimal	Hex	Character
47	2f	/	111	6f	o
48	30	0	112	70	p
49	31	1	113	71	q
50	32	2	114	72	r
51	33	3	115	73	s
52	34	4	116	74	t
53	35	5	117	75	u
54	36	6	118	76	v
55	37	7	119	77	w
56	38	8	120	78	x
57	39	9	121	79	y
58	3a	:	122	7a	z
59	3b	;	123	7b	{
60	3c	<	124	7c		
61	3d	=	125	7d	}
62	3e	>	126	7e	~
63	3f	?	127	7f	Delete

The hacking community has used the extended ASCII codes for decades to draw logos and other graphics in text files.

The standard ASCII codes cover alphabetic letters (a–z) in both lowercase and uppercase, numerals (0–9), and special characters, including punctuation. The extended ASCII codes (those above decimal 127 and not shown in Table 4.1) include accented characters and special graphical elements used for diagramming purposes. When you look at the data in a text file using a hex editor instead of a text editor, you can see the actual hex codes used to store the ASCII data.

Figure 4.2 shows a text file in Notepad++ (a popular free Notepad alternative), and Figure 4.3 shows the same text file viewed as hex codes. Notice the highlighted codes for the line breaks; they appear because the file was created in Windows, which inserts the 0a 0d codes to represent the Enter keystroke.

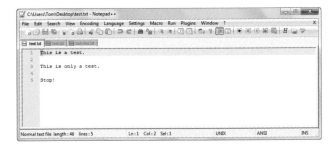

FIGURE 4.2 A text file in Notepad++

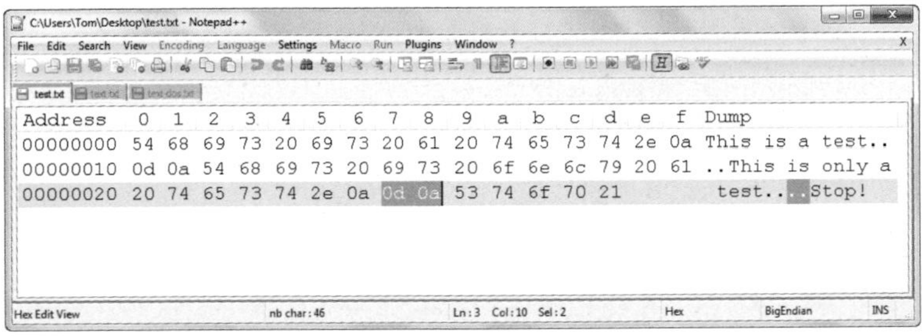

FIGURE 4.3 The same text file shown in hex view

WordPad, as previously mentioned, is a more advanced text editor. It supports enhanced formatting capabilities and can save the formatting information with the text data. WordPad, shown in Figure 4.4, allows you to save documents in the following formats:

- ▶ Rich Text Format (RTF)
- ▶ OpenDocument
- ▶ Open Office XML Document
- ▶ Text Document
- ▶ Text Document—MS-DOS Format
- ▶ Unicode Text

Unicode ASCII text is stored with two bytes of information for each character. One byte defines the character and the other byte is null or set to zeros.

The differences between the Text Document and Text Document—MS-DOS Format are minimal, but the latter format is more compatible with the Edit.com application in MS-DOS. Edit.com is no longer included in 64-bit editions of Windows, because it was developed only as a 16-bit application.

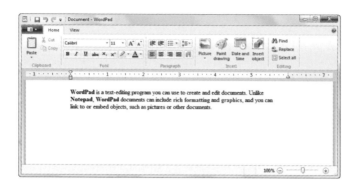

F I G U R E 4 . 4 WordPad as a text editor

WordPad provides the same features as Notepad and adds many more, including the ability to:

► Encode the text with varied fonts within the same file

► Save font style information, such as boldface, colors, and other formats

► Insert images and other objects

► Display an enhanced status bar with a built-in zoom control

► Send a document as an email directly from the application

Windows 7 introduces an additional text editing and note taking feature called Sticky Notes. This application lets you place multiple note windows on the Desktop. You can configure each note window to appear with one of six note colors: blue, green, pink, purple, white, or yellow. You can stack the notes on top of one another as well. To access the Sticky Notes application, click Start ➤ All Programs ➤ Accessories ➤ Sticky Notes.

Working with Images

Early versions of Windows provided a single application for image editing and management: Microsoft Paint. Today, Windows provides two primary applications out of the box. Microsoft Paint is still provided for creating and editing images. Also provided is Windows Photo Viewer, which is used only for image file viewing and management.

Paint is the traditional image viewing and editing application in Windows. The version of Paint that comes with Windows 7 has the following features:

- ▶ Uses the new Office ribbon bar interface
- ▶ Supports the JPEG, BMP, TIFF, GIF, and PNG file formats
- ▶ Allows image import directly from a scanner or camera
- ▶ Supports direct emailing from within the application
- ▶ Supports traditional drawing tools with a full color palette

The Windows Photo Viewer is not intended as an editor and lacks the drawing and editing functions of Paint. However, it is a useful tool for viewing images in various formats and supports the following features:

- ▶ Support for the BMP, JPEG, ICO, PNG, and TIFF formats
- ▶ The ability to send a file as an email from within the application
- ▶ Built-in zooming and image rotation functions
- ▶ The ability to print images or burn them to CD or DVD
- ▶ The ability to open images in other applications such as Paint or a third-party application (for example, the GIMP editor, an open-source image editor)

Performing Calculations

The Calculator application has been in Windows for several versions, but it has been updated in Windows 7 to include new features that many users will appreciate. The primary new features include:

- ▶ A new programmer mode that allows for easy conversion among formats, including decimal, octal, hexadecimal and binary
- ▶ Worksheets for common personal calculations

Figure 4.5 shows the new worksheet interface for calculating a mortgage payment. Additional worksheets include vehicle lease calculations and fuel economy calculations.

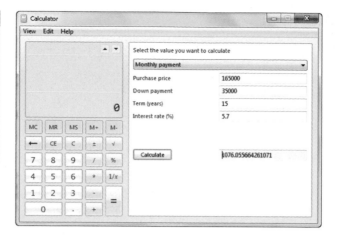

You can also turn on Digit Grouping on the View menu so that large numbers are displayed with commas and hex numbers are displayed with spaces.

FIGURE 4.5 The new worksheet views in the Calculator

Working with Internet Explorer

Internet Explorer was first introduced as an add-on to Windows 3.1 in the 1990s and was included with Windows 95 out of the box. Since that time, it has been the default web browser in the Windows OS. In this section, you will learn about the Internet Explorer interface and the Tools menu. As a Windows OS administrator, you must assist your users in utilizing tools like web browsers. This section will provide you with a basic overview of the web browser that ships with Windows 7 and the new features it provides.

Exploring the Browser Interface

Internet Explorer 9 was released after Windows 7 and is available as a free download. This book focuses on the included version 8 browser.

Internet Explorer 8 now ships with Windows 7. The Internet Explorer 8 browser introduces a vastly different interface from that of Internet Explorer 7 and earlier. The default browser interface is shown in Figure 4.6.

Internet Explorer 8.0 introduces several new features, among them:

Accelerators   Internet Explorer 8.0 and later accelerators allow you to perform common actions without navigating away from the current page. For example, you can highlight an address in a web page and then use an accelerator to automatically generate a map of the location. Four accelerators come with Internet Explorer 8.0, and more are available from the Internet Explorer gallery at www .iegallery.com.

FIGURE 4.6 The Internet Explorer 8.0 interface

Search Suggestions   The Internet Explorer 8.0 interface provides a search box in the upper-right corner of the browser. This search field can provide search suggestions from multiple search providers, such as Google or Bing. You can add more search providers as you desire.

SmartScreen Filter   The SmartScreen Filter is an engine that screens out potentially bad websites that may be used to perform social engineering attacks or malware infection attacks. SmartScreen Filter can work in two ways: entire site blockage or surgical blockage. When an entire site is blocked, no content from the specified location (for example, `www.someblockedsite12345.net`) can be loaded. When a surgical blockage is implemented, specific content at known valid sites may be blocked. Users can report potentially unsafe websites, and they can check a website as well.

InPrivate Browsing   When you want to browse a website and leave no record of your visit to that site on the local computer, you can use InPrivate Browsing. InPrivate Browsing may be used to access websites containing sensitive information, such as banking websites for the average user and special internal administrative websites for the support staff. You can enter InPrivate Browsing mode using the Safety ➢ InPrivate Browsing menu option or by pressing Ctrl+Shift+P.

In the new Internet Explorer 9.0 interface, the Search field is gone because you can simply type searches in the address field.

Social engineering attacks use human manipulation techniques to gain information from users or get users to perform desired actions.

Using the Tools Menu

The Tools menu is used to access the primary configuration interfaces in Internet Explorer. Figure 4.7 shows the contents of the Tools menu. From this menu, you can configure several items, including these:

A Domain Name System (DNS) server is used to resolve DNS hostnames, like www.sysedco.com, to IP addresses, like 67.35.12.18.

Diagnose Connection Problems   If you cannot connect to a web page, you can use this function to locate the cause of the problem. For example, Diagnose Connection Problems may determine that Internet connectivity is not available or that contact with the DNS server cannot be made.

Reopen Last Browsing Session   Use this option to open the browser windows that existed in the previous session. It can be useful in a scenario when the browser has crashed.

Pop-up Blocker   The Pop-up Blocker is used to prevent the loading of secondary browser windows. Such windows are often used to attempt the installation of malware. You can configure the browser to block pop-up windows and allow for exceptions on specified websites.

Manage Add-ons   Add-ons include search providers, toolbars and extensions, accelerators, and InPrivate Browsing configurations. The Manage Add-ons option allows you to add, remove, and configure these add-ons.

Work Offline   When working in offline mode, you can view cached website information, but you cannot navigate to online websites.

Compatibility View   Compatibility View is used to display websites as they would be displayed in an earlier version of Internet Explorer. This feature may allow for access to some web pages that would otherwise be inaccessible.

Full Screen   Use this menu option to toggle between full screen and windowed mode. It is important to remember the F11 shortcut key, which is used to return to windowed mode after switching to full-screen mode.

Toolbars   Use this menu option to select the toolbars you want to display. The toolbars include both the built-in toolbars and those that are installed as add-ons.

Explorer Bars   Three Explorer bars exist: Favorites, History, and Feeds. You can decide which, if any, of these bars you wish to display.

Developer Tools   The Developer Tools option provides an enhanced interface for viewing HTML and Cascading Style Sheets (CSS) code in web pages. It even includes a profiler that can organize and present all script functions used on a web page.

Suggested Sites The Suggested Sites feature allows Internet Explorer to track the sites you visit and then recommend similar sites that may be of interest to you.

Internet Options The Internet Options item provides access to a dialog where you can configure General, Security, Privacy, Content, Connections, Programs, and Advanced settings for the browser. If you cannot find the setting you want to change elsewhere, you'll probably find it here.

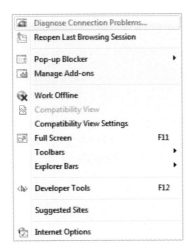

FIGURE 4.7 The Internet Explorer Tools menu options

Most of these Internet Explorer settings can also be configured through Group Policy. To locate the settings in a GPO, navigate to Administrative Templates ➢ Windows Components ➢ Internet Explorer.

Creating Screenshots

Taking screenshots is a common task for Windows users, and the Windows OS has always supported capturing the entire screen with keyboard shortcuts. It has also supported capturing the foreground window using keyboard shortcuts. However, Windows 7 finally introduces a screen capture utility with more flexibility, called the Snipping Tool. Both the keyboard shortcuts and Snipping Tool screen capturing methods are covered in this section. As an administrator, you can use these tools to capture screens for documentation of error messages or to provide step-by-step instructions for users to perform their tasks.

The phrases *screen capture* and *screenshot* are often used interchangeably. A screenshot is technically an image file, the result of a screen capture process.

Using the Print Screen Button

The simplest method used to create screenshots in any version of Windows is to use the Print Screen button (usually labeled as Prt Sc or Prt Scn on modern keyboards). To capture the entire screen:

1. Arrange the Desktop and open application windows as you desire them to appear in the screenshot.

2. Press the Print Screen key.

3. Open Paint or another image creation application or word processing application and press Ctrl+C to paste the image into the application.

As you can probably guess from the third step of this procedure, the Print Screen key actually copies the screen to the Clipboard. In addition to capturing the entire screen, you can capture only the foreground application windows using the following procedure:

1. Arrange the Desktop and open application windows as you desire them to appear in the screenshot.

2. Press the Alt+Print Screen keystroke combination.

3. Open Paint or another image creation application or word processing application and press Ctrl+C to paste the image into the application.

Working with the Snipping Tool

Windows 7 introduces a new screen capture application called the Snipping Tool. It is available in the Accessories group on the Start menu and is shown in Figure 4.8.

FIGURE 4.8 The Snipping Tool used to create screenshots

The Snipping Tool provides the following features:

▶ The user can capture the full screen, a window, a rectangular section, or a freeform section of the screen.

▶ Once a screen is captured, tools can be used to highlight it or mark it up.

▶ Images can be saved as PNG, JPEG, or BMP files.

▶ Images can also be saved in the single file HTML format (MHT).

▶ The capture can be emailed to someone.

Even with these enhanced features, many professional writers and technical document developers prefer third-party screen capture tools. These tools, such as TechSmith's Snagit, often provide much more powerful annotation tools, support more file formats, and provide extensive file management capabilities.

Using Media Applications

Computer video is an important application in modern business computing. Many e-learning products, marketing products, and customer service solutions include video or media support. Windows includes two primary applications used for video and audio: Windows Media Player (WMP) and Windows Media Center (WMC). In this section, you will learn about these applications and how to configure settings for the more popular of the two.

Understanding Media Applications

Two primary media applications exist in Windows 7. The first and most commonly used is the Windows Media Player. Windows 7 implements version 11 of WMP. The second application is Windows Media Center, which is primarily intended for the home entertainment market.

WMC can integrate with a TV tuner and other media hardware and software to act as the central hub for a home entertainment center. Figure 4.9 shows the WMC interface. It is usually used as a full-screen interface and is often navigated using a remote control. It is not intended for business use, which is where WMP comes into play. WMC is available in all editions of Windows 7 with the exception of the Starter edition.

WMP is a media player, as its name implies. It can play audio files and video files in practically any format. It includes playlists for queuing of media files for future play and is the engine used by many websites to embed media into their content. Figure 4.10 shows the new simplified default interface for WMP 11 in Windows 7 systems.

FIGURE 4.9 The Windows Media Center (WMC) interface

FIGURE 4.10 The new streamlined WMP interface

Configuring Windows Media Player

WMP can be configured using its Options dialog. To access this dialog, right-click an open area of the control bar (the one with the play button) and select Options. Alternatively, you can press Ctrl+M to enable the traditional menus and then use the Tools ➢ Options menu to access the dialog. Using either method, you should see a dialog like the one shown in Figure 4.11.

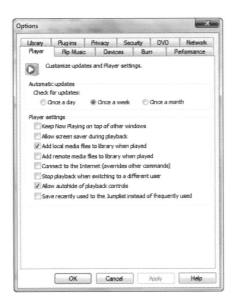

FIGURE 4.11 Using the Options
dialog to configure WMP 11

You can configure several important items in the Options dialog. First, the
Privacy settings can be adjusted on the Privacy tab. This includes the downloading of additional media information from the Internet. Some users may object
to this automatic downloading of information.

On the Performance tab, you can configure buffer settings for progressive download play items on the Internet. For example, on slower Internet connections, you
can extend the buffer to 20–30 seconds (instead of the default of 5 seconds), and
doing so may allow videos to play without pauses in the middle of playback.

Finally, on the Rip Music tab, you can specify the format to use for audio storage. While the default Windows Media Audio (WMA) format may be acceptable
if you plan to use the audio in WMP only, the MPEG-1 or MPEG-2 audio layer 3
(MP3) format may be preferable for portability to other media players.

The most widely
used audio format
for music storage
and playback today
is MP3.

Viewing Configuration Settings

It is important for support professionals and computer users to have a simple
method for viewing system configuration settings and properties. Windows provides two graphical tools for this: MSCONFIG and System Information. In addition, Windows PowerShell and Command Prompt tools are available for viewing
configuration settings. This section covers the tools you can use for configuration analysis.

Using MSCONFIG

A utility in Windows 7 called the System Configuration tool is used to view and manage various configuration settings. The tool has no shortcut on the Start menu, but you can access it by clicking Start and then typing either **msconfig** or **system configuration** in the Search field and pressing Enter. Figure 4.12 shows the System Configuration window.

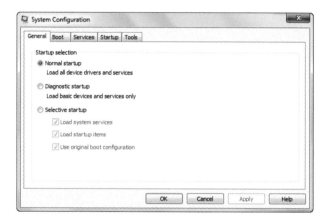

FIGURE 4.12 The System Configuration tool used to manage various configuration settings

The System Configuration tool (MSCONFIG) includes the following configurable settings:

▶ Startup selection of Normal, Diagnostic, or Selective. When the system is started under normal circumstances, the Normal option is used. The Diagnostic option provides more visual output during the boot process and a log file for analysis after booting. The Selective boot option allows you to pick and choose the extra boot-time diagnostic options you wish to use.

▶ Boot-time options such as safe boot, no GUI boot, and creating a boot log. These options are all covered in more detail in Chapter 14, "Backup and Recovery."

▶ Options for enabling and disabling services.

▶ Options for enabling and disabling applications that start up automatically when Windows starts.

▶ Options for launching various other information gathering and configuration tools, such as About Windows, Action Center, Computer

Management, Windows Troubleshooting, and Event Viewer. These tools can all be used to gather more information about your system's configuration and any errors that may be occurring.

Using System Information

System Information is a tool that provides exhaustive information about your system. You access it on the Start menu in the Accessories ➢ System Tools group. Advanced options are available by running it from the search field as MSINFO32.EXE. You can discover available command-line parameters for the System Information tool at the following web page:

http://technet.microsoft.com/en-us/library/bb490937.aspx

Figure 4.13 shows the graphical interface of the System Information tool.

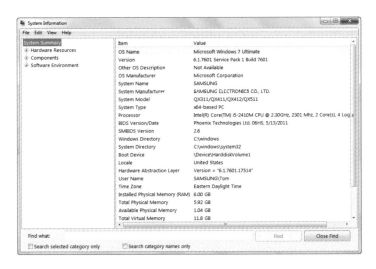

FIGURE 4.13 The System Information tool showing the System Summary page

Using the System Information tool, you can gather information about the following items:

► Hardware resources, including memory, interrupt requests (IRQs), direct memory access (DMA), and conflicts over resources

► Components such as display, network, ports, storage, and more

► Software environment items such as drivers, environment variables, running tasks, network connections, and startup programs and services

PowerShell and Command Prompt Information Gathering

The final information-gathering tools are the command-line tools. These include both PowerShell cmdlets and Command Prompt commands. The following PowerShell cmdlets are useful information-gathering tools:

▶ Get-Counter is used to view performance counters in PowerShell.

▶ Get-Event is used to display event log entries.

▶ Get-Process is used to display running processes.

▶ Get-Service is used to query services.

The following Command Prompt commands are useful information-gathering tools:

▶ Set is used to display environment variables.

▶ Whoami is used to display the currently logged-on user.

▶ Net stats and netstat are used to display networking statistics.

▶ Tasklist is used to display information about running tasks.

▶ IPConfig is used to display IP address configuration information.

Many more cmdlets and commands could be mentioned, but these commands are very popular for information gathering. For more information on Windows PowerShell commands, see my informational site www.MasterWindowsPowerShell .com. For more information on the Command Prompt, see my site www.Windows CommandLine.com.

THE ESSENTIALS AND BEYOND

In this chapter, you learned about the native applications in Windows. First, you learned about the text editing applications. These applications include Notepad for general text editing, WordPad for enhanced formatted text and images, and the Sticky Notes application for brief text notes displayed on the Desktop. Next you explored the image display and editing tools, which included Paint for image editing and Windows Photo Viewer for image display. Then you learned about the new Calculator application in Windows 7, which provides enhanced worksheet views and a programmer view.

(Continues)

THE ESSENTIALS AND BEYOND *(Continued)*

Internet Explorer was investigated next. You learned about the new interface in Internet Explorer 8.0 and its several new features, including InPrivate Browsing, Search Suggestions, and SmartScreen Filter. You also learned about the functions of the Tools menu.

Next you explored the screen capture methods available in Windows, including both the shortcut keys and the Snipping Tool application. You also learned about the media applications, which include Windows Media Center and Windows Media Player. Finally, you explored the various information-gathering tools available in both the GUI and command-line interfaces.

ADDITIONAL EXERCISES

▶ Download and install Notepad++ and then install the Hex Editor plug-in. Using this tool, view a text file generated in Notepad and locate the carriage return (0d) and line feed (0a) codes.

▶ Use the Snipping Tool application to create a screen capture of another application's window.

▶ Using several Command Prompt tools, view information about the IP network configuration, network statistics, and environment variables.

To compare your answers to the author's, please visit www.sybex.com/go/ osessentials.

REVIEW QUESTIONS

1. What application, included with Windows, is used more frequently in business settings to play files such as videos and sound files?

   A. Windows Media Center   **C.** Windows Media Player

   B. Windows Photo Viewer   **D.** Windows Paint

2. True or false. WordPad can save files in text format without losing the special formatting applied.

3. What hex characters are inserted into a text file when you press Enter in Notepad?

   A. 0d and 0a   **C.** 0a only

   B. 0d only   **D.** None of the above

4. What is the default encoding used by Notepad?

(Continues)

THE ESSENTIALS AND BEYOND (Continued)

5. What Windows 7 Command Prompt command can be used to view environment variables?

   A. Set

   B. System Information

   C. Tasklist

   D. Whoami

6. Define the System Configuration tool.

7. Define the WordPad application.

8. Which Internet Explorer Tools menu option is used to select and configure search providers?

   A. Search Providers

   B. Manage Add-ons

   C. Compatibility View

   D. InPrivate Browsing

9. What Internet Explorer 8 feature allows you to perform common tasks, such as blogging or viewing maps, without navigating away from the current page?

   A. Search Suggestions

   B. InPrivate Browsing

   C. SmartScreen Filter

   D. Accelerators

10. True or false. Internet Explorer 9.0 comes with Windows 7.

CHAPTER 5

Managing with the Control Panel

The Control Panel is the hub of configuration and administration for Windows operating systems, and it is very important for a technician or Windows user to understand its use. In this chapter, you will learn how the Control Panel works by investigating the various configuration tools and the important applets. You will explore the following specific topics:

▶ **Understanding applets**

▶ **Configuring Administrative Tools**

▶ **Configuring accessibility**

▶ **Using important applets**

Understanding Applets

The Control Panel consists of multiple components called *applets*. The Control Panel provides an organizational structure to the applets available on the system. In this section, you will learn what applets are and how to use the Control Panel interface to access them.

Defining a Control Panel Applet

Without applets, the Control Panel would be useless. The entire purpose of the Control Panel is to provide access to applets. A Control Panel *applet* is a special Windows application that is used to configure some aspect of the system and its add-on applications. Windows 7 ships with more than 40 Control Panel applets.

The modern Control Panel is a mixture of traditional applets and newer executable programs. Applets have a .CPL extension and executables have an .EXE extension. Many applets, dating back to Windows 3.*x* days, use the .CPL extension. For example, NCPA.CPL is still used to configure network adapter settings, and it was used as far back as Windows 95 and Windows NT 4.0. Windows 7 ships with at least 20 of these CPL files, as shown in Figure 5.1, which displays a directory listing from the Command Prompt.

```
C:\Windows\system32\cmd.exe

C:\Windows\System32>dir *.cpl
 Volume in drive C has no label.
 Volume Serial Number is D8EC-E40D

 Directory of C:\Windows\System32

07/13/2009  09:14 PM           649,216 appwiz.cpl
07/13/2009  09:14 PM           692,736 bthprops.cpl
07/13/2009  09:14 PM            83,968 collab.cpl
07/13/2009  09:14 PM           128,000 desk.cpl
07/13/2009  09:14 PM             4,608 Firewall.cpl
07/13/2009  09:14 PM           234,496 hdwwiz.cpl
07/13/2009  09:14 PM         1,466,368 inetcpl.cpl
06/10/2009  05:14 PM            34,120 infocardcpl.cpl
07/13/2009  09:14 PM           345,088 intl.cpl
07/13/2009  09:14 PM           418,816 irprops.cpl
07/13/2009  09:14 PM           138,240 joy.cpl
07/13/2009  09:14 PM           514,560 main.cpl
07/13/2009  09:14 PM           905,216 mmsys.cpl
07/13/2009  09:14 PM           100,352 ncpa.cpl
07/13/2009  09:14 PM           142,336 powercfg.cpl
07/13/2009  09:14 PM           326,656 sysdm.cpl
07/13/2009  09:14 PM           600,576 TabletPC.cpl
07/13/2009  09:14 PM           106,496 telephon.cpl
07/13/2009  09:14 PM           478,208 timedate.cpl
07/13/2009  09:14 PM         1,140,736 wscui.cpl
              20 File(s)      8,510,792 bytes
               0 Dir(s)  66,624,679,936 bytes free

C:\Windows\System32>
```

FIGURE 5.1 The directory listing of CPL files in the
`C:\Windows\System32` folder

If you install Microsoft Security Essentials or another third-party anti-malware solution, Windows Defender may be removed automatically.

In addition to the CPL files, many Control Panel tools are loaded from EXE files. For example, the Windows Defender item on the Control Panel is just a link to the Windows Defender configuration application (MSCASCUI.EXE). Other interfaces are nothing more than web pages shown within the Control Panel with links to the various EXE files used to perform the specified actions.

The point is simple: The Control Panel is no longer just a set of CPL files—it is a complex arrangement of CPL files, EXE files, and web pages. However, the file types aren't as important as what the various applets do, and this book will use the term *tool* to refer to CPL applets, EXE files, and web pages within the Control Panel.

Exploring the Available Applets

Sometimes a Control Panel tool is duplicated in more than one category, because it may provide functions for both categories.

When you open the Control Panel (by clicking Start and selecting Control Panel), you are presented with an interface that groups Control Panel operations into categories by default. This view is easiest if you know what you want to accomplish but don't know the name of the applet. Figure 5.2 shows the Control Panel in the Category view. Here's a summary of the available categories:

Appearance and Personalization   This category includes the ability to access Personalization, Display, Desktop Gadgets, Taskbar and Start Menu, Ease of Access Center, Folder Options, and Fonts. The focus of this category is on how things appear on your screen. For example, you can change system fonts used to display icon text and title bar text. You can also change the theme or the Desktop background.

Clock, Language, and Region   This category includes the ability to access the Date and Time as well as Region and Language options. The focus of this category is on settings related to your local region. For example, the local time depends on the zone in which you are located, and the language may differ as well.

Ease of Access   This category includes the ability to access the Ease of Access Center and Speech Recognition. The focus of this category is on accessibility. For example, you can configure speech recognition for OS commands instead of mouse or keyboard input. You can also launch the Narrator, which is a Windows 7 component that will read the text on the screen aloud to you.

Hardware and Sound   This category includes the ability to access Devices and Printers, AutoPlay, Sound, Power Options, and Display. The focus of this category is on the configuration and management of hardware devices, including sound devices. For example, you can add and remove hardware and also configure power management features related to the hardware installed.

Network and Internet   This category includes the ability to access the Network and Sharing Center, the HomeGroup feature, and Internet Options. The focus of this category is on network connectivity. The Network and Sharing Center provides tools for network troubleshooting and configuration, and the Internet Options section provides settings for configuring the Internet Explorer web browser. If you use an alternate browser, you will configure it from within the browser itself.

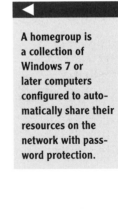

A homegroup is a collection of Windows 7 or later computers configured to automatically share their resources on the network with password protection.

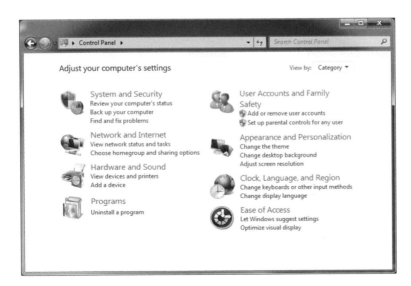

FIGURE 5.2 Viewing the Control Panel by category

Programs   This category includes the ability to access Programs and Features, Default Programs, Desktop Gadgets, and potentially other custom add-ons to the Control Panel. The focus of this category is on application management. For example, the Programs and Features section of this category is used to add and remove Windows OS features and to add and remove applications.

System and Security   This category includes the ability to access the Action Center, Windows Firewall, System properties, Windows Update, Power Options, Backup and Restore, BitLocker Drive Encryption, and Administrative Tools. The focus of this category is on Control Panel tools that allow you to secure your system and provide business continuity.

User Accounts and Family Safety   This category includes the ability to access User Accounts, Parental Controls, Windows CardSpace, and Credential Manager. The focus of this category is on Control Panel tools that allow you to configure and manage user accounts, account credentials, and the control of user account capabilities. Included in the User Accounts section of this category is the ability to change User Account Control settings.

You may prefer to select from a list of individual Control Panel tools. You can view this by changing the view from Category to either Large Icons or Small Icons. Figure 5.3 shows the Small Icons view of the Control Panel.

> The phrase *business continuity* is a fancy way of saying "continue to do business." Tools that provide business continuity allow you to continue using your system.

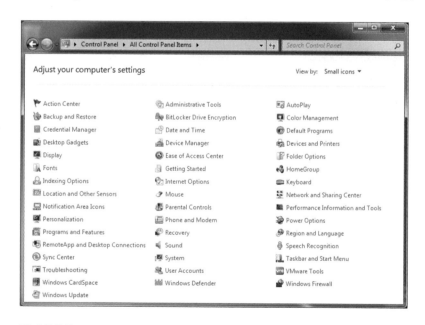

FIGURE 5.3 Viewing the Control Panel as Small Icons

You can launch Control Panel tools using several methods. First, you can open the Control Panel, navigate to the appropriate category or tool name, and then launch it using the appropriate link. Second, you can use the search field on the Start menu to type in the Control Panel tool name and then when the desired tool appears, select it from the list. For example, the following process will launch the System applet:

1. Click Start.

2. Enter **system** in the search field.

3. Select the item named System from the Control Panel section of the results list.

The third method used to launch Control Panel tools is to create shortcuts to them. You can create a shortcut to a Control Panel tool by navigating to the link location in the Control Panel and then dragging the link to the Desktop. The resulting icon can be used to launch the Control Panel tool directly at any time. Additionally, after creating the icon and naming it, you can use the search field on the Start menu to launch it quickly or you can pin it to the taskbar. Icons can be placed in locations other than the Desktop as well, such as folders hidden from view. The Start menu search functions will still work.

The fourth and final method for launching Control Panel tools is to learn the tool's filename and launch it from the Start menu. The following list provides the filenames for several Control Panel tools:

▶ Action Center: WSCUI.CPL

▶ System Properties: SYSDM.CPL

▶ Network Connections: NCPA.CPL

▶ Device Manager: DEVMGMT.MSC

▶ Display: DESK.CPL

▶ Power Options: POWERCFG.CPL

▶ User Accounts: NETPLWIZ.EXE

▶ Programs and Features: APPWIZ.CPL

▶ Task Scheduler: TASKSCHD.MSC

▶ Date and Time: TIMEDATE.CPL

◀

If you rename a shortcut icon to something more meaningful to you, then you can search with the Start menu based on this meaningful information.

For example, to quickly launch the System Properties dialog, follow these steps:

1. Click Start.

2. Enter **sysdm.cpl** in the search field.

3. Press Enter.

As you can see, you have great flexibility when accessing Control Panel tools. Using the methods just described, you can develop habits that allow you to manage systems more efficiently. You will find that a few of the tools are used more often than most, and these are the tools best accessed using faster methods like the search field on the Start menu.

THE SUPER CONTROL PANEL INTERFACE

Hidden within Windows 7 is a super Control Panel interface that allows you to search for items and browse through all of the tools as one extended list. This interface is sometimes called "God Mode" on the Internet simply because it places so much system configuration power at your fingertips.

To view this interface, you must create a special folder, and name it **text. {ED7BA470-8E54-465E-825C-99712043E01C}**, where *text* can be replaced with any text you wish to use to describe the folder, and the curly braces and the globally unique identifier (GUID) within them must be exactly as shown.

For example, to name the folder Super Control Panel, you would enter the following complete folder name: **Super Control Panel.{ED7BA470-8E54-465E-825C-99712043E01C}**. For example, here is the interface when created with the name Super Control Panel and displayed in the Small Icons view:

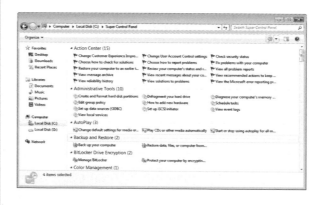

Configuring Administrative Tools

Now that you understand the basics of the Control Panel interface and how it works, it is time to explore specific tools. In this section, you will learn about Administrative Tools and the capabilities they offer.

Understanding the Administrative Tools Applet

Windows operating systems come with a special set of tools that have been traditionally called Administrative Tools. They are tools that typically require administrative privileges to operate, and they allow you to manage the system's configuration and important functionality settings.

These Administrative Tools have traditionally been located in a special Start menu group called Administrative Tools. They include tools like Computer Management, Event Viewer, and Services. In Windows 7, an additional access method is provided as the Administrative Tools Control Panel applet.

The applet can be accessed as follows:

1. Click Start ➢ Control Panel.

2. If in the Category view, select the System and Security category and then select Administrative Tools. If in the Small Icons or Large Icons view, select Administrative Tools.

Figure 5.4 shows the Administrative Tools applet. In addition to accessing this applet through the Control Panel interface, you can access it by searching for Administrative Tools on the Start menu. You can also have all Control Panel tools appear as menu items directly on the Start menu by following these steps:

1. Right-click the taskbar and select Properties.

2. Select the Start Menu tab.

3. Click the Customize button.

4. In the Control Panel section of the Customize Start Menu dialog, select Display As Menu and click OK.

5. Click OK again to close the Taskbar And Start Menu Properties dialog.

To have administrative privileges, you must be a member of an administrative group like the local Administrators group or the Domain Admins group in the domain.

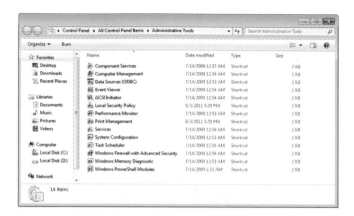

FIGURE 5.4 The Administrative Tools applet

Working with the Administrative Tools

A total of 14 tools exist in the Administrative Tools Control Panel by default. As a support professional or advanced Windows user, it is important for you to understand each of these tools. The following descriptions explain the purpose for each of the 14 tools:

> **COM, COM+, and DCOM are not likely to appear on any Microsoft OS certification exam, since they are not used as often today.**

Component Services   The Component Services tool is an administrative interface used to configure settings for the Component Services on the system. These components include COM+ objects and DCOM objects. The Component Object Model (COM) is a software development model that has existed in Windows for several versions. The concept allows for objects created in one environment to be used in another environment. It has been largely deprecated in favor of the new .NET development, but it and Distributed COM (DCOM) are still in use. This tool allows you to configure and manage settings for components.

Computer Management   The Computer Management tool is used to manage the computer, as its name implies. It provides access to System Tools, including the Task Scheduler, Event Viewer, Shared Folders, Local Users and Groups, Performance, and Device Manager. Many of these tools are also available as direct links from the Administrative Tools applet. Additionally, Computer Management provides access to Storage (Disk Management) and Services and Applications. Figure 5.5 shows this important Administrative Tool.

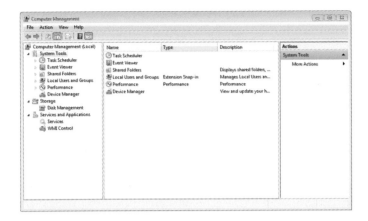

FIGURE 5.5 The Computer Management Administrative Tool interface

Data Sources (ODBC) The Data Sources (ODBC) tool launches the ODBC Data Source Administrator dialog, which is used to create data source names (DSNs). A DSN is simply a data connection configuration set that can be easily accessed as a single named element. User DSNs are available only to the user who created them. System DSNs are available to all users of the system. File DSNs are used to connect to file-based data sources, and these DSNs are also available to all users, like System DSNs.

The tool also allows for the management of data source drivers. For example, you can view the installed drivers. If you must add a driver for a data source that is not listed, you should go to the data source vendor (for example, Oracle for Oracle databases) to acquire the latest ODBC driver. Additionally, you can configure tracing to monitor the details of data access operations. Finally, you can enable connection pooling so that applications reuse open connection handles to improve efficiency. Figure 5.6 shows the ODBC Data Source Administrator dialog.

Event Viewer The Event Viewer is used to view the logs for the OS and applications installed on the computer. It is a useful tool for troubleshooting operations. The Event Viewer is covered in more detail in Chapter 13, "Windows Troubleshooting."

iSCSI Initiator This tool is used to configure and manage the Internet Small Computer Systems Interface (iSCSI) Initiator, which is a driver and service in Windows 7 that allows access to iSCSI-based storage area networks (SANs). The tool allows you to configure the connections to the SAN and to configure authentication parameters, if they are required.

The Open Database Connectivity (ODBC) solution provides access to various database systems through a standardized set of communication methods.

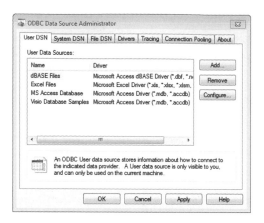

FIGURE 5.6 The ODBC Data Source Administrator dialog used to configure ODBC connections

Local Security Policy   The Local Security Policy tool allows you to easily access the security settings for the local computer. You can configure these settings through the local Group Policy Object (GPO) by running GPEDIT.MSC from the Start menu search field; however, this tool streamlines the process by showing only the security-related options.

Within the Local Security Policy tool, you can configure Account Policies, Local Policies, Windows Firewall policies, Network List Manager Policies, and additional advanced policy settings. Figure 5.7 shows the Local Security Policy interface. Any setting configured in Local Security Policy can be overridden by the domain-based Group Policy settings, if they exist.

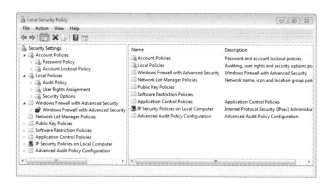

FIGURE 5.7 The Local Security Policy interface

Performance Monitor   The Performance Monitor tool is used to capture and view either live or archived performance data. The tool allows you to view performance information in two views: a graph view and a report view. In the graph view, you can observe the dynamic changes in performance with a line graph that is generated against live data or archived data. In the report view, you can view the specific numeric values of dozens of counters. A counter is simply a measurement of a specific performance metric.

Print Management   The Print Management tool provides a custom Microsoft Management Console that gives you direct access to all printers on the machine. Here you can view drivers and ports that are installed and the printers connected to them. You can launch the printer configuration dialogs and view and manage the print queues as well.

Services   This tool allows you to manage the services on your machine. Services typically run invisibly in the background and provide features and functions to the network and the local machine. You will learn more about services and service management in Chapter 7, "Managing Applications."

System Configuration   The System Configuration tool launches the MSCONFIG application directly. This application was covered in Chapter 4, "Using Native Applications."

Task Scheduler   The Task Scheduler tool is used to schedule tasks and manage scheduled tasks. Scheduled tasks are used to automate system maintenance procedures and possibly user processes. The Task Scheduler is a Microsoft Management Console and is covered in detail in Chapter 13.

Windows Firewall and Advanced Security   This tool is used to configure basic and advanced firewall policies. The Windows Firewall is a built-in firewall included with all Windows systems starting with Windows XP. A firewall is used to filter and control the communications coming into or going out of a system.

Using the Windows Firewall with Advanced Security tool, you can create Inbound Rules (those that filter incoming communications), Outbound Rules (those that filter outgoing communications) and Connection Security Rules (those that apply to specific connections between the local computer and another device or service). Additionally, you can use the Monitoring node to view any events that may have occurred, such as attempted communications that are disallowed. Figure 5.8 shows the Windows Firewall with Advanced Security dialog (which is called Windows Firewall and Advanced Security in the Administrative Tools applet).

Windows Memory Diagnostic   Windows Memory Diagnostic (WMD) is a special boot mode that allows Windows 7 to test and report on the functionality of internal RAM. When you launch it from the Administrative Tools applet, you can choose either Restart Now And Check For Problems or Check For Problems The Next Time I Start My Computer. Either way, the check occurs only when the system is booting. Figure 5.9 shows the Windows Memory Diagnostics Tool running at boot time.

Windows PowerShell Modules   The Windows PowerShell Modules tool simply runs a PowerShell session with all available modules loaded automatically. Once in the PowerShell interface that is launched, execute the `Get-Module` cmdlet to see a list of loaded modules. When executed with no parameters, `Get-Module` lists only the loaded modules. Next, you can use the `Get-Command` cmdlet with the `-Module` parameter to view the commands available for a specific module.

> **Some modules may not load, because of the script execution policy. You can change the policy with the `Set-Execution Policy` cmdlet.**

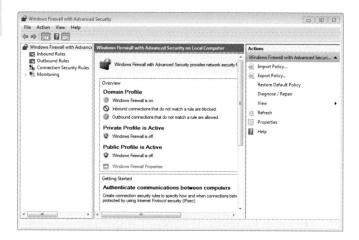

FIGURE 5.8 The Windows Firewall with Advanced Security dialog used to create and manage firewall rules

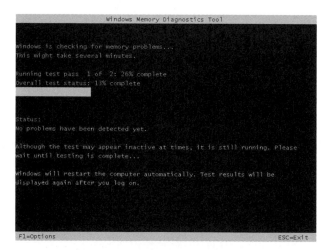

FIGURE 5.9 The Windows Memory Diagnostics Tool

Configuring Accessibility

Windows 7 includes features to assist those with accessibility needs. The goal of these features is to allow as many people as possible to have a useful experience with the Windows OS. In this section, you will learn about the accessibility features and how to use the Ease of Access Center.

Windows Accessibility Features

The Windows accessibility features include features for the visually impaired, the physically challenged, and the hearing impaired. The available features are described in Table 5.1.

TABLE 5.1 Accessibility features and descriptions

Accessibility Feature	Description
Narrator	Reads the text on the screen to users. Allows the visually impaired to better use the system.
High Contrast Theme	Make the screen more readable through higher-contrast color usage.
Magnifier	Increases the size of a selected area on the screen. Simply move the mouse over the area and it will be magnified as if under a magnifying glass.
Speech Recognition	Allows the computer to be used without a mouse or keyboard.
Mouse Keys	Allows the numeric keypad to be used to move the mouse pointer around on the screen.
Sticky Keys	Provides for multiple-key shortcuts to be entered one key at a time. For example, the Ctrl+C shortcut used to copy can be invoked by pressing and releasing Ctrl and then pressing and releasing C rather than requiring that they both be pressed and held together.
Toggle Keys	Plays a tone through the speakers when the user presses the Caps Lock, Num Lock, or Scroll Lock key. This helps to prevent accidental enabling of these keys.

(Continues)

TABLE 5.1 *(Continued)*

Accessibility Feature	Description
Filter Keys	Ignores or slows down accidental repeating of key presses that may be held down for slightly too long.
Sound Sentry	Provides a visual warning when the computer makes a sound. This allows the hearing impaired to receive the same alerts that are traditionally given through playing sound files.

Using the Ease of Access Center

The Windows accessibility features are all available within the Ease of Access Center. To access the Ease of Access Center, follow these steps:

1. Click Start ➢ Control Panel.

2. If in the Category view, select Ease of Access and then Ease of Access Center. If in the Small Icons or Large Icons view, select Ease of Access Center.

Figure 5.10 shows the Ease of Access Center. Notice that you can quickly enable several features, including Magnifier, Narrator, the On-Screen Keyboard, and High Contrast themes.

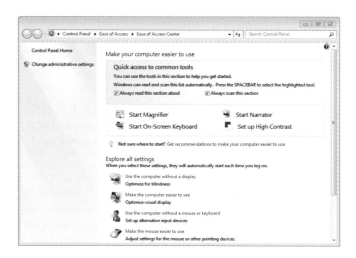

FIGURE 5.10 The Ease of Access Center

Table 5.2 provides instructions for locating the various features within the Ease of Access Center.

TABLE 5.2 Accessibility features and access instructions

Accessibility Feature	Access Instructions
Narrator	Use The Computer Without A Display ➤ Turn On Narrator
High Contrast Theme	Make The Computer Easier To See ➤ Turn On Or Off High Contrast When Left ALT + Left SHIFT + PRINT SCREEN Is Pressed
Magnifier	Make The Computer Easier To See ➤ Turn On Magnifier
Speech Recognition	Use The Computer Without A Mouse Or Keyboard ➤ Use Speech Recognition
Mouse Keys	Make The Keyboard Easier To Use ➤ Turn On Mouse Keys
Sticky Keys	Make The Keyboard Easier To Use ➤ Turn On Sticky Keys
Toggle Keys	Make The Keyboard Easier To Use ➤ Turn On Toggle Keys
Filter Keys	Make The Keyboard Easier To Use ➤ Turn On Filter Keys
Sound Sentry	Use Text Or Visual Alternatives For Sounds ➤ Turn On Visual Notifications For Sounds (Sound Sentry)

Using Important Applets

There are several additional Control Panel applets you should become familiar with, as they are used frequently when supporting and using Windows systems. These include the configuration of default programs, power management, and the System applet.

Configuring Default Programs

The Default Programs applet is a welcome addition to the Windows OS. For many years the settings configured in this applet were accessed through several different interfaces, and it was up to the user or support professional to locate and use them. This applet brings together the following four aspects of program management:

▶ Set Your Default Programs

▶ Associate A File Type Or Protocol With A Program

▶ Change AutoPlay Settings

▶ Set Program Access And Computer Defaults

Each of these four options, shown in Figure 5.11, provides access to important functions for default application management. They are described in the following list:

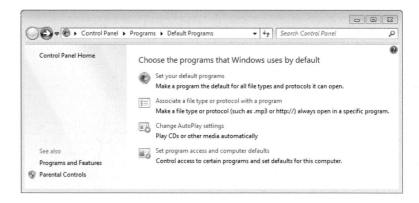

FIGURE 5.11 Using the Default Programs applet

Set Your Default Programs   This option is used to configure the default program for all file types and protocols that a program can open. When you click on a program, you will see the file types it can open, along with the number of types for which it could be configured as default compared to the number for which it is configured. For example, in Figure 5.12, you see that TheKMPlayer could be the default application for 68 file types, but it is the default for only 18 of them. To make it the default for all file types and protocols it supports, click the link that reads Set This Program As Default. Then, click the link that reads Choose Defaults For This Program.

Associate A File Type Or Protocol With A Program   This interface provides the more traditional method for managing file associations. You can select an individual file extension and then click Change Program to configure an alternate application as the default application for that file type.

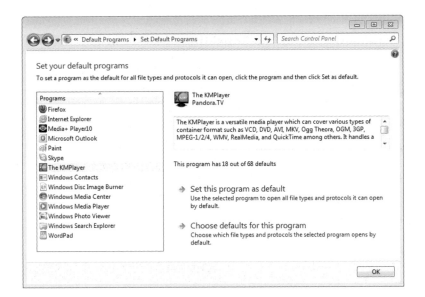

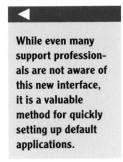

While even many support professionals are not aware of this new interface, it is a valuable method for quickly setting up default applications.

FIGURE 5.12 Using the Set Default Programs interface

Change AutoPlay Settings   The AutoPlay feature has been greatly enhanced in Windows 7. In this interface, you can not only turn AutoPlay on or off, but you can also configure it for many different scenarios. You can indicate the action to take based on the content of the AutoPlay source (CD or DVD). For example, when an audio CD is inserted, you can have one action occur, but when a blank CD is inserted you can have an entirely different action occur.

Set Program Access And Computer Defaults   This interface allows you to use one of three configuration sets to automatically configure the application defaults for file associations and protocol associations. The three configuration sets are Microsoft Windows, Non-Microsoft, and Custom. When you select Microsoft Windows, you will have all of the default settings that are used when Windows is first installed. When you select Non-Microsoft, the application will configure non-Microsoft applications for the default applications, if they are available. When you select Custom, you can choose the default applications for web browsers, email programs, media players, instant messaging applications, and Java virtual machines. Each one can be chosen individually as the Custom configuration set. If you revert to the Microsoft configuration set, your Custom configuration set is not lost.

Using the Power Management Tools

Windows Vista and then Windows 7 made great strides in their support for and configuration of power management settings. The Power Options applet is used to configure power settings in the GUI interface. A new tool named POWERCFG.EXE is available at the Command Prompt for power management as well.

Take these steps to access the Power Options applet:

1. Click Start ➢ Control Panel.

2. If using the Category view, select System and Security and then Power Options. If using the Small Icons or Large Icons views, select Power Options.

From the Power Options applet, as shown in Figure 5.13, you can perform any of the following actions:

- ▶ Require A Password On Wakeup
- ▶ Choose What The Power Button Does
- ▶ Choose What Closing The Lid Does (for laptops)
- ▶ Create A Power Plan
- ▶ Choose When To Turn Off The Display
- ▶ Change When The Computer Sleeps
- ▶ Select A Power Plan

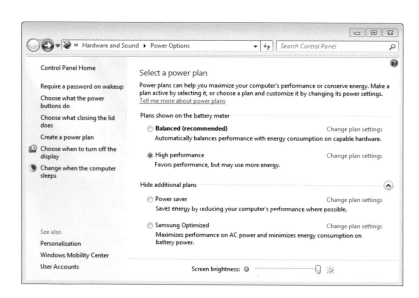

FIGURE 5.13 The Power Options applet

A power plan is a collection of power options that can be enabled by simply selecting the plan. All Windows 7 computers have the Balanced, High Performance, and Power Saver plans:

Balanced   The Balanced power plan is configured to turn off the display after 10 minutes and put the computer to sleep after 30 minutes. Additionally, it turns off the hard disks after 20 minutes.

High Performance   The High Performance power plan is configured to turn off the display after 15 minutes and never put the computer to sleep. Additionally, it turns off the hard disks after 20 minutes.

Power Saver   The Power Saver power plan is configured to turn off the display after 5 minutes and put the computer to sleep after 15 minutes. Additionally, it turns off the hard disks after 20 minutes.

A power plan can contain settings for the following options:

- ▶ Hard disk
- ▶ Desktop background settings
- ▶ Wireless adapter settings
- ▶ Sleep
- ▶ USB settings
- ▶ Power buttons and lid
- ▶ PCI Express
- ▶ Processor power management
- ▶ Display
- ▶ Multimedia settings

In addition to the three built-in power plans, many computer vendors create their own power plans that are preinstalled with the OS. In Figure 5.13, the power plan named Samsung Optimized is such a custom power plan. It came preinstalled on the laptop from which the screen was captured.

It is also important to know that computers with batteries, such as laptops, have dual options for each option—one setting for when the computer is running on battery and another for when it is plugged in. This allows you to configure power plans so that they work best for the current scenario—on battery or plugged in.

Finally, a power plan can be backed up to a file using the Command Prompt's powercfg command. The following command, for example, will export the Balanced power plan with the GUID of 381b4222-f694-41f0-9685-ff5bb260df2e:

```
powercfg -export balanced.pwr 381b4222-f694-41f0-9685-ff5bb260df2e
```

You can use the powercfg -l command to view the GUIDs for the different installed power plans. Figure 5.14 shows this command in action.

FIGURE 5.14 Using the powercfg command to export power plans

Understanding the System Applet

> You can quickly access the System applet by pressing the shortcut Windows key+Break.

The final Control Panel tool addressed in this chapter is the System applet, which is used to view and manage information that is global to the system. You access it in the Control Panel from the System and Security category. The System applet is used for the following tasks:

▶ View basic information about your computer

▶ Access the Device Manager

▶ Configure remote settings

▶ Configure system protection

▶ Access advanced system settings

The System applet displays the Windows Experience Index (WEI), which is a rating based on the lowest-performing factor in your system. The factors considered for the WEI are

▶ Processor

▶ Memory (RAM)

▶ Graphics

▶ Gaming Graphics

▶ Primary Hard Disk

Among these, the item with the lowest rating is the one from which the WEI will be derived. The scores for each item can range from 1 to 7.9 in Windows 7. Regardless of how well a component performs, it will never have a rating of more than 7.9. Microsoft will increase this upper limit as new versions of the OS are released.

◀

The only way to achieve a hard disk subscore of more than 5.9 is to install solid-state drive (SSD) technology.

THE ESSENTIALS AND BEYOND

In this chapter, you learned about the Control Panel, the primary interface for accessing system and user configuration and management settings. You learned that the different Control Panel tools consist of applets, executables, and web pages.

Next you learned about the specific tools exposed through the Administrative Tools applet and for what purpose each tool is used. Then you explored the Windows accessibility features made available through the Ease of Access Center. Finally, you learned about several additional important Control Panel tools, including Default Programs, Power Management tools, and the System applet.

ADDITIONAL EXERCISES

▶ Launch the Control Panel and use the three different views.

▶ Locate the files used to launch the following Control Panel tools: Sound, Internet Options, and Mouse Properties.

▶ Using the Power Options interface, create a custom power plan.

To compare your answers to the author's, please visit www.sybex.com/go/ osessentials.

REVIEW QUESTIONS

1. What file is associated with the Network Connections Control Panel applet?

   A. SYSDM.CPL   **C.** NETPLWIZ.EXE

   B. WSCUI.CPL   **D.** NCPA.CPL

2. True or false. Some Control Panel items are actually just web pages.

3. What option, within the Default Programs applet, should be used to most easily configure a Windows 7 machine to use Microsoft applications for all default programs wherever possible?

   A. Set Your Default Programs

   B. Associate A File Type Or Protocol With A Program

   C. Change AutoPlay Settings

   D. Set Program Access And Computer Defaults

(Continues)

THE ESSENTIALS AND BEYOND *(Continued)*

4. What Administrative Tool applet component is used to view the logs for a Windows OS?

5. Define Magnifier.

6. Define Sound Sentry.

7. Define Control Panel.

8. What command would be used in Windows PowerShell to view the available cmdlets provided by the AppLocker module?

   A. `Get-Module -Commands AppLocker`

   B. `View-Module -Commands AppLocker`

   C. `Get-Command AppLocker`

   D. `Get-Command -Module AppLocker`

9. What Command Prompt command is used to export power plans?

   A. `PowerMgmt`   **C.** `ConfigPwr`

   B. `PowerCfg`   **D.** `ManagePwr`

10. True or false. You can add shortcuts to Control Panel items on the Desktop.

CHAPTER 6

Mobility and Remote Management

*Mobility—the ability to work and communicate remotely—*has
become increasingly important for business users. To support mobility, modern
operating systems must have some method for synchronizing content with the
network. For this, Windows 7 provides the Sync Center. Laptops are used more
than ever today, and they support features that make them more mobile through
increased battery life and connectivity with other devices. The Windows Mobility
Center helps with this. Additionally, Windows 7 supports remote management
features through the use of Remote Desktop, Remote Assistance, the Microsoft
Management Console (MMC), and Windows PowerShell. Each of these features is
covered in this chapter, where you'll learn about the following topics:

► **Understanding mobility**

► **Using Remote Desktop**

► **Using Remote Assistance**

► **Understanding the MMC**

► **Working with Windows PowerShell**

Understanding Mobility

Mobility must be considered from two perspectives today. The first is the connectivity of your Windows 7 machine to networked file sources and the ability
to store networked files offline. The second is the use of mobility features in
laptop computers. Both perspectives are addressed in this section.

Using the Sync Center

The Sync Center, first introduced in Windows Vista, is a tool for managing
the offline files configured for your Windows 7 networked clients. Offline files

have existed for several versions of Windows, starting with Windows 2000. Using this feature, the user can designate files to be copied onto the local hard drive from the network shares. Then, when the remote user reconnects with the network, the local copy of the file needs to be synchronized with the network copy. In previous versions, no tool existed to manage the offline synchronization process with any real flexibility.

The Sync Center provides this much-needed management interface. Using the Sync Center, you can do the following:

▶ Start or stop synchronization processes.

▶ Create sync partnerships between the Windows 7 computer and a remote server.

▶ Resolve conflicts that occur during synchronization.

▶ View the status of existing sync partnerships.

▶ Schedule the times when synchronization should occur.

Using Windows Mobility Center

The Windows Mobility Center is used to configure settings that impact the performance and battery life of your computer. It also shows information about sync partnerships and the ability to connect to external displays or presentation devices such as LCD projectors. Figure 6.1 shows the Windows Mobility Center.

The Windows Mobility Center can be most easily accessed by keyboard shortcut; press the Windows key+X.

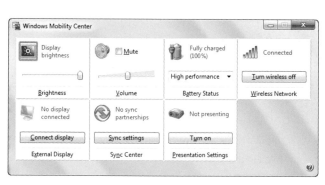

FIGURE 6.1 The Windows Mobility Center

The Windows Mobility Center provides the following configuration interfaces:

Brightness   This element is used to adjust the brightness of the display using a simple slider. You can also use the Power Options to adjust the brightness settings based on the selected power plan.

Volume   A slider is provided for the adjustment of the volume levels up or down. Interestingly, when the volume is greater it does consume more power as more is required to generate the energy.

Battery Status   This element displays the amount of battery charge remaining and also allows you to select a different power plan from the currently selected plan.

Wireless Network   The wireless network may be selected or you can disable the wireless network adapter to conserve power.

The wireless network adapter is usually one of the top three or four power consumers in a laptop.

External Display   If an external monitor is connected, you can configure how it is to be used.

Sync Center   You can access the Sync Center from here and also see information about existing sync partnerships.

Presentation Settings   This element allows you to enable or disable presentation settings. These settings represent a collection of settings you wish to enable when using your computer to run a presentation or a slide show.

Some computers, particularly Tablet PCs, have an additional element available in the Windows Mobility Center: a screen rotation status element.

To change the settings for any element in the Windows Mobility Center, click the icon in that section. For example, if you click the icon in the Presentation Settings section, you can customize some of the settings used when Presentation Settings are enabled.

UNDERSTANDING PRESENTATION SETTINGS

Presentation Settings represent a collection of settings that help you ensure a presentation goes smoothly. For example, when they are enabled, a laptop will stay awake and all system notifications will be disabled. This prevents disruptions during the presentation.

In addition, you can choose whether to do any of the following when Presentation Settings are enabled:

▶ Disable the screen saver

▶ Lock the speaker volume

▶ Change the Desktop background

With this feature, you have a simple method of placing your computer into presentation mode without having to remember to make several different changes. Additionally, it's much easier to revert to your nonpresentation settings when the presentation is over.

Using Remote Desktop

Windows servers and clients support two types of remote Desktop control without the use of third-party applications: Remote Desktop (RD) and Remote Assistance. Both are addressed in this chapter. In this section you'll learn about RD and how it is enabled and utilized.

Enabling Remote Desktop

For more information about Remote Desktop Services, see my book in this series titled *Microsoft Windows Server Administration Essentials* (Sybex, 2011).

The first thing you should understand is the difference between what Microsoft calls Remote Desktop and Remote Desktop Services. RD is a feature built into Windows servers and clients that allows administrators to connect to the machine and manage it from a remote client using the Remote Desktop Client software. RD does not require additional licensing; it is intended only for support purposes and not for the running of applications from remote computers. It uses the same Remote Desktop Protocol (RDP) as Remote Desktop Services, but it is much simpler to enable and configure. Remote Desktop Services is a larger-scaled infrastructure solution, running only on Windows Server operating systems, and is beyond the scope of this book.

In this section, you'll learn to enable RD for use on Windows 7 machines. To enable Remote Desktop on Windows 7, follow this procedure:

1. Click the Start menu, right-click Computer, and select Properties.

2. Click the Advanced System Settings link on the left menu of the System screen.

3. Select the Remote tab in the System Properties dialog box.

4. Choose either Allow Connections From Computers Running Any Version Of Remote Desktop or Allow Connections Only From Computers Running Remote Desktop With Network Level Authentication, and click OK.

Connecting to Remote Desktop

You can also click the Select Users button to add users who can access the Desktop remotely. By default, only Administrators may access the remote Desktop.

After enabling Remote Desktop on the machine, you can connect to it from another Windows client or server using the Remote Desktop Connection application and the following steps:

1. From a Windows 7 or Vista Desktop, select Start ➢ Accessories ➢ Remote Desktop Connection.

2. In the Remote Desktop Connection dialog, enter the computer name or IP address of the computer to which you wish to connect.

3. Click the Options drop-down arrow to customize the display and configure access to local resources, programs to execute upon connection, and the experience within the connection, such as the graphical richness of the connection.

4. On the General tab, enter the username with which you wish to connect, and then click Connect.

5. When prompted for credentials, enter the password for the username you entered in step 4.

6. If you see a prompt that says The Certificate Cannot Be Verified, do not be alarmed. This indicates that the server is using a self-signed certificate. If you know you can trust the server, click Yes to connect.

◄

The username you enter must have the rights to connect using Remote Desktop.

After completing this procedure, you will be connected to the remote computer's Desktop and can interact with it as if you were sitting in front of the machine with a monitor, keyboard, and mouse. The remote connection allows full utilization of the system from the perspective of keyboard and mouse input.

Using Remote Assistance

Remote Assistance (RA) provides a solution for users or administrators to receive help from someone else using a request and response engine. The user with access to the local Desktop interface must request help from another individual before that individual can connect. In a client computing RA scenario, the requesting user is known as the novice and the responding assistant is known as the expert.

RA can be used to allow either remote viewing or remote control. When remote control is allowed, the RA assistant can interact with the requesting user's Desktop. When it is disabled, the assistant can only view the user's actions. Remote viewing is useful when you need someone to see your actions and correct errors in those actions but you do not have the required trust to allow that individual access to control your machine.

Enabling and Configuring Remote Assistance

On Windows 7 computers, there is no need to install or enable RA. It is installed by default. In some situations, you may have to enable support for RA in Windows Firewall; however, if you do not perform this action before requesting assistance the first time, the request wizard will detect the Windows Firewall blockage and reconfigure it for you automatically.

Requesting Assistance

The first step in using RA is to request assistance. Use the following procedure to request assistance:

1. Log on to the machine as the requesting user.

2. Click Start and type **Windows Remote Assistance** in the search field and press Enter.

3. In the Windows Remote Assistance dialog, select Invite Someone You Trust To Help You.

4. If you see the notice The Computer Is Not Setup To Send Invitations, click Repair to allow the wizard to automatically repair the problem and then relaunch Windows Remote Assistance beginning with step 2.

5. Select Save This Invitation As A File.

6. Provide a filename and location in the Save As dialog and click Save.

7. The Windows Remote Assistance application window will appear and display a password, which the remote assistant will need to access your machine, as shown in the following image.

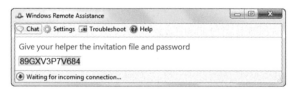

At this point the assistance request process is complete. You should email the invitation file to the individual who will provide assistance. Alternatively, you could place it on a shared network location, such as a share on a Windows Server machine. On computers with Microsoft Outlook installed, you can even choose to send the invitation as an email in step 4 of the preceding procedure.

Responding to a Request

When the assistant receives the invitation generated in the preceding section, she can initiate a connection and enter the password provided. To initiate the connection from a supporting Windows client machine, the assistant simply double-clicks the invitation file and then enters the appropriate password as provided by the requestor.

When the assistant initiates the connection, the requestor must respond by clicking Yes in the prompt that appears when the assistant connects. If the assistant wants to control the Desktop, he must request control, and the requestor must grant this control. Figure 6.2 shows the RA client connected to a Windows 7 machine from another Windows 7 client computer.

FIGURE 6.2 Using the RA client to connect to a remote Windows 7 machine

Understanding the MMC

The Microsoft Management Console (MMC) was first released as an add-on for Windows NT and Windows 95. It has been included in every version of Windows since Windows 2000 out of the box. One key feature of many MMC snap-ins is that they can be used to access remote computers as well as the local computer. This section will introduce the MMC interface and the methods used to create custom MMC consoles.

Snap-ins are modules that load into an MMC interface to provide functionality. The MMC, by itself, is nothing more than a shell for snap-ins.

Exploring the MMC Interface

No shortcut to an empty MMC application exists on the Start menu. To access an empty MMC, simply click Start, type **mmc** into the search field, and press Enter. You will see an application similar to the one in Figure 6.3.

FIGURE 6.3 The MMC interface elements

You should understand each section of the MMC interface in order to best know how to use it in building custom consoles. The leftmost section is the console tree. It begins with the console root and will include various nodes depending on the snap-ins added to the console. The middle section is the display area. It will display the view selected in the console tree. The rightmost section is the Action panel. This panel will change depending on the node selected in the console tree.

The OS comes with several prebuilt consoles. For example, when you right-click the Computer icon on the Start menu and select Manage, you are loading a console with the Computer Management snap-in (among other snap-ins) preloaded.

The Computer Management snap-in is one of the most important for remote computer management.

Creating Custom Consoles

Ultimately, the MMC is most useful for creating custom consoles. To create and save a new console, follow these steps:

1. Click Start, type **mmc** in the search field, and press Enter.

2. In the MMC window, click File ➢ Save.

3. Provide a filename for the console and click Save.

At this point, you will have an empty custom console. This alone does not provide much value. Next, you will want to add one or more snap-ins to the console. To add a snap-in to the console, follow these steps:

The MMC defaults to saving custom consoles in the Administrative Tools group on the Start menu.

1. Press Ctrl+M or click File Add/Remove Snap-in to display the Add Or Remove Snap-ins dialog.

2. Scroll through the Available Snap-ins list to select the first one you wish to add and click the Add button.

3. If you are presented with a screen asking you to choose the local computer or a remote computer, make the appropriate selection to continue.

4. Repeat steps 2 and 3 until all desired snap-ins are added. You can add more than one instance of the same snap-in when connecting to remote computers.

5. When all desired snap-ins have been added, click OK.

You can create as many custom consoles as you require. It is not uncommon for support professionals to create several custom consoles for different purposes. For example, you may create a custom console with the Event Viewer snap-in loaded several times—once for each remote machine you support. You can do the same in another console for the entire Computer Management snap-in. Creating custom consoles with snap-ins configured for connectivity to remote computers is the primary way that the MMC is used for remote management.

Working with Windows PowerShell

Windows PowerShell, as you learned in Chapter 1, "Windows Operating Systems Overview," is a command-line interface. It is designed to provide scripting and the power to accomplish administrative tasks with consistency. Why not simply use the Command Prompt? One reason is that its commands, unlike those of PowerShell, sometimes use dashes for switches, or forward slashes, or even double dashes. This inconsistency can make it difficult to master. The introduction of Windows PowerShell provides a consistent interface across all utilities and administrative tasks.

On versions of Windows earlier than Windows 7, you will have to download and install Windows PowerShell. You can search at www.microsoft.com for "PowerShell download" to locate the download files. Windows 7 includes PowerShell 2.0 without requiring a separate download and installation procedure.

As you begin to work with Windows PowerShell as an administrator, there are two aspects you must understand. The first is the concept of a *cmdlet*; to know which one best suits the task at hand, you have to know how to get information on the available cmdlets and their uses. And to provide technical support you'll also need to know how to execute PowerShell commands remotely. Both topics are addressed in the following sections.

Understanding Cmdlets

Instead of using executables, like the Windows Command Prompt, Windows PowerShell uses cmdlets. Cmdlets are verb/object constructs. This simply means that a verb is combined with an object to form a command. Verbs include *get*, *set*, *new*, *write*, *update*, *invoke*, and *clear*, among others. The objects may be the contents of a file, the list of running processes, or a history object, among others. This construction of cmdlets makes it easy to conceptualize and remember the various commands.

To see a list of all available cmdlets, open a Windows PowerShell session and execute the command Get-Command -commandtype cmdlet. Figure 6.4 shows a partial output of this command.

You can also view only the cmdlets available as part of a PowerShell module by using the -module parameter.

FIGURE 6.4 Output of the get-command cmdlet

When you browse through the list of cmdlets, you are likely to locate one that performs the function you desire. However, to be sure of its purpose and use, you can use the Get-Help cmdlet. Simply execute get-help followed by the name of the cmdlet you want to read about, and the help will be displayed on the screen. For example, to get complete help for the Get-Command cmdlet, execute the command

```
get-help get-command -full
```

The -full parameter indicates that get-help should provide all available help, including examples. You can alternatively use the -details and -examples parameters to indicate that you want only the full details or only the examples respectively.

An important feature of PowerShell is the ability to pipe the output of one cmdlet into another cmdlet as an object. For example, you can use the Out-File cmdlet with the other cmdlets to save information into a file. The Get-Process cmdlet is used to list running processes. You can dump the output of the Get-Process cmdlet to a text file using the Out-File cmdlet with the following command:

```
get-process | out-file processes.txt
```

To learn more about the specific Windows PowerShell cmdlets, visit my informational website at www.MasterWindowsPowerShell.com.

Executing Remote Commands

One important feature of Windows PowerShell that you will likely use as a support professional is remote execution. That is, you can enter cmdlets on one computer to be executed on a remote computer. To do this, you must first enable Windows Remote Management (WinRM) on both the support computer and the target computer. WinRM is a service framework that allows access to remote computers for administration and management purposes. It is used by Windows PowerShell to invoke remote commands, and it is also used by the Event Viewer to subscribe to remote events. To enable WinRM, execute the following command at a Windows Command Prompt with administrative privileges:

```
winrm quickconfig
```

You will be asked to enable changes that allow WinRM to work. Press Y to indicate that the changes should be made.

After enabling WinRM, you can use the Invoke-Command cmdlet to execute remote cmdlets. For example, to get a list of running processes on the remote computer named CPU0013, execute the following command in a Windows PowerShell window:

```
Invoke-command -computername cpu0013  -scriptblock {get-process}
```

The -computername parameter specified the remote computer name and the -scriptblock parameter can be followed by any valid Windows PowerShell command enclosed in curly brackets.

THE ESSENTIALS AND BEYOND

In this chapter, you learned about mobility and remote management of computers. You learned about the Sync Center and Windows Mobility Center and the roles they play in providing support for mobile computers such as laptops and tablet PCs. You then explored Remote Desktop and Remote Assistance and learned how they can be used to connect to and support remote desktops and laptops. Next, you learned how to use the Microsoft Management Console (MMC) to create custom consoles for management of remote computers using snap-ins. Finally, you learned how to discover and use Windows PowerShell cmdlets and the tools available for remote computer management with Windows PowerShell.

ADDITIONAL EXERCISES

▶ Use the Windows Mobility Center to configure power management and customize presentation settings.

▶ Create a custom MMC console that includes links to several technical websites. Use the Link to Web Address snap-in to accomplish this.

▶ Enable Windows Remote Management so that a support professional can invoke PowerShell commands against your machine.

To compare your answers to the author's, please visit www.sybex.com/go/osessentials.

REVIEW QUESTIONS

1. What parameter is used with the Get-Command cmdlet to retrieve only cmdlet commands and not functions, aliases, filters, scripts, or applications?

   A. Get-Command -module cmdlets

   B. Get-Command -commandtype cmdlets

   C. Get-Command - noview functions; aliases; filters; scripts; applications

   D. None of the above

2. True or false. An MMC console can include one and only one snap-in.

3. Which of the following cmdlets is used to gather information about running processes?

   A. Get-Running   **C.** Tasklist

   B. Get-RunningProcess   **D.** Get-Process

(Continues)

THE ESSENTIALS AND BEYOND *(Continued)*

4. What can you use to create custom administration interfaces for different support professionals?

5. What shortcut key can be used to add a new snap-in to an MMC console?

   A. Windows key+X

   B. Ctrl+M

   C. Ctrl+A

   D. Alt+X

6. Define a snap-in.

7. Define Remote Assistance.

8. You are viewing the status of offline file synchronization processes. What specific tool are you using?

   A. Remote Assistance

   B. Microsoft Management Console

   C. Windows Mobility Center

   D. Sync Center

9. Which of the following are PowerShell cmdlets? (Choose all that apply.)

   A. Get-Process

   B. Tasklist

   C. IPconfig

   D. Invoke-Command

10. True or false. The winrm quickconfig command can be used to easily enable Windows Remote Management.

CHAPTER 7

Managing Applications

We do not run operating systems for the simple joy of having an operating system. Instead, we run them so that we have an interface to manage our data and applications. In this chapter, you will learn about the application management options available for Windows 7. The following topics are included:

▶ **Planning for local and network applications**

▶ **Installing, configuring, and removing applications**

▶ **Using Group Policy for application control**

▶ **Understanding application virtualization**

▶ **The difference between services and standard applications**

Planning for Local and Network Applications

Applications can be installed locally or they can run from the network. In this section, you will learn about both application types. In organizations today, local applications are still the most common, but network application use is growing through the implementation of cloud-based computing.

Using Localized Applications

Localized applications are programs that are installed and run on the local machine. These applications are the traditional application types and they are accessed through shortcuts or by directly accessing the application program files.

Application shortcuts can be created on the Desktop, on the Start menu, or in any other folder. In Chapter 3, "Managing the Desktop," you learned to create shortcuts. These shortcuts can point to many different types of targets, including

▶ Executable files with an .exe or .com extension

▶ Batch files with a .bat or .cmd extension

▶ Document files of any type (DOC, DOCX, PPT, PPTX, PDF, and so on)

▶ Web pages and other Internet-based locations

If a document type does not have a configured application association, when you run its shortcut you will be asked how to open the file.

Local applications can also be launched directly. You can search for them, as you've seen throughout this book, on the Start menu. You can browse for them using the Explorer interface and then launch them by double-clicking.

The most important thing to remember about localized applications is their default installation location. It is common to run 64-bit versions of Windows 7, and this version has two different locations for applications. The 32-bit applications are stored in one location by default, and the 64-bit applications are stored in another.

32-Bit Applications   On 64-bit systems, 32-bit applications are installed in the C:\Program Files (x86) folder by default. On 32-bit systems, they are installed in the C:\Program Files folder.

64-Bit Applications   On 64-bit systems, 64-bit applications are installed in the C:\Program Files folder by default. On 32-bit systems, 64-bit applications cannot be installed.

Remember that 64-bit versions of Windows 7 cannot run 16-bit applications directly, but 32-bit versions can.

An application can be installed to any location, but by accepting the default of installing to the Program Files or Program Files (x86) folders, you bring more consistency to your installations.

Using Networked Applications

Networked applications fall into two categories:

▶ Networked applications with client-based components installed

▶ Networked applications executed entirely from the network

In Microsoft's SQL Server database system, these functions stored in the database are called *stored procedures*.

When the networked application requires a client component, the client must be installed on the local machine just like a localized application. However, it will call on network-based functions, routines, and programs to perform much of the work. An example of such a networked application is a line-of-business application that uses functions stored in a database server to perform business calculations but has a client interface installed for the users to access these database functions.

When networked applications execute from the network without any localized client components, they may run as cloud-based applications or they may download to the memory of the local machine each time they are launched. As an example, you can access an entire collection of tools at live.sysinternals.com. When you click on one of the tools, like PROCMON.EXE, and select to run it, what it really does is download the self-contained executable file to the local machine and then launches it. A self-contained executable file is a program that does not require any other components, such as DLL files or configuration files, to run.

Cloud-based applications run on networked computing infrastructures, and you see the results of their execution. The applications are not downloaded to your local machine. The Microsoft Office 365 applications are an example of cloud-based applications. Google Documents are another example. In both cases, a web browser with the appropriate plug-ins or add-ons is required, but no additional application components must be installed on the local machine. Figure 7.1 shows the Office 365 version of Microsoft Word running in the Internet Explorer web browser.

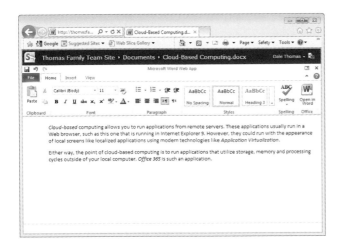

FIGURE 7.1 Microsoft Office 365 Word running in the cloud

Installing, Configuring, and Removing Applications

Now that you know the basic differences between local and networked applications, you need to understand the various methods used to install applications on the local machine. In this section, you will learn how to install applications, configure them, and remove or uninstall them when they are no longer required.

Understanding Installation Methods

Applications can be installed interactively or automatically. Interactive installations require that the support professional or user run the installation process and answer any questions asked by the installation. Common information that must be provided when installing applications includes the following items:

▶ Name of the user

▶ Product ID keys or serial numbers

▶ Installation locations

▶ For whom the application should be made available

When you are installing applications, it is common to be asked whether the application should be available for the current user only or for all users.

Interactive installations can be based on custom-coded installation routines or they can use the Windows Installer engine. Custom-coded installation routines have become less common, but they do still exist. A custom-coded installation routine does not take advantage of the Windows Installer engine; instead, it manually copies files to the target installation folder and configures appropriate Registry settings. If a custom installation routine does not also provide a clean uninstallation routine, it can be difficult to fully uninstall and clean up after such an application.

Windows Installer is an installation and application configuration service that runs on Windows operating systems. Windows Installer provides several advanced features for application management, including these:

▶ The ability to install multiple patches to the OS or applications with a single routine, without requiring multiple reboots

▶ The ability to install multiple installation packages as a single transaction, allowing for a rollback to the previous state if any of the individual installation packages fail

▶ The ability to advertise applications and features according to the OS so that only available features are shown

▶ Standard application installation features, such as copying files, creating and modifying Registry entries, configuring application settings, and creating shortcuts

Most Windows Installer deployments use the MSI file format. These files can be launched directly, and they can also be installed from the network using Group

Policy. For extensive details on the Windows Installer service, its features, and capabilities, see

```
http://msdn.microsoft.com/en-us/library/windows/desktop/cc185688
(v=vs.85).aspx
```

Group Policy provides an infrastructure for application deployment. If you want to use Group Policy for application deployment, the following elements must be in place:

► The Windows clients must be members of an Active Directory Domain Services (AD DS) domain.

► The MSI files to be deployed must be located in a network share that the users can access with at least read permissions.

► A Group Policy Object (GPO) must be created in the AD DS domain to deploy the applications.

Figure 7.2 shows the interface, within a GPO, for application deployment. When an application is deployed through Group Policy, it can either be published or assigned. An application that is published is made available but is not necessarily installed automatically. When an application is assigned, it installs automatically the next time the user logs onto the machine. When you deploy a Windows Installer application (MSI file) through Group Policy, it will install without user interaction. Later in this chapter, in the section "Deploying Applications with Group Policy," you will see step-by-step instructions for this process.

It is possible to install an application based on file associations. When the user attempts to run an associated file, the application will be installed at that time.

FIGURE 7.2 The Group Policy software deployment interface

Configuring Applications

After installing an application, you may be able to configure it using the installation engine that was used to install it initially. If the installation engine supports reconfiguration of the installation, you will see a Change button available in the Programs and Features Control Panel. To check for this option for a specific application, follow this procedure:

1. Click Start ➢ Control Panel.

2. Select the Programs category.

3. Click on the Programs and Features link.

4. Scroll through the list of installed applications and click on the one you want to reconfigure.

5. If a Change button appears, click it to reconfigure the application (see Figure 7.3).

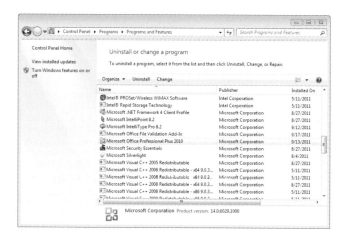

FIGURE 7.3 Using the Programs and Features Control Panel to reconfigure an application

When you use this process, you are using the installation engine to reconfigure the application, but the Programs and Features Control Panel applet provides access to the engine for this purpose.

Removing Applications

You can also use the Programs and Features applet to uninstall or remove an application. To remove an application using Programs and Features, follow these steps:

1. Click Start ➢ Control Panel.

2. Select the Programs category.

3. Click the Programs and Features link.

4. Scroll through the list of installed applications and click the one you want to uninstall.

5. Click the Uninstall button to launch the installation engine for application removal.

In some cases, the application may not show up in the Programs and Features applet. This means that it was installed using a custom installation engine that did not place the uninstall information into the system Registry. The application may have a custom uninstallation engine as well. Check the application's installation directory in such cases. If an uninstallation engine is available, it will most likely be located in the application directory or folder. If no such uninstallation engine is available, the application will have to be removed manually. To do so:

1. Delete all shortcuts to the application, including Start menu folders that may have been created.

2. Delete all files in the application's folder and the folder itself.

3. Delete Registry entries that refer to the application.

Removing an application manually must be done with great caution. It is possible that the application files are shared by another application you wish to continue using. In such cases, you cannot remove the application without causing disruption to the other application you want to keep. Additionally, when you delete items from the Registry, you must do so very carefully to avoid accidental deletion of Registry keys that are needed for other applications and the OS.

Always export a Registry key before deleting it. This way, you can recover it if you determine that it is still required.

CAUTION: REGISTRY AT WORK

The Windows Registry is a sensitive portion of the OS. It is easily corrupted and damaged when you are not fully aware of its structure and functionality. Great caution should always be taken when working in the Registry, and you should make backups of any keys where you plan to make changes or deletions.

To create a backup of a Registry key, perform the following steps:

1. Launch the Registry Editor by searching for regedit on the Start menu and pressing Enter.

2. Navigate to the key where changes or deletions are to be made.

3. Right-click the key and select Export.

4. Provide a filename and location, and click Save.

(Continues)

> **CAUTION: REGISTRY AT WORK** *(Continued)*
>
> If you need to restore the Registry key at a later time, you can double-click the REG file that was created by the export routine to restore it.
>
> Finally, as a best practice, always modify the Registry through application interfaces if they are available. These interfaces include the Options, Settings, and Preferences dialogs within various applications. Certainly, some situations require direct Registry access, but most actions can be taken through safer application interfaces.

Using Group Policy for Application Control

Group Policy plays a significant role in application management and control. This section shows you how to restrict application installation and access to removable media using Group Policy. You'll also learn the steps required to deploy applications using Group Policy Objects.

Restricting Application Installation

You can use Group Policy to restrict application installations directly in two ways. First, you can remove the Programs and Features page so that users cannot add Windows OS features that are not already installed on their machines. Second, you can explicitly restrict access to installation routines using AppLocker. Both methods are covered in this section.

To remove the Programs and Features page, follow these steps on a local machine:

1. Click Start and search for **gpedit.msc** and press Enter.

2. Expand User Configuration ➢ Administrative Templates ➢ Control Panel ➢ Programs.

3. Enable the policy named Hide "Programs and Features" Page.

AppLocker is a new feature in Windows 7 (Enterprise and Ultimate Editions only) that provides for advanced software restrictions, including the control of Windows Installer routines. If you want to use AppLocker, the following must be true:

▶ You must be running Windows 7 Enterprise or Ultimate Edition on all clients you wish to control through AppLocker.

▶ The Application Identity service must be configured to start automatically when the Windows 7 clients start.

You can also enable this Group Policy setting through a domain-based GPO so that it automatically applies to AD DS domain users.

Figure 7.4 shows the AppLocker interface within a GPO on Windows Server 2008 R2. Notice the Windows Installer Rules section. This section is used to restrict installation routines. If you right-click the Windows Installer Rules node and select Create Default Rules, the following recommended default rules are created:

- ▶ Allow everyone to run all digitally signed Windows Installer files

- ▶ Allow everyone to run all Windows Installer files in the %*systemdrive*%\Windows\Installer path

- ▶ Allow administrators to run all Windows Installer files

The variable %*systemdrive*% refers to the drive where the Windows folder is located, which is typically C:.

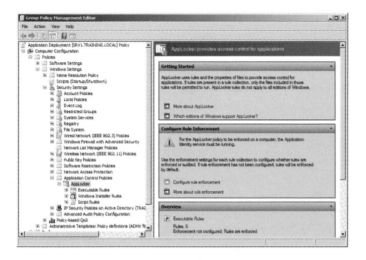

FIGURE 7.4 AppLocker running on Windows Server 2008R2

In addition to these rules, you can create your own allow or disallow rules for specific Windows Installer files or folders. The condition type is used to identify the Windows Installer file to which a rule should apply. The following three condition types can be used to build a rule:

- ▶ Publisher

- ▶ Path

- ▶ File Hash

The Publisher condition is used to allow or disallow all Windows Installer files from a specific publisher. For example, you may have a license with a publisher to run all of their applications. You can create a rule that allows the users to install an application from this publisher.

The Path condition is used to allow or disallow all Windows Installer files from a specific folder. This is useful for allowing users to run Windows Installer files from a specific network share. You can place the MSI files in this share that you want users to install. If no other rules exist, the users can install from the specified share, but not from any other location.

Of the three types, the File Hash is the most specific to a file. The odds that two Windows Installer files would result in the same hash digest are so unlikely as to be considered impossible. A hashing algorithm is a mathematical algorithm that takes a variable-length input and generates a fixed-length output. For example, you can pass a 500-megabyte file to a hashing algorithm and it may generate a 160-bit hash digest (which is really just 160 1s and 0s or bits). If you pass a 500-byte file to the same algorithm, it will still generate a 160-bit hash digest. However, the digest will be different for each file. When you want to guarantee that your rule applies to one specific file only, use a hash rule.

The most important thing to remember about AppLocker is this: If no rules are created and AppLocker is enabled, users can run any executables and use any Windows Installer files or run any scripts. For this reason, you should always create the default rule sets. If you create a single rule for each of the three categories (Executables, Windows Installer, and Scripts), users will be allowed to do what that rule specifies and nothing more. These two facts are important to consider when you are planning AppLocker deployment.

An older technology known as Software Restriction Policies also exists and can be used to block Windows installation routines. However, Software Restriction Policies are not truly aware of Windows Installer files and treat them like any other application. They can still be used to restrict application installations on Windows 7 editions other than Enterprise or Ultimate and on older versions of the OS.

COMPLETELY DISABLING WINDOWS INSTALLER

As an alternative method, you can block all access to Windows Installer. This setting is found in the GPO in the Administrative Templates ➢ Windows Components ➢ Windows Installer location. The policy setting name is Disable Windows Installer. By setting this policy to Always, you effectively disable Windows Installer use. Other custom installation methods can still be used, but the majority of modern installation processes, which are based on Windows Installer, will not work. Although it is rare to completely disable Windows Installer, Microsoft provides this option because many organizations create Windows clients that are entirely locked down. They do not want any installations running on them. An example of this would be a kiosk that is provided for public use and that the support staff want to control and limit to reduce support problem occurrences on the machine.

Disabling Access to Removable Media

One method users often employ to install applications is to launch the installation from removable media. Several policies exist for controlling removable media, and they are located in the Administrative Templates ➢ System ➢ Removable Storage Access section of the GPO. Figure 7.5 shows the Group Policy Management Editor with the Removable Storage Access policy settings displayed.

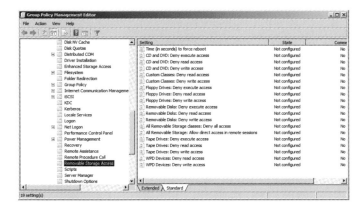

FIGURE 7.5 The Removable Storage Access policy settings in a GPO

In the past, you could either deny or allow access to removable storage devices. You could also restrict access based on drive letters. In Windows 7, you can provide access to removable storage, but only for read or write access and not for execute access. This allows users to access documents and other data on removable media, but does not allow them to install applications or run applications from the removable media. It also enables administrators to configure removable media restrictions for any of the following media types independently:

- ▶ CD and DVD
- ▶ Floppy drives
- ▶ Removable disks (like USB drives)
- ▶ Tape drives
- ▶ Custom classes

Using custom classes, you can disable specific removable media types based on the GUID for the device. The device GUID can be located by connecting the device to a computer and then opening the Device Manager. There you can view the properties for the specific device, access the Details tab, and inspect the value of the Device Class GUID property, as shown in Figure 7.6. After retrieving the

GUID, you can enter it as a custom class in the GPO, and that device can then be restricted according to your needs.

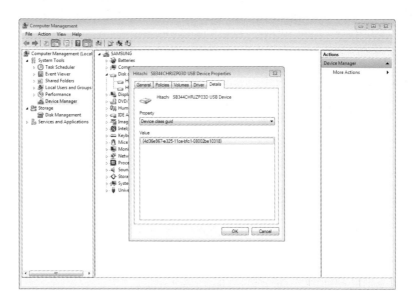

FIGURE 7.6 Viewing the GUID value for a device in Device Manager

Deploying Applications with Group Policy

Earlier in this chapter, you learned that Group Policy can be used to deploy applications. While you may not have access to a Windows Server running AD DS to perform these steps, it is important to understand the basic process used to deploy applications in this way. The following steps will create a GPO to deploy an application named BUSINESSAPP.MSI located in the \\server1\apps share:

> **Chapter 10, "Network Shares," covers the concept of network shares and how to create them.**

1. Log onto the Windows Server domain controller as an administrator.

2. Click Start ➢ All Programs ➢ Administrative Tools ➢ Group Policy Management.

3. Expand the Domains container and then the target domain for application deployment, as shown in Figure 7.7.

4. Right-click the Group Policy Objects container within the target domain and select New.

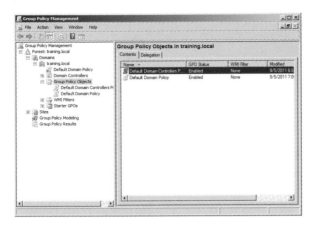

FIGURE 7.7 The Group Policy Management Console
with the Domains container expanded

5. In the New GPO dialog, provide a name for the GPO, such as
Application Deployment, and click OK.

6. Right-click the newly created GPO and select Edit.

7. Expand Computer Configuration ➢ Policies × Software Settings to
deploy to the computers or expand User Configuration ➢ Policies ➢
Software Settings to deploy to users.

8. Right-click Software Installation and select New ➢ Package.

9. In the Open dialog, enter **\\server1\apps\BusinessApp.msi** in the
File Name field and click Open.

10. In the Deploy Software dialog, choose Published, Assigned, or Advanced
and click OK. If you choose Published or Assigned, you are returned to
the Group Policy Management Editor. If you choose Advanced, you will
be taken to the Properties dialog for the application immediately, as
shown in Figure 7.8.

◀

**When deployed to
users, the applica-
tion applies only to
the users who are
targets of the GPO.
When deployed to
computers, it applies
regardless of the
user logging on.**

After creating the Software Installation object in the GPO, you can right-click
it and select Properties to adjust any settings required. Exiting the Group Policy
Management Editor causes your changes to the GPO to be saved. Now, any container (domain, site, or organizational unit) in AD DS to which you link the GPO
will receive this new application.

FIGURE 7.8 The application's Properties
dialog for Group Policy software distribution

Understanding Application Virtualization

Application virtualization is a solution that allows applications or even entire
Desktops to run on servers or in the cloud while appearing as local applications
or Desktops to the users. Microsoft offers two solutions to assist with application
virtualization: Med-V and Virtual Desktop Infrastructure (VDI). Both are covered in this section.

Understanding Med-V

Microsoft Enterprise Desktop Virtualization (Med-V) allows legacy applications,
including Internet Explorer–based applications, to run on Windows 7. Med-V
workspaces are created and deployed to Windows 7 clients so that users can run
previous versions of Internet Explorer for application compatibility or other legacy applications that worked on Windows XP but do not work on Windows 7.
The benefits of Med-V include the following:

▶ No additional infrastructure services are required, as Med-V workspaces
can be deployed using existing application deployment solutions, such
as Group Policy software deployment.

▶ Passwords can be saved so that automatic sign-on occurs when users
run Med-V applications, making the implementation transparent to
the users and allowing them to feel as if the applications are standard
installed applications.

▶ Applications can take advantage of the local My Documents, Desktop, and networked printers just like standard installed applications.

▶ Internet Explorer redirection options can be used to automatically redirect web browsing to a legacy version of Internet Explorer through Med-V.

▶ Med-V applications show up on the local Start menu just as standard installed applications. When the application runs, it has a visual display that looks like Windows XP instead of Windows 7, but otherwise it appears to be a standard application.

To be clear, Med-V is a management interface or layer used by technology support professionals to manage and deploy workspaces for application compatibility. It depends on Windows Virtual PC, as a Windows XP virtual machine runs in the background to allow the applications to operate. Med-V offers additional features not found in Windows XP Mode, but it is based on similar technology. You can download Windows XP Mode from the Microsoft website and install it on any machine. Effectively, Med-V is managed Windows XP Mode with the additional features just listed.

MED-V VS. APP-V

Do not confuse Med-V with App-V. Application Virtualization (App-V) is used to provide applications to users without actually installing them on their machine as normal applications. Med-V requires that Windows Virtual PC be installed on the clients, and App-V does not.

App-V uses a special client to run the applications. This client provides the following virtualized components for the App-V applications:

▶ Virtual drives or file systems

▶ Virtual registry

▶ Virtual COM objects

▶ Virtual services

▶ Virtual fonts

▶ Virtual INI files

▶ Virtual process environment

(Continues)

MED-V VS. APP-V *(Continued)*

Effectively, the applications think they are installed and running natively on the computer but they are not. The App-V client runs the applications in a guarded environment that keeps the client clean from all normal changes that applications make. You can learn more about App-V here:

www.microsoft.com/windows/enterprise/products/mdop/app-v.aspx

Understanding VDI

The Microsoft Virtual Desktop Infrastructure (VDI) is a bundling of multiple Microsoft technologies together into a single licensing package for organizations seeking to deploy virtual desktops. Virtual desktops are virtual machines running on servers and made available to Windows clients or thin clients across the network. Microsoft provides a standard license and a premium license for VDI. The Microsoft VDI Standard Suite license includes the following:

▶ Hyper-V Server 2008 R2 for running the virtual machines

▶ System Center Virtual Machine Manager 2008 R2 for the management of virtual machines

▶ System Center Operations Manager 2007 R2 and System Center Configuration Manager 2007 R2 for centralized control and management of the virtual desktops

▶ App-V through the Microsoft Desktop Optimization Pack (MDOP)

▶ Windows Server 2008 R2 Remote Desktop Services for connection brokering and session management

The Microsoft VDI Premium Suite license includes the following:

▶ Everything in the Standard Suite license

▶ Full Remote Desktop Services capability for session-based desktops as well as virtual machine desktops

▶ App-V for Remote Desktop Services

For more information on Microsoft VDI, see

www.microsoft.com/windows/enterprise/solutions/virtualization/
default.aspx

The Difference between Services and Standard Applications

A *service* is a special kind of application that runs on Windows computers. This section introduces services and their management on Windows 7 machines. Additionally, it describes some of the most important services that come with Windows 7 to help you better understand why they exist and the functions they perform. This section also introduces you to service management using service accounts and the Services console.

Defining Services

A service is an application or operating system component that runs on a computer and provides services to the local machine, the networked devices, or both. In most cases, services run in the background, meaning that they do not have a visual interface that you can see on the computer's Desktop. While a few services may be exceptions to this rule, they are also exceptions to the common practice of service development. The service itself should not be confused with the service management tools or interfaces that allow administrators and users to configure the service.

Windows comes with many services built in. You can install additional services so that they can provide functions or capabilities to networked computers or the local computer. In many cases, you will not even have to install a service to meet your needs. Dozens of services are installed on Windows 7 computers by default, and they require only that you enable them to use them. This is true for both Windows servers and Windows clients. In fact, many services are shared between the Windows servers and clients and perform the exact same functions for each.

Additional services may be added to Windows computers either by purchasing them and installing them or by downloading free services from the Internet.

Most services run in the background without a visible interface, but you will encounter some applications that also provide service-like functions.

Windows 7 clients and Windows servers run many of the same services because they run the same basic operating system code and share many features and services.

SERVICE INSTALLATION PROCESSES

Services may be installed in several ways on a Windows machine. They may require installation procedures similar to applications on client computers, or they may be installed through specialized interfaces.

Services that are installed as supporting components for your computer and that come with the operating system are installed through the Programs and Features Control Panel interface. After adding the service, you may be required to configure it before it can begin running on the machine.

(Continues)

SERVICE INSTALLATION PROCESSES *(Continued)*

Services that come preinstalled with the operating system need only to be enabled. You can configure these services to start automatically when the operating system loads, or you can start them manually each time you wish to use them. In most cases, preinstalled services cannot be removed from the operating system.

Third-party services typically use installation procedures similar to standard application installations. You may be provided with a configuration interface during installation so that the services installed are enabled immediately after the installation is complete.

Additionally, many services require a system reboot after installation. If the installation procedure indicates that you must reboot the machine, it is best to do so before attempting to use or configure the service. While you may be able to interact with the service, unpredictable results may occur. For example, your configuration may not be saved, or the system may become unstable.

Windows 7 installations have many services preinstalled, as shown in Figure 7.9. Covering each service in great detail is beyond the scope of this book, but it is important that you understand the purpose of several services. The following services have been selected for detailed coverage because of their fundamental importance to the operation of a Windows machine. They are listed in alphabetical order so that no unintended level of importance can be placed on any single service.

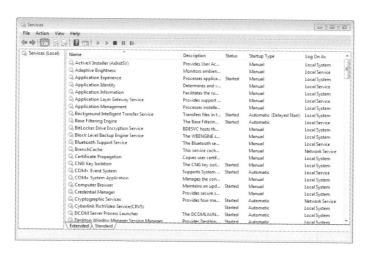

FIGURE 7.9 The Services management interface showing the services installed on a Windows computer

Application Identity   The Application Identity service is required for AppLocker policies to be processed. AppLocker is a new software control solution first made available in Windows 7 and Windows Server 2008 R2. It can be used to disallow the execution of specified applications through rules configured within Group Policy.

Background Intelligent Transfer Service (BITS)   BITS is a service that allows data to be transferred across the network in the background. The data is transferred during idle times so that the transfers do not interfere with user-requested network operations.

Cryptographic Services   The Cryptographic Services service provides for the management of certificates. Certificates are used to provide authentication and encryption in secure systems. The service is used frequently in the Windows operating systems because it is needed to validate the digital signatures of signed device drivers.

DHCP Client   The DHCP Client service is used to acquire an IP configuration from a Dynamic Host Configuration Protocol (DHCP) server. The client is needed on Windows XP and earlier operating systems even if static IP addresses are used, because the DHCP Client service is also responsible for registering the computer's hostname with the dynamic DNS servers used by Active Directory Domain Services on these older versions. Windows Vista and later clients use the DNS Client service to register with the Dynamic DNS servers.

The Active Directory Domain Services (AD DS) service runs on Windows Server installations and provides the network domain services.

Disk Defragmenter   The Disk Defragmenter service is new to Windows 7 and Windows Server 2008 R2. It provides disk defragmentation functions as a scheduled process. When a third-party defragmentation solution is used, this service should be disabled.

DNS Client   The DNS Client service is responsible for Domain Name System (DNS) name resolution. It resolves domain names to IP addresses. This service does not register the local computer's hostname with a dynamic DNS server on Windows Server XP and earlier versions of Windows. It does perform the hostname registration task on Windows Vista and later versions.

Encrypting File System (EFS)   The EFS service provides the functionality required to implement encryption on the NTFS files system. If the service is not running, users will be unable to access data encrypted with EFS.

Extensible Authentication Protocol (EAP)   First added in Windows Vista and Server 2008, the EAP service provides port-based 802.1X authentication for wired and wireless networks, virtual private networks (VPNs), and network access protection (NAP). NAP is used to test the health (such as the existence of antivirus software) of a computer before allowing it access to the network.

Group Policy Client   Windows Vista and Server 2008 introduced new Group Policy capabilities called Group Policy Preferences. The newly introduced Group Policy Client service provides support for these enhancements and other new features that are not supported in earlier versions of the Windows client and server operating systems.

IKE and AuthIP IPSec Keying Modules   The IKE and AuthIP IPSec Keying Modules (IAIKM) service provides modules for Internet Key Exchange (IKE) and the Authenticated Internet Protocol (AuthIP). The modules are used for key exchange and authentication when the IP Security (IPSec) protocol is used for network communications security. This service is required for proper IPSec operations.

IP Helper   The IP Helper service was first introduced in Windows Vista and Windows Server 2008 and provides tunnel connectivity using IP version 6 (IPv6) transition solutions, including 6-to-4, Intra-Site Automatic Tunnel Addressing Protocol (ISATAP), and Teredo. Tunneling solutions simply allow IPv6 communications to be transmitted across IPv4 networks.

▶

Replay attacks occur when an attacker reads a network packet off the network and then plays the packet back onto the network with possible alterations to the packet contents.

IPSec Policy Agent   Windows Server operating systems include a Microsoft Management Console (MMC) snap-in called the IP Security Policies snap-in. With this tool, you can create IPSec policies for network-level authentication, data integrity, data source authentication, encryption, and protection from replay attacks. Windows clients also process these policies for IPSec secure connections.

Link-Layer Topology Discovery Mapper   In the Network and Sharing Center, you may view a map of your network. The feature is disabled by default on AD member computers, but it can be enabled by the administrator through Group Policy. The Link-Layer Topology Discovery Mapper service is responsible for building this map. It collects PC and device topology (infrastructure devices such as switches and routers) information and descriptive data related to each PC and infrastructure device.

Netlogon   The Netlogon service is used to log into an AD DS domain. Without this service, you cannot join a machine to a domain. Computers installed as part of a workgroup or homegroup network do not require this service.

Print Spooler   The Print Spooler service is used to provide local and network printing queues so that a single printer can handle more print jobs than its internal memory would allow. On machines that do not provide printer sharing and from which you rarely print locally, this service can be safely stopped. You can later start the service, if you need to print, and all installed printers will still be available.

Remote Desktop Services   The Remote Desktop Services service must be running to allow a user to control the Windows Desktop across the network. Through this service, a user can log onto the Windows Desktop using the Remote Desktop Connection client. The user can control the Desktop using her keyboard and mouse as if she were sitting at the server locally.

Remote Registry   The Remote Registry service has been available since Windows 95 and Windows NT 4.0 were released in the mid-1990s. The service allows remote access to the Windows Registry, which is the central configuration database for the operating system and applications. Using the Registry Editor, you can connect to other remote computers running the Remote Registry service, if you have the appropriate permissions.

Server   The Server service allows for sharing of printers, files, and named pipes across the network. This service implements the Server Message Block (SMB) protocol. It is the server peer to the client Workstation service. Both the Server service and the Workstation service are typically enabled on all Windows clients and servers.

Task Scheduler   The Task Scheduler service monitors for scheduled tasks and executes them at the defined time. Many scheduled tasks are built into the Windows operating system. For example, by default, every Wednesday at 1:00 a.m., the disks are defragmented. Additionally, every 14 days, a power efficiency analysis is executed to discover potential conditions causing overconsumption of power.

Volume Shadow Copy   The Volume Shadow Copy service provides the background backup processes used by shadow copies and other backup services. Shadow copies of files allow for recovery of previous file versions. Volume Shadow Copy was first introduced in Windows XP and Windows Server 2003.

Windows Event Log   The Windows Event Log service is used to log events that are viewed with the Event Viewer application; however, it does much more than this. The Windows Event Log service is also responsible for querying events, subscribing to events on remote machines, archiving event logs based on archive settings, and managing event metadata.

Windows Firewall   The Windows Firewall service is a client firewall that runs on Windows server and client operating systems. The Windows Firewall supports using IPSec rules for security as well as basic application and protocol filtering. The Windows Firewall functions will not be active if this service is disabled.

Windows Management Instrumentation   Windows Management Instrumentation (WMI) is to Windows operating systems what the Simple Network Management Protocol (SNMP) is to networked devices. SNMP allows administrators to monitor settings and states on network devices like switches and routers; WMI does the same for Windows operating systems. WMI was first introduced with Windows XP and Windows Server 2003. The WMI service provides access to the management information exposed by the WMI model.

Windows Remote Management   One of the most important new features in Windows Vista and Windows Server 2008 was Windows Remote Management (WinRM). The service that provides WinRM is the Windows Remote Management service. WinRM provides access to remote computers including the WMI data and allows for event collection with Event Viewer. The WinRM service may be configured locally or through Group Policy.

Windows Update   The Windows Update service uses either the Windows Update or Microsoft Update Internet service to download and install updates on the local system. The service must be running to check for, download, and install updates even if automatic updates are disabled.

Workstation   The Workstation service is responsible for network connections to Server Message Block (SMB) servers. Without this service, you cannot connect to shares on other Windows machines.

Configuring Service Settings

Services can be configured with many different settings. The settings impact the way a service starts and recovers. They also impact the privileges the service will have. The first thing you should understand is the various service startup types.

Services can be configured to start automatically or manually. Figure 7.10 shows the dialog used to configure service startup settings. They may also be configured as disabled. Table 7.1 lists the service startup types and the meaning of each type. Use this table as a reference to determine the proper startup type for a specific service.

Services can be configured only by users who are members of the Account Operators, Domain Admins, Enterprise Admins, or local Administrators group.

TABLE 7.1 Service startup types

Startup Type	Description
Automatic	Services configured to start automatically start when the operating system starts.
Automatic (Delayed Start)	Services configured to Automatic (Delayed Start) will start after all services configured for Automatic start.

Startup Type	Description
Manual	A manual startup type indicates that the service will not start automatically; however, it may be started when needed by a user or by an application that requires its use.
Disabled	A disabled service is one that will not be started automatically and cannot be started manually.

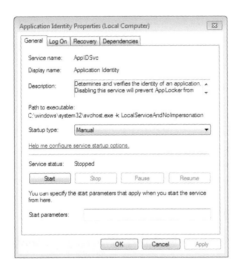

FIGURE 7.10 Configuring service startup settings

Like all applications, services may fail. If a service fails, the Windows Server operating system supports recovery actions. These actions include restarting the service, running a program, restarting the computer, or doing nothing.

In addition to the four optional reactions to a failure, you can determine what happens on the first, second, and subsequent failures. On the first failure, for example, you can simply restart the service. On the second failure, you can choose to run a program, which may be a script or batch file that you create to perform maintenance on the service and attempt to prevent future failures. On the subsequent failures, you can choose to restart the entire machine. You can set a reset fail counter so that the first and second failure must be within a given time frame in order to escalate through the first, second, and subsequent failure actions. Figure 7.11 shows the service's Recovery tab.

Services may be in one of several states at any given time. These include stopped, started, and paused.

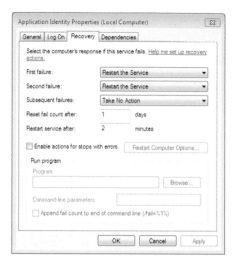

FIGURE 7.11 Using the service's
Recovery tab to configure recovery options

Managing Service Accounts

Service accounts may be used to run services in the context of a user account. In most cases, service accounts are created specifically for the services that use them, and real users never log on with those accounts. From a service trouble-shooting perspective, it's important to remember that a service must be able to do what it is designed to do. Services may attempt to perform any of the following operations:

► Read and write from or to the filesystem

► Read and write Registry data

► Access remote servers

► Access internal system hardware

Although services can do more than this list indicates, I chose those actions to show the capabilities that a service may require. For example, if a service requires access to remote servers, you must run the service in the context of a user account with access to those remote servers. If the service must read and write filesystem data, you must run the service as a user with those capabilities.

At the same time, it is important that you not give the service more capabilities than it requires. As explained in the sidebar "When You Want the Least and Not the Most," it is always best to abide by the principle of least privilege.

Service accounts are configured using the following procedure:

1. Click Start, search for SERVICES.MSC, and press the Enter key.

2. Double-click the service for which you wish to configure the service account.

3. Select the Log On tab and configure the desired account settings, as shown in Figure 7.12.

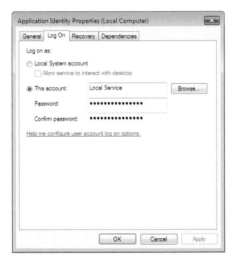

FIGURE 7.12 Configuring the service Log On settings

You should always configure a service's account through the service configuration tools if they provide this option. Doing so will ensure proper permissions for the service.

WHEN YOU WANT THE LEAST AND NOT THE MOST

The principle of *least privilege* states that users and systems should have no greater access than is required to perform their intended duties. This definition means that systems should be allowed to do what they need to do and nothing more. Other systems can access the secured system to perform their intended operations and can do nothing more. Least privilege is essential for secure network operations.

If you have a service configured with privileges beyond what it requires, and that service received requests from the network, it is possible that an attacker could take advantage of a vulnerability (a security flaw) in the service and force it to execute commands for him. If the service is running with privileges greater than those required to perform its duties, the service is unnecessarily exposing your system and network. If it were running with

(Continues)

WHEN YOU WANT THE LEAST AND NOT THE MOST *(Continued)*

least privilege, in the worst case scenario, the attacker could do whatever the service could do and nothing more.

Least privilege is achieved through a three-step process. First, you must determine the actions the service will need to take. Second, you must define the permission required to take those actions. Third, you must create an account with those permissions and configure the service to run in the context of that account. By doing so, you will increase the security of your network and systems.

Understanding Service Dependencies

If you have used Microsoft Office, you know that you can use the various applications in the suite together. For example, you can take a graph generated in Excel and load it into PowerPoint. Even though the graph is in PowerPoint, you can double-click it and edit it as if it were still in Excel. To perform these actions, both Excel and PowerPoint must be installed on the computer. They depend on each other to provide this functionality.

In a similar way, services may depend on other services. If a dependency service is not running, the dependent service may fail to start or simply not function correctly. If you suspect a service dependency problem, you can use the following procedure to view service dependencies:

1. Click Start, search for SERVICES.MSC, and press the Enter key.

2. Double-click the service for which you wish to view dependencies.

3. View the service dependencies in the upper pane labeled This Service Depends On The Following System Components.

> ▶
>
> **You can also see other services that depend on the selected service on the Dependencies tab of a service's Properties dialog.**

CLARIFYING SERVICE DEPENDENCIES

Service dependencies may be considered from two perspectives. From the depending service's perspective, the service dependencies are the services on which it depends. From the providing service's perspective, the service dependencies are the other services that depend on it.

(Continues)

> ## CLARIFYING SERVICE DEPENDENCIES *(Continued)*
>
> If you stop a service on which other services depend, severe problems could result. It is always best to look at the service dependencies before stopping a service. Look at the section of the Dependencies tab that reads The Following System Components Depend On This Service and ensure that no critical components will be impacted.

Stopping, Starting, and Restarting Services

The primary tasks related to service management are stopping, starting, and restarting services. Services may be stopped using one of three methods:

- ▶ The Services GUI interface
- ▶ The Windows CMD command-line interface
- ▶ The Windows PowerShell command-line interface

To stop a service using the GUI interface, you must first launch the Services management MMC. You can do this easily on Windows machines by clicking Start, typing **services.msc** into the search field, and pressing the Enter key.

You must first select the service you wish to stop so that you can stop it. Once it is selected, you can stop the service in any of several ways: by clicking the Stop button on the toolbar; selecting Stop from the Action menu; right-clicking the service and selecting Stop; or by double-clicking the service and then clicking the Stop button on the General tab of the service's Properties dialog.

If you want to stop a service at the CMD command-line interface, you must know the service name. The service name is displayed in the Service Name field of the General tab in the service's Properties dialog.

After you have determined the name of the service, you can stop it at the CMD command-line interface with the following steps:

1. Click Start ➢ All Programs ➢ Accessories ➢ Command Prompt.

2. Execute the following command:

   ```
   net stop spooler
   ```

3. When it is completed, execute the **exit** command, to exit the Command Prompt.

You can also launch the Command Prompt by searching for *cmd* in the search field on the Start menu.

You can also stop services at the Windows PowerShell command-line interface using these steps:

You can also launch Windows PowerShell by searching for *powershell* in the search field on the Start menu.

1. Click Start ➢ All Programs ➢ Accessories ➢ Windows PowerShell ➢ Windows PowerShell.

2. Execute the following command:

   ```
   stop-service spooler
   ```

3. Execute the **exit** command, when completed, to exit the Command Prompt.

Services can be started using the same three methods you learned in the preceding section for stopping them.

To start a service in the Services GUI, use the following procedure:

1. Click Start, search for SERVICES.MSC, and press the Enter key.

2. Select the service you wish to start and click the Start button on the toolbar, right-click the service and select Start, click the Start option on the Action menu, or double-click the service and click the Start button on the General tab.

To start a service at the CMD Command Prompt, use the following procedure:

1. Click Start ➢ All Programs ➢ Accessories ➢ Command Prompt.

2. Execute the following command:

   ```
   net start spooler
   ```

3. Execute the **exit** command, when completed, to exit the Command Prompt.

To start a service in the Windows PowerShell command-line interface, use the following procedure:

1. Click Start ➢ All Programs ➢ Accessories ➢ Windows PowerShell ➢ Windows PowerShell.

2. Execute the following command:

   ```
   start-service spooler
   ```

3. Execute the **exit** command, when completed, to exit the Command Prompt.

Sometimes a service will stop responding. When you look at the service status in the SERVICES.MSC application, it may show Started as the status even though it is no longer responding. In such cases, you should try restarting the service to get it running properly again. You can restart a service in the GUI MMC interface by clicking the service and then clicking the Restart Service button. You can also select the Action menu and choose the Restart option.

To restart a service at the CMD Command Prompt, you will need to perform a stop-and-start procedure. You must first use the net stop command to stop the service and then use the net start command to start it again. There is no restart option with the net command. You may alternatively use the Command Prompt sc command, but it also requires one command to stop the service and another to start it.

In Windows PowerShell, you can use the restart-service command to restart a service. It works just like the start-service and stop-service commands. Use the following procedure to restart a service in Windows PowerShell:

1. Click Start ➢ All Programs ➢ Accessories ➢ Windows PowerShell ➢ Windows PowerShell.

2. Execute the command **restart-service spooler**.

3. Execute the **exit** command, when completed, to exit the Command Prompt.

◄

Do not be alarmed when you receive no feedback after stopping a service with the Windows PowerShell stop-service **command. The command simply stops the service, and you receive feedback only if a problem occurs.**

THE ESSENTIALS AND BEYOND

In this chapter, you learned how to work with applications on Windows computers. First, you learned about the differences between local and networked applications. Next, you learned how to install, configure, and remove applications. You then explored various application virtualization solutions. Finally, you saw how to configure and manage services on Windows operating systems.

ADDITIONAL EXERCISES

▶ Download and install an application on Windows 7.

▶ Using Group Policy, disallow access to CD and DVD drives for execute actions.

▶ View the service dependencies for the DHCP Client service.

To compare your answers to the author's, please visit www.sybex.com/go/osessentials.

(Continues)

THE ESSENTIALS AND BEYOND *(Continued)*

REVIEW QUESTIONS

1. When configuring recovery options for Windows services, how many recovery actions can be set based on first failure, second failure, and so on?

    A. 1   **C.** 3

    B. 2   **D.** 4

2. True or false. Med-V is a management interface used to configure and deploy virtual machines that run on the client computers.

3. What is the name of the Group Policy setting that disables the Programs and Features Control Panel applet?

    A. Hide "Programs and Features"

    B. Disable "Programs and Features"

    C. Disable "Programs and Features" Applet

    D. Hide "Programs and Features" Page

4. What are the three states that a Windows service can be in at any given time?

5. Where are 64-bit applications installed on 32-bit editions of Windows 7?

    A. `C:\Program Files`   **C.** `C:\Program Files (x64)`

    B. `C:\Program Files (x86)`   **D.** They cannot be installed.

6. Define VDI.

7. Define a service account.

8. What cmdlet is used in Windows PowerShell to start a service?

    A. `net start`   **C.** `start-service`

    B. `service-start`   **D.** `net begin`

9. What command can be used at the Windows Command Prompt to stop a service?

    A. `net quit`   **C.** `service quit`

    B. `net stop`   **D.** `service stop`

10. True or false. AppLocker rules apply to Windows 7 Professional, Enterprise, and Ultimate editions of the operating system.

CHAPTER 8

Controlling Malware

Malware includes any software that is designed to cause harm or hassles for computer users. It includes viruses, worms, Trojans, and spyware. Malware has become an increasingly severe problem over the years. Today, it is essential for networked computers to run antivirus software and possibly other anti-malware solutions. This chapter introduces malware and the various protection methods used to prevent infection and infiltration. The topics covered include:

▶ **Understanding malware types**

▶ **Planning for malware protection**

▶ **Understanding Microsoft protection methods**

Understanding Malware Types

Malware comes in two basic forms: software and wetware. Wetware is a colloquial term that refers to human brain cells. Stated differently, malware in the form of wetware is simply the attack of one human intelligence against another. Phishing, covered later in this section, is an example of a wetware attack. Software-based malware includes viruses, worms, Trojans, and backdoors, all of which are covered in this section.

Understanding Viruses and Worms

A computer program with the ability to regenerate itself is called a *virus*. A virus may or may not harm the infected computer. Viruses may lie dormant for some time before they attack the infected host machine. A *worm* is a self-replicating application that requires no user action for reproduction. Viruses usually require human interaction in some way, whereas worms do not.

To define viruses more clearly, consider that they typically have three components:

▶ A mission

▶ A trigger

▶ Self-propagation

The mission is the "why" of the virus. It is the reason it was created; this reason can include destruction of data, denial-of-service (DoS) attacks, and many other ill results. The trigger is the "when" of the virus. It determines what will cause the virus to execute. It may be a specific date or time. It may be anytime an infected program is launched, but some trigger is associated with the virus. Finally, the self-propagation is the "how" of the virus; it occurs through either attachment to other files or attachment to boot sectors. Either way, the virus can spread rapidly throughout any environment.

While viruses depend on a carrier to spread, worms do not. Worms can be self-contained, self-propagating programs. However, the results of a worm's actions are the same as those of a virus: data destruction, DoS attacks, and so on.

THE VIRUS TEAM

In the 1990s, I worked for a large organization in the United States. We had more than 60 locations and over 25,000 employees. When the Word and Excel macro viruses came on the scene in the mid-90s, we were running antivirus software, but it did not detect these macro viruses. They were a new breed of virus, and it took the antivirus vendors some time to catch up.

We assembled a team of seven people to investigate the problem of macro viruses (as well as other viruses) and develop a solution to clean our Microsoft Office documents as well as removable media, which were floppy disks in those days. As the team moved forward, we tracked the progress and found that we were cleaning more than 2,500 infected documents each day. Thankfully, the process was automated, but this was still a lot of infected documents.

The number slowly dropped, but it was more than six months before it fell below 100 cleaned documents each day. The problem was simple. We would clean documents, but a user would bring in another floppy disk from home and open an infected document. Then he would open other documents, which would be reinfected because the application itself was infected from the document brought from home. As he attached the newly infected business documents to emails and sent them out, many more people would get infected.

This is the reality of malware. Thankfully, we have a better grip on it today than we did in those early days, but it shows the importance of running anti-malware solutions before an infection occurs.

Defining Trojans and Backdoors

Another type of malware is the Trojan horse. Named after the fabled gift of ancient fame, the Trojan horse enters the computer under the guise of a useful program or utility. Once in the machine, it may infect the machine with a virus or worm, or it may download other Trojans.

Similar to the Trojan horse is the spyware or adware villain. Spyware is installed on your computer and reports back to the source. Adware is installed on your computer and causes unwanted ads to display on your screen. Additionally, spyware and adware combinations are common.

Both Trojan horses and spyware applications may infect your computer with backdoor applications. Backdoors are applications installed on the computer to provide the attacker with a way back into the machine at a later time. They may also be used to gain access to the network even though the firewall would not otherwise allow it.

Avoiding Phishing Attacks

Phishing attacks are used to manipulate individuals into taking actions they should not take or providing information they should not provide. They are often implemented through email or text messaging (also called instant messaging or Short Message Service [SMS]). The attacker may use different methods, but the following are common:

Phishing attacks fall into a larger category of attack known as social engineering. Social engineering uses human manipulation to circumvent security.

Impersonating Someone   With the impersonation method, the attacker first gains information about people you know and possibly trust. Next, he sends you a message and makes it appear to come from that person. Because you know the person, the message has greater initial legitimacy. The attacker may then go on to ask you to send money or provide banking information so that he can place money into your account. Of course, his real goal is to take money out of the account.

Spoofing a Website   When spoofing a website, the attacker will create a site that looks just like one you are familiar with, such as a banking website or a site like PayPal. Next, she will send you an email asking you to log into the site and verify your profile information or some such action. The link provided is to the spoofed website, and when you log into it, you are just giving your logon information to the attacker.

Creating a False Scenario   The original phishing attacks fell into this category. The attacker devises a scenario in which he has access to millions of dollars that he needs to store somewhere. If you let him store it in your account, he will let you keep the interest earned on the account. Of course, once again, he just wants to steal the money from your account. Other scenarios exist, but this has been the most common over the years.

The first step to avoiding a phishing attack is simply being aware of them. Anytime you receive an email that asks for personal information, banking information, or updates to a website you use, you should question the authenticity of that email. Most online service providers have now taken a position of not sending out links but telling you to go to the site and log on. This way, it is up to you to enter the valid URL in your web browser.

In general, the following tips will help you to avoid phishing attacks:

▶ Be suspicious of any scenario where you are asked for money or financial information.

▶ Don't click links within emails; instead, manually navigate to the known site in your web browser.

▶ Scan all downloaded applications for worms and Trojans; downloaded applications may be used to gather information.

▶ Do not enter personal information in pop-up screens on websites, as they may be the result of an attack on the website and not legitimate code.

▶ Verify that you are using a secure website (the URL should begin with HTTPS://) when submitting credit card information online.

▶ Update your web browser to ensure that all security patches are applied.

In addition to these actions, it is beneficial to report phishing attacks to the website at www.antiphishing.org. You can also forward phishing attack emails to spam@uce.gov. Finally, you can notify the Internet Crime Complaint Center at www.ic3.gov.

> **Pharming is a new kind of attack where the information is gathered through malicious programs installed on your computer.**

Planning for Malware Protection

Now that you understand the problem, you can learn about the solutions. In this section, you will first learn about the concept of security itself. Security is defined and then three important topics are addressed:

▶ Configuring and using User Account Control (UAC)

▶ Selecting anti-malware solutions

▶ Protecting the Windows Registry

Security Defined

Security is a difficult concept to define as it relates to computers and information systems. Why is the term so hard to define for so many people? It may be because the term *security* represents an impossible dream. Consider the definition of security as found in The Oxford American College Dictionary:

> *The state of being free from danger or threat.*

Can this state of freedom really be achieved? When it comes to computers, many think it cannot. Even in everyday life we cannot really be free from danger or threat. We can only manage the level of risk we accept in relation to dangers and threats. The same is true for computer and network security. So let's use the following as our working definition of security in relation to Windows OS security:

> *Security is the state in which an acceptable level of risk is achieved through the use of policies and procedures that can be monitored and managed.*

With the phrase "acceptable level of risk," we establish a foundation that is both achievable and measurable. We can achieve the acceptable level of risk by creating and documenting policies, implementing procedures in compliance with these policies, and ensuring the adherence to the policies through auditing and enforcement.

A DEFINITION THAT WAS HARD TO COME BY

To illustrate the difficulty of defining the term *security*, consider an exploratory adventure I went on just before writing this paragraph. I pulled out two different Security+ certification study guides to see how security was defined in their glossaries. Each book indeed had a glossary. Each was designed to prepare candidates for a certification that has one single word in the title, and that word is *security*. Yet, neither book defines security in the glossary. The word is simply missing from the list.

I didn't want to give up here, so I pulled out the study guide for another certification. This time, the certification was the CCNA Security exam from Cisco Systems. The book, again, has a glossary. Do you want to guess whether the word *security* was defined? If you guessed that the word was missing from this glossary, too, you were correct. Those who know me well know that I don't give up easily. I left the certifications with the word *security* in

(Continues)

A Definition That Was Hard to Come By *(Continued)*

the certification name and decided to look at other resources. After seeking through the glossary of 11 books on the topic of security, I finally found one that included the word in the glossary. It was the *Certified Ethical Hacker (CEH) Prep Guide*, by Ronald L. Krutz and Russell Dean Vines (Wiley, 2008). Now, I'm sure that many other security books on the market include a definition for the term in the glossary, but I was surprised at the effort it took to find one in my library of more than 1,100 books on computer-related topics (yes, I love books and have a library of more than 4,000 books in total).

Just in case you're wondering, the definition in *The CEH Prep Guide* book was, "Measures and controls that ensure the confidentiality, integrity, availability, and accountability of the information processed and stored by a computer." I agree with this specific computer-related definition and have found this book exceptional in its coverage of hacking techniques, whether you're interested in gaining the CEH certification or not.

The importance of security varies by organization, depending on the differing values placed on information and networks within organizations. For example, organizations involved in banking and healthcare will likely place a greater priority on information security than organizations involved in selling greeting cards. However, in every organization there exists a need to classify data so that it can be protected appropriately. The greeting card company will likely place a greater value on its customer database than it will on the log files for the Internet firewall. Each of these data files has value, but one is more valuable than the other and should be classified accordingly so that it can be protected properly.

The information classification process is at the core of information security; it can be outlined as follows:

1. Determine the value of the information in question.

2. Apply an appropriate classification based on that value.

3. Implement the proper security solutions for that classification of information.

For example, suppose your organization chooses to classify information in three categories: internal, public, and internal sensitive. Information classified as internal may require only appropriate authentication and authorization. Information classified as public may require neither authentication nor authorization. The internal sensitive information may require authentication, authorization, and storage-based encryption.

You can see why different organizations have different security priorities and needs from this very brief overview of information classification and security measures. It is also true, however, that every organization is at risk of certain threats. Threats like DoS, worms, and others are often promiscuous in nature. The attacker does not care what networks or systems are damaged or made less effective in a promiscuous attack. The intention of such an attack is often only to express the attacker's ability or to serve some other motivation for the attacker, such as curiosity or need for recognition. Since many attacks are promiscuous in nature, it is very important that every organization place some level of priority on security, regardless of the intrinsic value of the information or networks it employs.

Various organizations perform surveys and gather statistics that are useful in gaining an understanding of the need for security. *InformationWeek* magazine performs an annual security survey. A recent survey showed that complexity is the greatest difficulty in securing systems. A whopping 62 percent of respondents cited complexity as the biggest security challenge. Administrators are dealing with many different data types and that data is often unclassified. Without classification, it's difficult to determine how to protect the data. Good news exists, however, in *InformationWeek*'s survey: solutions exist that can help reduce the likelihood of a security incident. According to the survey, the following solutions were selected by the indicated percentage of respondents:

- ▶ Firewalls (63 percent)
- ▶ Antivirus (59 percent)
- ▶ Encryption (46 percent)
- ▶ VPNs (45 percent)
- ▶ Strong passwords (40 percent)
- ▶ Spam filtering (35 percent)
- ▶ Email security (34 percent)

The Computer Security Institute (CSI) is another organization that reports on the state of information and systems security. CSI has performed their annual security survey for more than 10 years and the statistics show that security should be a very important part of any organization's budget and plans. In a five-year period, the results showed a drop in the average organization's losses due to cybercrime; however, recent surveys reported a significant rise in estimated losses. The only good news is that the spike in the recent survey results in financial losses that are still lower than those reported in earlier surveys. This continued lower financial loss rating may indicate that we are doing a better job of securing our data and assets, or it may only indicate that we are spending less on hardware and software and therefore losing less when these assets are stolen or compromised.

The following statistics represent just a few of the important reports from the CSI Computer Crime and Security Survey:

▶ 25 percent of responding organizations spend between 6 and 10 percent of the annual IT budget on security.

▶ 61 percent of responding organizations still outsource no security functions.

▶ 46 percent indicated that they had experienced a security incident in the previous 12 months and 10 percent indicated that they were unsure.

▶ 26 percent of the total responding pool indicated that there had been more than 10 incidents in the previous 12 months.

▶ Only 36 percent indicated that they accrued no losses due to insider threats, which means that 64 percent experienced an insider attack that led to losses.

▶ The most common type of attack was the simple abuse of Internet access by valid users.

▶ Viruses were also a common attack problem, with 52 percent reporting such attacks.

▶ Only 5 percent reported telecom fraud and 13 percent reported system penetration; however, it is important to know that some experts estimate as many as 85 percent of all attacks go undetected.

It is very clear from these statistics that threats are real and security is important and actions should be taken to improve the security of our systems, including our database systems. The statistics show us what is happening, but the theory can help us gain an understanding of why these attacks occur.

Configuring and Using UAC

The User Account Control (UAC) feature was first introduced in Windows Vista. It is an entirely new way to think of running applications in Windows operating systems. The purpose of UAC is to allow administrators to run as standard users until they need administrative access. Doing this makes it more difficult for viruses and other malware to infect the system. However, when UAC was first introduced in Windows Vista, users and administrators had one major complaint: It nagged them too much. In other words, it seemed to continually be asking for approval for even mundane tasks. Microsoft resolved this issue in Windows 7 by removing several items from the list of tasks requiring administrative rights. The following tasks required an administrator in Windows Vista but do not in Windows 7:

▶ Installing updates from Windows Update

▶ Installing drivers downloaded from Windows Update or included with the OS

▶ Pairing a Bluetooth device with the computer

▶ Resetting the network adapter and performing other network diagnostics tasks

▶ Viewing Windows settings

To fully understand UAC, you must grasp the difference between a standard user and an administrative user. A standard user account is one that belongs to no administrative groups. Every Windows machine includes a local group named Administrators. In a Windows domain environment, which includes Windows servers acting as network authentication servers, the Domain Admins and Enterprise Admins groups are also administrators.

An administrative user account is one that belongs to one of the mentioned administrative groups and can therefore perform administrative actions. When default UAC settings are used and an administrator logs onto the machine with an admin account, she runs as a standard user until an administrative action is performed. When the administrative action is performed, the user is asked to elevate privileges to perform the action. The request for elevation is called an elevation prompt; Figure 8.1 shows an example. The elevation prompt asks for permission to elevate, by default, when an administrator is logged on. When a standard user account is logged on, the prompt will ask for administration credentials to perform the task.

The user is still prompted for elevated privileges when changing Windows settings.

The term *elevate* simply refers to using administrative permissions or rights for the requested action.

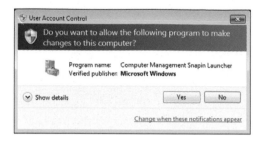

FIGURE 8.1 The UAC elevation prompt
for signed code

> **Signed code is
> application code that
> is digitally signed
> with a certificate.
> Microsoft allows
> code it has signed to
> function differently
> than code it has not
> signed.**

UAC displays different elevation prompts depending on the type of user logged onto the machine and the settings for UAC. Figure 8.1 showed the elevation prompt for an administrative user when signed code is executed. Figure 8.2 shows the elevation prompt when unsigned code is executed.

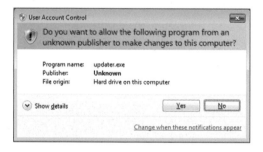

FIGURE 8.2 The UAC elevation prompt
for unsigned code

When an administrative user account logs onto a Windows 7 machine with UAC enabled, she receives two access tokens for the network. The access token identifies her and the groups to which she belongs. The first access token is a standard user access token with no administrative rights. The second access token is a full administrator access token with administrative rights. After the access tokens are assigned, EXPLORER.EXE loads to display the Desktop and Start menu user interface.

When a standard user account logs onto the same machine, only a standard user access token is provided and then EXPLORER.EXE loads. Standard users who are also configured as admins in UAC must always provide their administrative credentials (typically a username and password) when asked to elevate privileges.

Finally, it is important to understand the prompts and UAC levels in more detail. Additionally, you should know how to change the UAC levels using the Control Panel.

Two general types of prompts exist: consent prompts and credential prompts. Consent prompts are used only when administrative users are logged on. They simply ask for permission to elevate privileges. Credential prompts ask for a username and password of an administrative user. They are used when standard users are logged on.

Three different colors are used for the banners in elevation prompts: red, blue, and yellow. The red banner indicates a blocked publisher. In this case, the network administrator has blocked the publisher in Group Policy, and the result is that the user cannot select to elevate privileges. The only option is to close the UAC prompt, as shown in Figure 8.3. Blocked publishers are those explicitly declared as untrusted in Software Restriction Policies within Group Policy.

FIGURE 8.3 UAC prompt for an untrusted publisher

The blue banner indicates that the application requesting administrative access is either signed by Windows or is an explicitly trusted publisher in Group Policy. The yellow banner indicates that the publisher is simply unknown. The publisher is not blocked, it is not a Windows signed application, and it is not explicitly trusted.

You can adjust the UAC level for prompts in the Control Panel. To do so, follow these steps:

1. Log onto the machine as an administrative user.

2. Click Start ➢ Control Panel.

3. In the Category view, select System and Security.

4. In the Action Center group, select Change User Account Control Settings.

5. If prompted to elevate privileges, click Yes.

6. Drag the slider to adjust the settings as desired, as shown in Figure 8.4. Refer to Table 8.1 for an explanation of the four available settings.

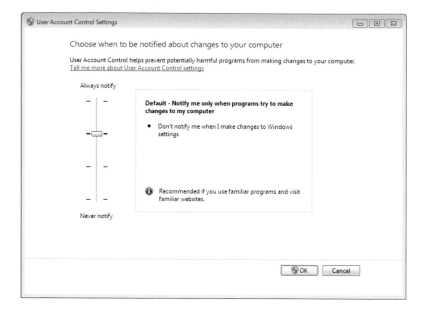

FIGURE 8.4 The UAC Settings dialog

TABLE 8.1 UAC level settings

UAC Level	Description
Always Notify Me	Any action requiring administrative rights results in an elevation prompt.
Notify Me Only When Programs Try To Make Changes	Only actions requiring administrative rights and executing nonsigned code result in an elevation prompt.
Notify Me Only When Programs Try To Make Changes (Do Not Dim My Desktop)	The same as the previous option, except the Desktop remains available during the display of the elevation prompt.
Never Notify Me	The UAC feature is effectively disabled.

Additional customizations can be made to the behavior of UAC through Group Policy settings. You can make these additional modifications through the Local Security Policy or through the domain-based Group Policy settings. For more information, see

`http://technet.microsoft.com/en-us/library/dd446675(WS.10).aspx`

Microsoft suggests that the UAC feature can help to prevent malware infections in the following ways:

▶ Standard users have insufficient privileges to install software.

▶ Malware cannot silently install itself even when administrators are logged on as long as default UAC settings are used.

▶ All tasks requiring administrative user privileges must be explicitly enabled to run.

Each organization will have to decide on the best way to configure UAC settings. The driving factors will be security and usability. The more restrictive settings are more secure, but they make the system more difficult to use. The less restrictive settings are easier to use, but they make the system less secure. On the spectrum between security and usability, most organizations will be able to find the best settings for their needs.

Selecting Anti-Malware Solutions

To protect your network from the many types of malware applications, you will need to run antivirus and antispyware applications. There are two basic types of anti-malware applications: ingress and host-based. Ingress applications reside at the entry point of the data, and host-based anti-malware applications run on the host devices. An example of an ingress anti-malware application would be an email server scanner. This software would scan email messages as they enter (and possibly exit) the email server. If malware is detected, the message can be rejected, flagged as malware-infected, or passed on without attachments.

Host-based anti-malware solutions run on the Windows computer. Several commercial applications are available from many vendors besides Microsoft, including these:

▶ Symantec

▶ TrendMicro

▶ McAfee

▶ Panda Security

In addition to these commercial anti-malware providers, several free solutions are available from Microsoft as well as third-party companies.

Antivirus software must be maintained. You will need to download and apply new definition files frequently. Many antivirus applications include automatic update features so that the definitions can be maintained without the need for user interaction. The definition file includes the signatures that are used to identify known malware.

Protecting the Windows Registry

The Windows Registry is the centralized configuration database for the OS, applications, and user settings. Protecting the Registry is very important. The simplest way to back up the Registry is to create a system restore point using System Restore, which is covered in detail in Chapter 14, "Backup and Recovery." For now, it is important to understand the sections of the Registry that may be exploited by malware.

In most cases, malware will be installed and configured so that it starts each time your system starts. The Registry includes locations that contain applications and services that should start automatically when the system starts. You can view Registry data using the Registry Editor application. No shortcut exists for this application, but it can be accessed by searching for **regedit** in the Start menu search field. Figure 8.5 shows the Registry Editor. The following locations should be checked for malware applications if you suspect such applications are on the system:

- ► HKEY_LOCAL_MACHINE
    - ► SOFTWARE\Microsoft\Windows\CurrentVersion\Run
    - ► SOFTWARE\Wow6432Node\Microsoft\Windows CurrentVersion\Run
    - ► SYSTEM\CurrentControlSet\services
- ► HKEY_CURRENT_USER
    - ► SOFTWARE\MICROSOFT\Windows\CurrentVersion\Run

Some malware applications will block access to the Registry and tools like MSCONFIG, and this can be a sign of infection as well.

In addition to the Registry, applications may start up automatically through the Start menu's Startup folder. Any shortcuts located in the Startup folder will run automatically on system startup, so you should check this location as well when you suspect a malware infection. You can also use the MSCONFIG application to view the list of programs that start automatically when the system is started. This application can be found by searching in the Start menu's search field for **msconfig**. MSCONFIG is shown in Figure 8.6 with the Startup tab displayed, showing all applications configured to run automatically on startup.

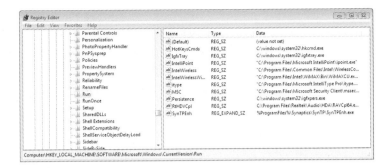

FIGURE 8.5 The Registry Editor showing the Run subkey contents

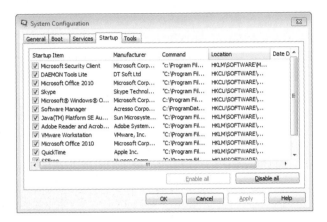

FIGURE 8.6 MSCONFIG (System Configuration)
showing the Startup tab

Understanding Microsoft Protection Methods

In this section, you will learn about the various tools that Microsoft provides to help protect you from malware and remove malware should it infect your systems:

▶ The Action Center

▶ The Malicious Software Removal Tool

▶ Windows Defender

▶ Microsoft Security Essentials

▶ Microsoft Forefront

Some of these are included with Windows 7 and others must either be downloaded or purchased before use. Remember that third-party vendors also create similar applications, but this book is focused primarily on the Microsoft solutions related to Windows operating systems, so those solutions are presented in more detail here.

Working with the Action Center

The Action Center does not actually protect your system from malware, and it has no ability to clean the system of malware should it become infected. However, it does provide notifications related to anti-malware software installation and update status. The Action Center will warn you if you have no anti-malware software installed or if the definitions are old.

You can access the Action Center by clicking on a Notification Area notification balloon, should one be displayed, or through the Control Panel. To access it through the Control Panel, follow these steps:

1. Click Start Control Panel.

2. In the Category view, select System and Security.

3. Click the Action Center link on the System and Security page.

Figure 8.7 shows the Action Center interface.

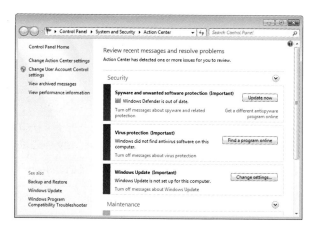

FIGURE 8.7 The Action Center showing notifications

In the Security section, the Action Center will notify you about the status of the following security features:

► Windows Update

► Internet Security Settings

▶ Network Firewall

▶ Spyware and Related Protection (Windows Defender)

▶ User Account Control

▶ Virus Protection

You can change the notification settings by clicking Change Action Center Settings on the left panel. On the Change Action Center Settings page, you can disable both security and maintenance notifications, as shown in Figure 8.8.

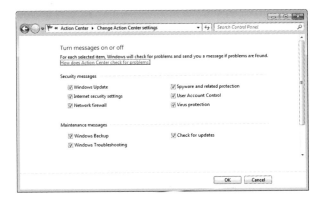

FIGURE 8.8 Changing Action Center default notification settings

Understanding the Malicious Software Removal Tool

The Malicious Software Removal Tool (MSRT) is a free download from Microsoft that removes many known malware applications. The tool can remove more than 160 malware applications. A complete list of removable malware is maintained at

`http://www.microsoft.com/security/pc-security/malware-families.aspx`

Two installation types of MSRT exist:

▶ The Microsoft Update and Windows Update version runs in the background once each month and reports if a malware infection is found.

▶ The installation available from the Microsoft Download Center can be executed as often as needed.

Regardless of the installation type used, Microsoft releases a new version of the tool on the second Tuesday of each month and as needed in response to security

This second Tuesday of the month has come to be called Patch Tuesday among the user community.

incidents that may occur. Figure 8.9 shows the MSRT application performing a custom scan on a Windows 7 machine.

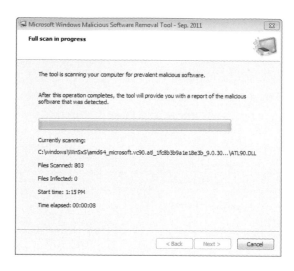

FIGURE 8.9 Performing a custom scan with MSRT

Using Windows Defender

Windows Defender is a preinstalled application on Windows 7 computers that detects spyware and other potentially unwanted software. Microsoft considered Windows Defender an operating system component, but it can be disabled should you choose to use a different antispyware solution. Some anti-malware solutions will completely remove Windows Defender, such as Microsoft Security Essentials, and others will simply disable it. Windows Defender can protect a computer in two ways:

Real-Time Protection   With real-time protection, Windows Defender monitors software installation attempts and warns you when it suspects that an attempt is made to install unwanted software. Additionally, it may alert you when applications attempt to make changes to administrative-level Windows settings.

Scanning   On-demand scans allow you to perform a scan of all the data on your drives at any time. If a file is suspected as spyware or other unwanted software, you will be notified. You can schedule scans to occur on a regular basis as well.

You can execute Windows Defender by selecting Start and searching for **Windows Defender** in the search field. Figure 8.10 shows Windows Defender indicating the need for a definition update. If you use the Microsoft Security Essentials software and some other third-party software applications, Windows Defender will be disabled as it is not required.

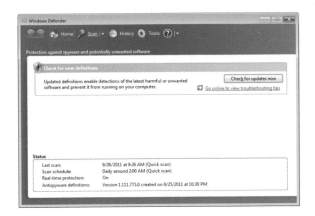

◀

Like antivirus software, Windows Defender uses definitions to detect unwanted software based on signatures. The definitions must be updated regularly.

FIGURE 8.10 Windows Defender indicating the need for an update

Using Microsoft Security Essentials

Microsoft Security Essentials is not included in Windows 7 or any other Windows OS; however, it is available as a download from the Microsoft website. Microsoft Security Essentials is a free anti-malware application. Once installed, it actively monitors the system processes and files scanning for malware. Figure 8.11 shows the Microsoft Security Essentials Home tab, which is used to launch on-demand scans and view the status of the application.

FIGURE 8.11 The Microsoft Security Essentials Home tab

Like Windows Defender, Microsoft Security Essentials can be used for real-time protection and scanning-based protection. On the Settings tab, you can configure the scanning schedule and the default actions to take should unwanted software be discovered. Figure 8.12 shows the Settings tab.

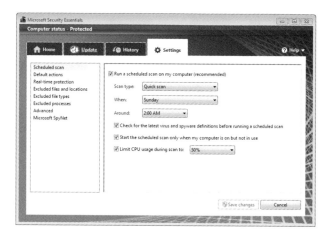

FIGURE 8.12 The Microsoft Security Essentials Settings tab

Microsoft Security Essentials also scans inside archives, such as ZIP and CAB files, by default. This allows the tool to locate even malware that may be embedded in downloads. You can optionally enable automatic scanning of removable drives like flash drives as well.

Understanding Microsoft Forefront

Threat management servers are used to detect and hopefully prevent security attacks on your network. Microsoft offers the Forefront server solution for threat management. Forefront can integrate with other Microsoft products to provide security for these products. The products that can be integrated include:

- ► Exchange Server
- ► SharePoint
- ► Office Communication Server
- ► Endpoints (computers running Windows operating systems)

Microsoft Forefront Threat Management Gateway 2010 offers several features to help protect your users. These features include:

HTTPS Inspection   Provides the ability to inspect the contents of SSL encrypted traffic to look for potential malware.

Email Security   Scans email messages for potential malware.

Network Inspection System (NIS)   Scans network traffic looking for malware and other types of attacks.

Web Malware Detection   Scans standard HTTP traffic for malware.

VPN Support   Allows VPN connections to be created for site-to-site connections and remote access VPN connections. Site-to-site VPN connections are made between two networks to allow traffic from multiple users to traverse the VPN.

Microsoft Forefront Threat Management Gateway is just one example of a threat management server. Several companies offer competing products.

THE ESSENTIALS AND BEYOND

In this chapter, you learned about malware and the important tools and techniques used to manage and combat it. You began by exploring the various types of malware, including viruses, worms, Trojans, and backdoors. Next, you investigated the planning of malware protection, which included gaining an understanding of the concept of security, using the built-in User Account Control (UAC), selecting protection software, and protecting the Registry. Finally, you learned about the Microsoft malware solutions.

ADDITIONAL EXERCISES

▶ Research new viruses online at the McAfee virus information site located at http://home.mcafee.com/virusinfo.

▶ Download and install Microsoft Security Essentials and perform a system scan.

▶ Use the Malicious Software Removal Tool to scan your computer for malware.

To compare your answers to the author's, please visit www.sybex.com/go/osessentials.

REVIEW QUESTIONS

1. When does Microsoft release a new version of the Malicious Software Removal Tool?

    A. First Tuesday

    B. Second Tuesday

    C. Third Tuesday

    D. Fourth Tuesday

(Continues)

THE ESSENTIALS AND BEYOND (Continued)

2. True or false. When an unknown application is executed with default UAC settings as a standard user, the banner color is red.

3. What specific type of application is often installed on a computer to provide a method of re-entry for an attacker?

    A. Virus   **C.** Phish

    B. Worm   **D.** Backdoor

4. Where are the alerts from the Action Center displayed?

5. You receive an email asking you to update your account at PayPal.com with a link to the update page. What kind of attack is most likely included in this email?

    A. Virus   **C.** Trojan

    B. Worm   **D.** Phishing

6. Define data classification.

7. Define a virus.

8. What application runs once each month by default and displays notifications only if malware is found?

    A. Windows Defender   **C.** Malicious Software Removal Tool

    B. Microsoft Security Essentials   **D.** Microsoft Forefront

9. What specific type of application is installed as if it were used for a specific purpose but is really a method for installing malware?

    A. Virus   **C.** Trojan

    B. Worm   **D.** Frontdoor

10. True or false. Forefront Threat Management Gateway is used to scan for malware in network traffic.

CHAPTER 9

File Management

Files are used to store data, application execution code, and anything else that needs to be stored. File management tools are an important collection of features in any OS. Windows operating systems provide support for multiple filesystems, the use of data encryption and compression, and a special management feature called *libraries*. This chapter introduces all of these topics:

▶ **Understanding filesystems**

▶ **Working with encryption**

▶ **Using libraries**

Understanding Filesystems

Filesystems are used on storage devices and media. You will learn more about storage device management in Chapter 12, "Storage Management."

Originally, Microsoft's OS was called the Disk Operating System (DOS), and the very name of the OS indicated its primary function: providing access to disks and the data stored on them. Of course, over the years the OS has evolved to offer many features unrelated to disk management, but that is still a primary feature of all versions. In this section, you will learn about the purpose of a filesystem, the various filesystems supported by Windows, and the issues related to 32- and 64-bit systems.

Exploring the Purpose of a Filesystem

A filesystem defines the methods used to store and retrieve data using storage devices. The filesystem usually includes the following features or components at a minimum:

▶ A defined structure for storing data on the storage unit

▶ A method for referencing the location of the data on the storage unit

▶ Constraints on factors such as file sizes, number of files, and filenames

Beyond those minimum requirements, when selecting a filesystem you must ensure that you use one that meets your needs. For example, if a filesystem does not support long filenames and you require them, you would not select that filesystem. If a filesystem does not support permission management and you require this feature, you would not select that filesystem. These are the important issues to keep in mind as you choose the appropriate filesystem for your installation and storage locations.

The first component of a filesystem is the defined structure for storing data. For example, the filesystem may store data in allocation units or clusters. If an allocation unit size is 4 kilobytes, and a 7 kilobyte file is written to the disk, 8 kilobytes will be consumed because an entire allocation unit is required for storage. Many filesystems allow for variable allocation unit sizes that can be configured at the time of formatting the storage media.

The second component is the referencing method for locating data on the storage unit. This is essentially a database that indicates the filename and the physical drive sectors where the file is stored. It is used by the OS to look up and retrieve the physical data for a file when it is required by an application.

The third component is the set of constraints that limit file sizes, the total number of files, and the filenames that can be used. Some filesystems are case sensitive, for example, and you can name one file Horse.txt and another file horse.txt while placing them in the same folder or directory. Other filesystems do not allow this. Windows filesystems are case preserving but they are not case sensitive by default; however, you can create multiple files with the same names but with different capitalization. If you do this, in most applications, you will be able to access only one of the files. As for the file size limit, this is mostly related to the bit level of the filesystem. For example, 32-bit filesystems can support larger files than 16-bit filesystems, and so on.

Comparing Windows Filesystems

Windows 7 supports several filesystems. Some of these filesystems are well known; others are legacy systems still used even though many advanced support professionals are not aware of their existence. The following filesystems are supported in Windows 7, where the number indicates the bit level of the filesystem:

- ▶ FAT12
- ▶ FAT16
- ▶ FAT32
- ▶ NTFS
- ▶ CDFS
- ▶ UDFS

Of these filesystems, 12-bit File Allocation Table (FAT12) is probably the biggest surprise to most support professionals. This is the original version of FAT, and it is still used in Windows 7 and Windows Server 2008 R2 today. When a drive or volume smaller than 16 MB is formatted in Windows, it will be formatted with FAT12.

FAT16 is also still used, but only for backward compatibility with older systems that still require it. Such older systems include Windows 3.1 and DOS. If you do not require compatibility with these older systems, FAT32 should be used instead whenever the FAT filesystem is needed. FAT32 supports much larger drives than FAT16 (up to 32 GB compared to only 4 GB) and uses more efficient storage allocation units for larger drives.

The New Technology Filesystem (NTFS) could also be called NTFS64, as it is a 64-bit filesystem. Today, Microsoft simply calls it NTFS and does not indicate that the acronym is still applicable. In addition to supporting very large volumes, NTFS provides support for enhanced features like compression, encryption, and file-level permissions.

The Compact Disk Filesystem (CDFS) and Universal Disk Format System (UDFS or simply UDF) are used on CD and DVD media. UDFS may also be used on additional media types.

In most cases, you only have to choose the filesystem when formatting internal or removable drives larger than a few megabytes (16 MB to be specific). When making your choice, consider the factors in Table 9.1. As you can see from the table, NTFS supports the largest volume sizes, file sizes, and number of files. For this reason alone, it would be a preferred filesystem on larger volumes; however, it also adds enhanced features, as previously mentioned, beyond just the enhanced file size support.

The most common use of FAT12 today is for formatting floppy disks, although even this is becoming less common.

TABLE 9.1 Comparing Windows filesystems

Factor	FAT16	FAT32	NTFS
OS compatibility	MS-DOS, all versions of Windows	Windows 95 and later as well as Windows NT 4.0 and later	Windows NT 4.0 with Service Pack 4 and later can all access the same NTFS volumes
Volume size	Up to 4 GB	Up to 32 GB	2 TB recommended, though larger sizes are supported
Files per volume	65,536	4,177,920	4,329,967,295
Maximum file size	4 GB	4 GB	16 TB minus 64 KB

Windows 7 also introduces several new features to NTFS, including the following:

▶ Files can now be read from a disk at the same time that data is being flushed to the disk using the disk cache manager, which enhances overall system performance.

▶ Short filenames can now be disabled on a volume basis, whereas earlier versions required that they be disabled globally or not at all.

▶ Filesystem metadata related to sparse files and the Encrypting Filesystem (EFS) can now be defragmented.

Metadata is data that describes other data. For example, it may include encryption keys used by EFS.

Contrasting 32-Bit and 64-Bit Systems

When you looked at Table 9.1, you probably noticed a relationship between the bit level of a filesystem and the file size and volume size it supported. If you did, you made a very astute observation. A 64-bit filesystem supports more files and larger file sizes, as well as increased volume sizes, than the 32-bit or 16-bit filesystems.

However, it is important to understand that although NTFS uses a 64-bit structure for file storage, this does not in any way constrain its use to 64-bit editions of the filesystem. It may be used on 32-bit editions as well as 64-bit editions. It simply uses a 64-bit structure for the tracking and management of files.

Think of the MFT as a database used to track the files on the disk and the locations of those files.

The NTFS filesystem uses a Master File Table (MFT) to store information about the data on the storage device instead of the file allocation table used by the FAT filesystem. Two copies of the MFT are maintained on each volume. One is stored at the beginning of the volume and the other is stored at an alternate location on the volume. This allows for recoverability should the primary MFT become corrupted. By default, 12.5 percent of the volume space is reserved for the MFT. If very large files are stored on the volume and the reserved space is required for other data storage, it will be made available. This space is initially reserved in order to help prevent fragmentation within the MFT file itself.

As files are stored on the NTFS volume, detailed information about the files is included in the MFT or in external space described by the MFT, including

▶ File size

▶ Time and data stamps

▶ Data content

▶ Permissions

Working with Encryption

One of the enhanced features available through the use of NTFS is encryption. This is the process of converting data from its normal state to a state that is unreadable without a corresponding translation key. The unreadable state is known as *ciphertext* (or *cipherdata*), and the readable state is *plaintext* (or *plaindata*). The usual way to encrypt something is to pass the data through an algorithm using a key for variable results. For example, let's say we want to protect the number 161. Here is our algorithm for protecting numeric data:

original data / crypto key + (3 × crypto key)

Using this algorithm to protect (encode or encrypt) the number 161 with a key of 7, we come up with this formula or algorithm:

$$161 / 7 + (7 \times 3) = 44$$

To recover the original data, you must know both the algorithm and the key. Needless to say, modern cryptography algorithms are much more complex than this and keys are much longer, but this overview gives you an idea of how data encryption works.

Encryption is used in Windows operating systems to encrypt files and folders individually and also to encrypt entire drives. Additionally, Windows offers compression options, which cannot be used in conjunction with encryption. This section provides essential information for understanding and using encryption solutions with your data in Windows environments.

Encrypting Files and Folders

When you want to encrypt files and folders, the target volume must be formatted with NTFS. If you attempt to perform the file encryption process and the option is not available, this typically indicates that the volume is formatted as FAT16 or FAT32. The encryption system that allows for individual file and folder encryption on NTFS volumes is called the Encrypting Filesystem (EFS).

EFS works by generating an encryption key, called the *file encryption key (FEK)*, and then encrypting the data with the FEK. Next, the FEK is itself encrypted with the user's public key (which is provided in a file encryption certificate that is either automatically generated or created by the network administrator) and stored along with the data. When the user accesses the encrypted file, the FEK is first decrypted with the user's private key, and then the data is decrypted using the FEK.

All of this can get quite confusing, so remember this: An encryption key is nothing more than a number used in an encryption algorithm. Encryption algorithms come in two primary forms: symmetric and asymmetric. Symmetric algorithms use the same key to both encrypt and decrypt the data. Asymmetric algorithms use one key to encrypt the data and another key to decrypt the data. The two keys used by an asymmetric algorithm are known as a key pair because they must be used together.

In general, asymmetric algorithms provide enhanced security management, but they are more CPU-intensive. This is why symmetric encryption is used to encrypt the actual data (it is faster) and asymmetric encryption is used to encrypt the FEK (it is easier to manage). In most cases, the asymmetric encryption keys are provided in a certificate; you'll learn more about certificates in the section "Managing Encryption Keys," later in this chapter.

To encrypt an individual file on an NTFS volume, follow these steps:

1. Navigate to the location where the file is stored.

2. Right-click the file and select Properties.

3. On the General tab, click the Advanced button.

4. Check the Encrypt Contents To Secure Data option, as shown here:

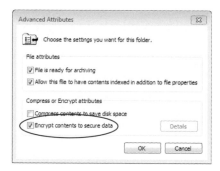

5. Click OK to close the Advanced Attributes dialog and then click OK again to close the Properties dialog.

When you complete these steps, by default on Windows 7 systems you will see the Encryption Warning dialog. This dialog warns you that it can be dangerous to encrypt individual files instead of the entire folder containing the files. This warning is needed because of the way in which many applications work with their files. For example, if you open a spreadsheet in Microsoft Excel to edit it, a copy is made of the spreadsheet as a temporary file. To enhance recoverability, this temporary file is maintained for active changes until you choose to save your changes. The problem is that the temporary file will be encrypted only if the folder is marked for

You incur no added security risk by encrypting an individual file if you know that the application does not use temporary files in this way.

encryption instead of the individual files. For this reason, Microsoft suggests that you never encrypt an individual file.

To encrypt an entire folder and its contents:

1. Navigate to the location where the folder is stored.

2. Right-click the folder and select Properties.

3. On the General tab, click the Advanced button.

4. Check the Encrypt Contents To Secure Data option.

5. Click OK to close the Advanced Attributes dialog and then click OK again to close the Properties dialog.

After completing these steps, you will receive no warning that prevents the action; however, if it is the first time you have ever used EFS, you will see a balloon notification in the Notification Area telling you that you should back up your encryption keys. Specifically, it is suggesting that you back up the public and private keys stored in your file encryption certificate, which were discussed earlier. If you click the icon in the Notification Area, you will see a dialog like the one in Figure 9.1. You should use this dialog immediately to back up your file encryption certificate and key to a safe location to ensure that you can recover your data later should the key on the hard drive become damaged.

FIGURE 9.1 The EFS backup notification dialog

To perform the backup, follow this procedure:

1. If you haven't already, click the notification icon in the Notification Area to open the dialog shown in Figure 9.1.

2. Click Back Up Now (Recommended).

3. In the Certificate Export Wizard dialog, click Next.

4. Choose the Personal Information Exchange - PKCS # 12 (.PFX) format as shown in Figure 9.2 and click Next.

> Don't be confused by this cryptic format name. It is simply the format used to store the certificates needed by EFS.

FIGURE 9.2 Selecting the key export format

5. Enter and confirm a password to secure the backed-up certificate and click Next.

6. Browse for the location and filename you wish to use to save the backup. You should consider storing this on a USB flash drive or some other external storage location rather than your internal drive. After selecting the location and providing a filename, click Save and then click Next in the Certificate Export Wizard.

7. On the Completing The Certificate Export Wizard page, click Finish to complete the backup process.

If you are wondering how you would decrypt files or folders after encrypting them, do not be alarmed. The decryption and encryption happens automatically as long as the user who initially indicated that the data should be encrypted is logged onto the machine. However, this also introduces an important security concern. If you feel that the data is sensitive enough to warrant encryption, you must ensure that the user is logging on with very strong authentication. Passwords will probably not suffice, and you'll likely need to use something stronger like biometrics or smart card authentication.

Understanding BitLocker Encryption

Unlike EFS, BitLocker encrypts the entire volume. BitLocker was first introduced with Windows Vista and has been enhanced in Windows 7. BitLocker can be used to encrypt the following volumes:

- ► Storage-only volumes that do not contain operating system files
- ► The operating system volumes
- ► USB flash drive volumes

The ability to encrypt flash drive volumes is new in Windows 7 and is called BitLocker to Go. Flash drives encrypted with BitLocker to Go can be accessed on Windows Vista machines with full read/write capabilities as long as the user knows the password used to encrypt the drive. On Windows XP systems running Service Pack 2 or later, BitLocker to Go drives can be accessed only in read-only mode.

In addition to these requirements for BitLocker to Go, it is important that you understand the requirements of BitLocker for the encryption of internal drives. To encrypt storage-only volumes, BitLocker has the following requirements:

- ► A Trusted Platform Module (TPM) chip for storage of encryption keys or a USB flash drive for storage of encryption keys
- ► Windows Vista or later operating system

In addition to these requirements, to encrypt the operating system volume, a separate volume of approximately 100 MB must exist for access to important files needed at boot time and before the operating system volume has been decrypted. This 100 MB volume is created for you automatically during the installation of Windows 7, unless you override this behavior by partitioning the disk before starting the installation process.

To encrypt a volume of a flash drive with BitLocker on a system that meets the requirements previously listed:

1. Click Start ➤ Control Panel.

2. Select the System and Security category.

3. Select BitLocker Drive Encryption.

4. For the drive you wish to encrypt, choose Turn On BitLocker and follow the prompts in the BitLocker Drive Encryption Wizard.

As you work through the wizard, you will be asked for either a password or a smart card to use as the unlock mechanism for the drive. You will also be asked to save recovery information so that you can restore the drive and access the

If you encrypt the OS volume, you should use a TPM chip so that the loss of USB drives does not result in the inability to boot the computer.

encrypted data. If the drive is an internal drive, you will also have the option to automatically unlock the drive so that a password is not required each time.

Managing Encryption Keys

Earlier in this chapter, you learned the importance of backing up your encryption key. For small businesses with just a few users, the simple backup of the local encryption keys may be all that is required. In larger enterprises, you will need to understand the concepts of certificates and a Public Key Infrastructure. You should also have a plan to back up Active Directory domains, but that is beyond the scope of this book. In my book *Microsoft Windows Server Administration Essentials* (Sybex, 2011), you can learn more about Active Directory backups.

Encryption keys are often generated and managed using certificates. This is particularly true when managing encryption as it relates to secure websites. A certificate can be defined as "a digitally signed statement that contains information about an entity and the entity's public key" (*Dictionary of Information Security*, Syngress Publishing, 2006). Certificates may be generated internally if the generating organization has implemented a Public Key Infrastructure (PKI), or they may be acquired externally through third-party organizations.

A PKI is an internal set of servers responsible for the creation, distribution, management, and destruction of certificates. Organizations that require hundreds or even thousands of certificates will typically implement a PKI. The certificates generated from the PKI are useful for internal web servers. They are still not as beneficial for external users, as the certificates will not be trusted by those users' machines.

Third-party vendors offer certificates, and they are usually trusted by the clients on the Internet. In order for a certificate provider to be trusted, the provider's certificate must be installed in the client machine. Popular certificate providers, such as VeriSign and Thawte, have their certificates in most operating systems out of the box.

A third type of certificate could also be used. This is a self-signed certificate. If you use a self-signed certificate, all users will receive a security warning the first time they visit the site. However, users may install the certificate into their local store on the first visit and then will not receive future warnings.

▶

When a user accesses an HTTPS website, her machine validates the certificate. If it is from an untrusted party, the user receives a security warning.

Using Compression

You may be wondering what compression has to do with encryption. If so, you are right to be curious. The issue is really simple: You cannot both encrypt data using EFS and compress data using NTFS compression at the same time. If you access the Advanced Attributes dialog, you will see two check boxes in the Compress or Encrypt Attributes section. The first reads Compress Contents To Save Disk Space, and the second reads Encrypt Contents To Secure Data. You cannot check both options at the same time. This is an imposed limitation in order to prevent the major performance problems that would result from both encrypting data and compressing it each time the files are accessed.

However, if saving space is more important, you can certainly compress data on NTFS volumes. When you encrypt data using EFS, the files or folders change to a green color to indicate that they are encrypted. When you compress data, the files or folders change to a blue color to indicate that they are compressed. This is a useful method for quickly identifying encrypted or compressed data. After compressing data, you can see the space saved by viewing the properties of the file. On the General tab, as shown in Figure 9.3, you will see the Size attribute as well as the Size On Disk attribute. The difference between the two is the amount of savings provided by the compression.

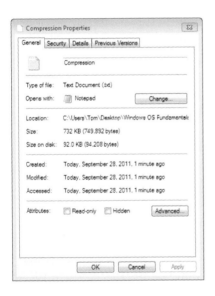

FIGURE 9.3 Viewing the properties of a compressed file

Using Libraries

You may have visited a library or two in your time. Libraries are used to store large amounts of information in a central location. This information may include books and magazines and other items. Windows 7 introduced a new feature that provides for library type functions within the windows operating system. This new feature is aptly named *libraries*. Libraries can be created for each project or for each category of documents and data that you wish to track. Four default libraries—Documents, Music, Pictures, and Videos—exist as soon as you finish installing Windows 7. In this section you will explore library features and functionality and learn how to organize with libraries, create new libraries, and configure library properties.

Library Features and Functionality

A library is nothing more than a collection of documents and folders that you want to combine into a single interface. Using libraries you can better organize your data and the different documents that you use for all of your applications. Libraries include the following important features and functionality:

▶ Tagging features so that picture items can be easily organized and located

▶ Custom arrangement options so that you can view a library by folder, date modified, author, data type, name, or custom tags assigned by the user

▶ The ability to include multiple folders in a single library

▶ The ability to optimize each library for the type of included data so that indexing is more efficient and searching is faster

Remember that making network locations available offline could cause extra strain on your network.

It is important that you understand several things related to libraries. First, note that you can include networked locations in a library. However, if you include a networked location in the library, that location must be either indexed or made available for offline use. When you make it available offline, it is automatically indexed. You can also trick the machine into allowing a network location to be included in a library, using the Command Prompt MKLINK command, but this method is not supported by Microsoft.

As an alternative to using offline files, you can install Windows Search 4.0 or later on the machine that actually stored the network share in question. If you index the share with Windows Search 4.0 (which will work on older versions of Windows as well), the data will be indexed and can be made available as part of a library.

You should also understand that only one of the folders in a multifolder library can be the default save location. When you drag a file to the library, it is saved in the default save folder. To see the current default save folder for a library, take the following steps:

1. Open Explorer.

2. Right-click the target library in the panel and select Properties.

3. Note the folder with the checkmark next to it, My Documents in Figure 9.4, as this folder is the default save location.

FIGURE 9.4 Viewing the default save location for a library

4. If you want to change the default save location, simply click the desired folder in the library's Properties dialog and click the Set Save Location button.

Organizing with Libraries

When you change the optimization settings for a library, it changes the arrangement options for that library as well. For example, if a library is optimized for Music, you can arrange it by any of the following attributes:

▶ Album

▶ Artist

▶ Song

▶ Genre

▶ Rating

▶ Folder

When you optimize the library for Pictures, you can arrange it by any of the following attributes:

- ► Month
- ► Day
- ► Rating
- ► Tag
- ► Folder

When you optimize the library for Videos, you can arrange it by any of the following attributes:

- ► Year
- ► Type
- ► Length
- ► Name
- ► Folder

When you optimize the library for Documents, you can arrange it by any of the following attributes:

- ► Author
- ► Date modified
- ► Tag
- ► Type
- ► Name
- ► Folder

Finally, when you optimize it for General Items, you can arrange it by any of the following attributes:

- ► Date modified
- ► Tag
- ► Type
- ► Name
- ► Folder

Creating a New Library

For many users, the existing libraries, Documents, Music, Pictures, and Videos, may be sufficient. Other users will want to create custom libraries. To create a library, follow this procedure:

1. Open Explorer.

2. Right-click Libraries in the left panel and select New ➢ Library.

3. Enter a name for the new library and press Enter.

4. Click on the newly created library to display the notification screen that indicates the library is empty, as shown in Figure 9.5.

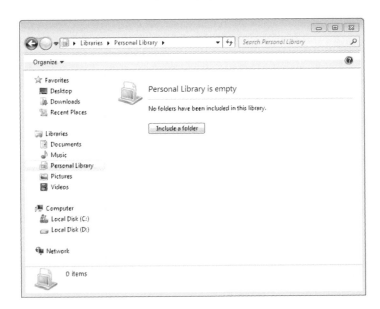

FIGURE 9.5 Viewing the empty library after creation

5. Click the Include A Folder button to add a new folder to the library.

6. Browse for the desired folder, select it, and click Include Folder.

If you want to include multiple locations in the library, click the link that says 1 Location just under the library name in Explorer. You will see the dialog shown in Figure 9.6. Here, you can click Add and add as many additional folders to the library as you desire.

FIGURE 9.6 The Library Locations dialog used to add folders to or remove them from a library

Configuring Library Properties

After you create a library, you can configure its properties to meet your needs. Figure 9.7 shows the Properties dialog for a custom library. As you can see, you have a limited number of properties that can be configured for a library through this interface. You can configure any of the following settings:

▶ Library locations

▶ The default save location

▶ Library optimization setting

▶ Whether to show the library in the navigation pane

▶ Whether to share the library when a homegroup is used with the Shared option

▶ Whether to restore the defaults of the libraries that are preconfigured

If you want to deploy custom libraries to user computers, you will need to first create the library file. It is an XML file, and the schema (structure) for this file is defined here:

```
http://go.microsoft.com/fwlink/?LinkId=159581
```

FIGURE 9.7 The Personal Library
Properties dialog

Next, you can install the library file to the *%userprofile%*\Appdata\romaing\
Microsoft\Windows\Libraries directory. You can do so using logon scripts
or through Group Policy Preferences, which you can use to install files on the
computer.

Additionally, you can easily hide default libraries. This may be an option in
an enterprise setting where you do not want the average user using a Pictures
library. First you need to hide the library file itself, with batch file code similar
to the following:

```
@echo off
%systemdrive%
cd\
cd %appdata%\Microsoft\Windows\Libraries
attrib +h Pictures.library-ms
```

The library filenames for each default library are as follows:

- ▶ Documents: DOCUMENTS.LIBRARY-MS

- ▶ Pictures: PICTURES.LIBRARY-MS

- ▶ Videos: VIDEOS.LIBRARY-MS

- ▶ Music: MUSIC.LIBRARY-MS

◀

The *%userprofile%*
variable references
the specific user's
profiles path so
you do not have to
manually enter it.

Figure 9.8 shows the contents of the VIDEOS.LIBRARY-MS file in the Notepad application. As you can see, it is an extensible markup language (XML) file even though it does not have an .XML extension.

FIGURE 9.8 Viewing the contents of the VIDEOS.LIBRARY-MS **XML file**

Next you need to configure the Library as hidden in the User Configuration\ Administrative Templates\Start Menu and Taskbar policy setting location. The policy settings that can be enabled to hide links to these libraries include the following:

▶ Remove Documents Icon From Start Menu

▶ Remove Music Icon From Start Menu

▶ Remove Pictures Icon From Start Menu

▶ Remove Videos Link From Start Menu

THE ESSENTIALS AND BEYOND

In this chapter, you learned about the file management features available in the Windows OS. You started by learning about filesystems and the features they commonly offer. Then you compared the different filesystems that are available in Windows and learned why NTFS is the most common filesystem used. Next, you learned how to use encryption and compression features in Windows 7. Finally, you learned how to work with and manage libraries.

(Continues)

THE ESSENTIALS AND BEYOND *(Continued)*

ADDITIONAL EXERCISES

▶ Research the extra features offered by the NTFS filesystem beyond those covered in this chapter.

▶ Compress a file and then view the space savings provided through the use of NTFS compression.

▶ Create a custom library and include at least two folders in the library.

To compare your answers to the author's, please visit www.sybex.com/go/osessentials.

REVIEW QUESTIONS

1. What must be available to use BitLocker encryption on the operating system volume?

   A. An unencrypted 100 MB system volume

   B. A PKI

   C. A smart card reader

   D. An AD DS domain

2. True or false. Logon scripts may be used to hide default libraries, such as Documents and Pictures, from the Explorer view.

3. You want to provide permission management at the file level for a new volume you are formatting. What filesystem should you use to provide this feature?

   A. FAT12

   B. FAT16

   C. FAT32

   D. NTFS

4. What is the maximum volume size available for FAT32 volumes as implemented in the Windows OS?

5. What filesystem is used to access CDs in Windows 7?

   A. NTFS

   B. FAT32

   C. CDFS

   D. FAT16

6. Define a PKI.

7. Define MFT.

(Continues)

THE ESSENTIALS AND BEYOND *(Continued)*

8. In what directory or folder are library setting files maintained?

    A. *%userprofile%*\Appdata\roaming\Microsoft\Windows\
    Libraries

    B. *%userprofile%*\Appdata\roaming\Libraries

    C. *%system%*\Libraries

    D. *%systemdrive%*\Windows\Libraries

9. What Command Prompt command is used to hide libraries from the Explorer view?

    A. ATTRIB   **C.** HIDELIB

    B. LIBHIDE   **D.** DIR

10. True or false. You can use Group Policy to remove links to default libraries from the Start menu.

CHAPTER 10

Network Shares

One of the primary reasons for implementing a network is to share data. Windows 7, like all Microsoft operating systems, has the capacity to share data as well. In fact, it has the same capabilities for sharing data as Windows Server, with the exception that Windows Server can handle many more concurrent connections. In this chapter you will learn about creating network shares and in the process explore the following topics:

▶ **Planning for file sharing**

▶ **Creating file shares**

▶ **Understanding NTFS and share permissions**

▶ **Sharing printers**

Planning for File Sharing

Computers that participate on a network communicate with each other using network hardware and software. The connection between the computers is called the *communication channel*. To share files with each other, two users must be using computers that have an active communication channel. This section introduces you to networking hardware, protocols, and network types so that you can implement network shares. The most difficult part of file sharing is planning the actual network on which the sharing will take place.

Understanding Network Hardware

A local area network (LAN) is a group of devices connected using high-speed connections and sharing a locally managed network infrastructure. When you are building a LAN, you use specific hardware devices to allow for communications on your network. These devices include hubs, switches, and routers. Together, they make up the network infrastructure, or the internal building blocks, that allow the network to function:

Hubs Hubs are devices used to connect multiple other computing devices together. A hub sends all received communications out all its ports. For this reason, hubs are used less often on modern networks. Sending all communications to all devices does not result in the best performance.

Switches   Switches have sometimes been called "smart hubs," because they send communications out only on ports required to reach the intended destination. Switches maintain a list of connected devices and the ports to which they are connected so that they can direct communications out the appropriate port.

Protocols are used to provide a standard method for communications between network devices.

Routers   Routers are used to allow for communication between network segments or between entire networks. The most common communications method used on modern networks is the Transmission Control Protocol (TCP)/Internet Protocol (IP) protocol suite. Most routers provide IP routing and allow one IP network to talk to another IP network.

When networks are designed, they may include all three of these components. In most modern networks, only switches and routers are used from this list of devices. The switches provide the point of connection to the local network, and the routers provide connections between networks.

In addition to the infrastructure devices, it is important to understand the network device in each computer. The network adapter is the interface to the network. Each server and client computing device on your network must have a network adapter. The network adapter is also known as a network interface card (NIC). The NIC has several important characteristics that you must define for your networking needs:

Speed   Today, most new computers come with 1 Gbps NICs—some even come with 10 Gbps NICs—but some do still ship with 100 Mbps adapters. Be sure to select the speed you require.

Form Factor   NICs come as PCI, PCI Express, CardBus, and USB adapters. You will need to select the form factor required by your connecting device. Most motherboards also include a built-in network adapter.

Operating System Support   Some adapters come with only Windows drivers. If you want to use another operating system, be sure to stay away from such adapters.

Understanding TCP/IP

TCP/IP is the most commonly used network protocol suite today. It is the protocol suite used to communicate on the Internet, and it is the default protocol suite used on Windows computers. It is called a *suite* of protocols because it consists of multiple protocols for communications. The Transmission Control Protocol (TCP) is used to establish connections and ensure the integrity and delivery of data. The Internet Protocol (IP) is used to establish network addresses (identifiers) and provides the ability to route information on the network. You could say that TCP is the automobile and IP is the road on which it drives.

Another protocol used on TCP/IP networks is the User Datagram Protocol (UDP). Unlike TCP, which ensures that the communications are delivered, UDP simply sends the data and hopes for the best. TCP is called a connection-oriented protocol because it establishes and maintains connections during a communication. UDP is called a connectionless protocol because it sends the data and forgets about it.

UDP is used when fast delivery is more important than accurate delivery. TCP is used when the opposite is true. For example, UDP is used to carry voice communications on voice over IP (VoIP) networks because the speed of delivery is very important. TCP is typically used to transfer files because the accuracy of the data is very important.

Whether TCP or UDP is used for the data transmission, IP must be used for the addressing. IP comes in two versions today: IP version 4 (IPv4) and IP version 6 (IPv6). IPv4 uses 32 bits to represent the network address, and IPv6 uses 128 bits. IPv4 addresses are usually displayed as four 8-bit numbers separated by dots, like this:

- ▶ 17.23.56.8

- ▶ 10.12.25.142

- ▶ 172.16.87.91

This format is known as *dotted decimal* notation because you use decimal values (what most people think of as numbers) separated by dots.

IPv6 addresses are usually represented using hexadecimal values, like this:

- ▶ 3ffe:1900:4545:0003:0200:f8ff:fe21:67cf

- ▶ fe80:0000:0000:0000:0200:f8ff:fe21:67cd

The good news is that IPv6 is mostly self-configuring with the exception of the routers, and you will rarely have to enter one of these long addresses into a Windows 7 computer's configuration.

Even IPv4 addresses are usually configured dynamically today using a service called the Dynamic Host Configuration Protocol (DHCP). DHCP configures the computer IP address, the default gateway (the IP address of the router), the subnet mask, and the DNS server IP address for the clients. The subnet mask is used to define the network or subnetwork on which the computer operates. It helps to determine when the router is needed and when it is not.

It is useful to know the difference between a public and a private IPv4 address. Public addresses are used on the Internet. Private addresses cannot communicate directly with the Internet. If you see a computer configured with an IPv4 address beginning with any of the following numbers, it is using a private address:

- 10
- 169
- 172.16–172.31
- 192.168

For example, all of the following addresses are private addresses:

- 10.4.15.8
- 172.16.23.41
- 172.23.18.78
- 192.168.100.100

> **Addresses starting with 127 are also private addresses, but they are not used for host addresses. The 127.0.0.1 address is a loopback address into the local host.**

If your computer uses a private IP address, a device must be used between your computer and the Internet to allow for communication on the Internet. This device is a special kind of router known as a Network Address Translation (NAT) device. Its job is to translate between the private network addresses and the public Internet addresses. Most home Internet routers act as NAT devices, and enterprise-class routers from companies like Cisco can also implement NAT functionality. An alternative to a NAT device is a web proxy or Internet proxy server. These servers access the Internet on behalf of the internal hosts and forward Internet responses to the internal network.

WHAT'S UP WITH THE 169?

If you have ever had to troubleshoot a computer that was not able to connect to the network or the Internet, you may have encountered an IP address that starts with 169.254. If so, you have seen Automatic Private IP Addressing (APIPA) in action. APIPA is used to configure an IP address for a Windows client when a DHCP server cannot be contacted and the client is configured to use DHCP for its IP settings. APIPA assigns an address in the range from 169.254.0.1 to 169.254.255.254.

(Continues)

WHAT'S UP WITH THE 169? *(Continued)*

If you connect two Windows 7 computers to a switch and the switch is not connected to anything else, APIPA is useful because it allows these two computers to communicate. If you are on a network with routers and DHCP servers, the fact that APIPA is configuring the IP settings is bad news. Something is wrong in the network communications. In Chapter 13, "Windows Troubleshooting," you will learn to use several tools that can help you analyze why your computer is not communicating properly on the network.

Working with Network Types

Windows 7 computers can participate in three network types:

► Workgroup

► Homegroup

► Domain

As a support professional or user, you need to understand each type.

The workgroup is one the oldest network types, dating back to the days of Windows for Workgroups 3.11, which was a special version of Windows 3.*x* with enhanced networking capabilities. Workgroups are used for network communication when a central authentication server is not available. Windows 7 computers can participate in a workgroup that includes older Windows operating systems, such as Windows 2000, XP, Vista, and even Windows 95. All nondomain Windows 7 computers must belong to a workgroup if they have networking capabilities. The following characteristics define a workgroup:

◄

A workgroup is defined as a collection of peer-to-peer networking partners that share resources with each other.

► Workgroups are not password-protected.

► Each computer has a local set of user accounts. Only users with accounts on the target computer can access resources on that target computer through the workgroup.

► All computers are peers, indicating that no single computer has control over the others.

▶ All computers are typically on the same LAN subnet, such as 10.10.0.0 255.255.0.0 or 192.168.12.0 255.255.255.0.

▶ Although there is no limit to the number of computers that can participate in a workgroup, Microsoft recommends connecting no more than 20 computers in this way.

The homegroup is the newest network type available in Microsoft operating systems. You could say that the homegroup is an enhanced workgroup with automatic sharing and security capabilities. Only Windows 7 and later machines can participate in a homegroup. Homegroups, unlike workgroups, are password-protected so that only authorized computers may participate in the network. You can share files as read-only or with modification capabilities as you desire. The following characteristics define a homegroup:

▶ Homegroups are password-protected.

▶ Computers participating in the homegroup can easily share data with other people without a need for complex permissions screens.

▶ Homegroup computers must also be part of a workgroup if they are not joined to a domain.

▶ Domain-joined computers may access resources in a homegroup, but they cannot share their libraries or printers on the homegroup.

The domain is the most secure and manageable of the network types, but it requires at least one centralized authentication server, called a domain controller (DC). The DC must run Windows Server and not a Windows client OS. Versions from Windows 3.*x* all the way to the Windows 7 client can participate in a Windows domain that is configured to support the appropriate authentication protocols. The following characteristics define a domain:

▶ Domains require access to an administrative account to join to and participate in the network.

▶ Domains require a dedicated server for account management and authentication processes.

▶ Only those with a user account in the domain can log onto domain-joined computers.

▶ Domains can support thousands of computers.

The term *domain-joined* simply refers to a Windows computer that is part of a Windows domain network.

▶ Domains allow computers to be on different LAN subnets.

▶ Domains provide centralized management and configuration options for the domain clients through the use of Group Policy and logon scripts.

Participating in a Workgroup

To participate in a workgroup, a computer only needs to exist on the same network and have the same workgroup name. To configure the workgroup name on a Windows 7 computer, follow this procedure:

1. Click Start, right-click Computer, and select Properties.

2. In the System Control Panel page, scroll down if necessary and click Change Settings in the Computer Name, Domain, and Workgroup Settings section, as shown in Figure 10.1.

FIGURE 10.1 Using the System Control Panel page to access the workgroup name settings

3. In the System Properties dialog, click the Change button.

4. In the Computer Name/Domain Changes dialog, enter the desired workgroup name in the Workgroup field, as shown in Figure 10.2, and click OK.

FIGURE 10.2 Entering a
workgroup name

Creating a New Homegroup

When Windows 7 is first installed and connects to a network, you will be asked
about the network type to which you are connected. Figure 10.3 shows the dialog used to select the network type.

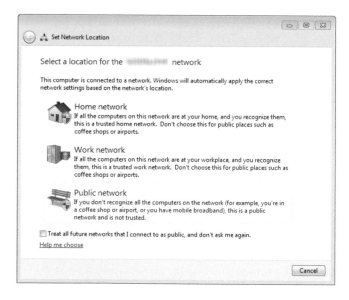

FIGURE 10.3 The Set Network Location dialog used to
define the type of network to which you are connected

If you choose the Home Network option and a homegroup does not exist on your network, you will be prompted to create one. If you choose the Home Network option and a homegroup does exist, you will be asked if you wish to join the existing homegroup or create a new one. Figure 10.4 shows the screen that is displayed when no existing homegroup is detected after selecting Home Network in the Set Network Location dialog. Notice that you can select to share your Libraries (Documents, Pictures, Music, and Videos) and Printers.

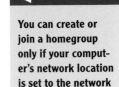

You can create or join a homegroup only if your computer's network location is set to the network type of Home.

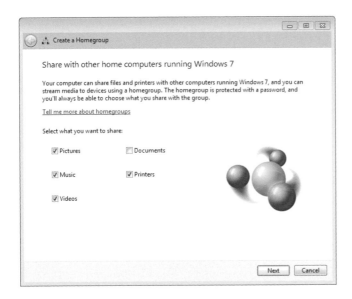

FIGURE 10.4 The Create A Homegroup dialog used to define what should be shared on the homegroup

Finally, you are presented with the password for the homegroup, as shown in Figure 10.5. This password must be used to join other computers to the same homegroup. Additionally, using the final screen of the Create A Homegroup wizard shown in Figure 10.5, you can print both the password and instructions for joining the homegroup from another Windows 7 computer.

You can view the homegroup password again at a later time on any machine that participates in the homegroup. To do so:

1. Click Start ➢ Control Panel.

2. Select the Network and Internet category.

3. Choose the Homegroup link.

4. Click View Or Print The Homegroup Password in the Other Homegroup Actions list.

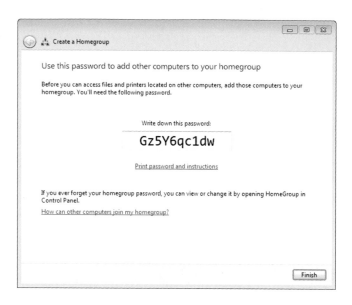

FIGURE 10.5 Viewing the homegroup password at the completion of the Create A Homegroup wizard

In some instances, you may want to leave a homegroup and no longer participate in it. You can do this by clicking the link Leave The Homegroup in the Other Homegroup Actions list on the Homegroup Control Panel page. When you select to leave a homegroup, you will be offered three choices:

▶ Leave The Homegroup

▶ Don't Leave, And Don't Change Anything

▶ Don't Leave, But Change What I'm Sharing

To leave the homegroup, you must click the Leave The Homegroup option. The system will take a moment to process the request and then notify you that your files are no longer shared with the homegroup.

If you do not want to leave the homegroup but simply want to change the resources you are making available to the homegroup, you can select the Don't

Leave, But Change What I'm Sharing option. This option allows you to remain in the homegroup but remove shared items like documents or printers.

Joining a Windows Domain

If you want to participate in a Windows domain, you must use the Work network type. The various network types (Home, Work, and Public) not only allow you to connect to homegroups and domains, but also specify important firewall settings. For example, the Windows Firewall is more restrictive when connected to a Public network than it is when connected to a Home or Work network. Do not confuse these three network types with the big picture network types we are discussing, such as workgroups, domains, and homegroups. These network types—Home, Work, and Public—are network setting profiles that determine what you can do on your network connection.

To join a domain, you must have the credentials of an account in that domain with the ability to join computers to the domain. By default, any authenticated users can join a computer to the domain as long as a computer account exists in the domain for that computer; however, only administrative-level users can create the computer accounts in the domain.

Assuming you have administrative credentials and want to both create the computer account in the domain and join the computer to the domain at the same time, follow these steps:

1. Click Start, right-click Computer, and select Properties.

2. In the System Control Panel page, scroll down if necessary and click Change Settings in the Computer Name, Domain, and Workgroup Settings section.

3. In the System Properties dialog, click the Change button on the Computer Name tab.

4. Select the Domain option, enter the name for the domain you wish to join, and click OK.

5. Enter the administrative username and password to create the computer account and join the computer to the domain.

If you receive an error message indicating that the domain controller could not be contacted, check your DNS server settings.

Creating File Shares

> A shared folder is simply a folder on a Windows computer that has been configured for availability on the network.

You create network shares to allow users to access local resources across the network. It is important to understand how to create shares and choose among the various sharing types. It is also helpful to know how to map drives to network shares using the GUI and the Command Prompt. In this section, you will learn how to create and map network shares.

Creating Share Types

Windows 7 supports three network share types: public shares, basic shares, and advanced shares. The first step in file sharing is determining the type of share you need to create. The following descriptions explain the share types:

Public Shares   Public shares, or public folders, are created automatically in your libraries. They are enabled by default when you participate in a homegroup. Anything you place in the Public folders (such as Public Documents, Public Music, and so on) will automatically be shared with other homegroup users. If the Windows 7 computer is part of a domain or workgroup only, Public Shares must be turned on.

Basic Shares   Basic shares must be individually created, but they are easily configured using a wizard and predetermined sets of permissions. Basic shares are the default method used to create shares in Windows 7.

Advanced Shares   Advanced shares allow you to set permissions on the share with more granularity and to configure all the details for the share. You must enable the ability to use advanced sharing, because it is disabled by default in Windows 7.

If you are using a homegroup, public sharing will be enabled by default. If you are not using a homegroup, you can follow these steps to enable public shares:

1. Click Start ➢ Control Panel.

2. Choose the Network and Internet category.

3. Select the Network and Sharing Center.

4. Click the Change Advanced Sharing Settings link in the left panel.

5. Expand either the Home Or Work section or the Public section.

6. In the Public Folder Sharing subsection, choose Turn On Sharing So Anyone With Network Access Can Read And Write Files In The Public Folders.

Be very careful when enabling this option, because it does provide full read/write capabilities to all network users.

7. Click Save Changes to apply the new configuration.

After performing this procedure, you will have enabled public shares. Now, you can place any files you want to share with everyone in the various Public folders within your libraries.

When you need to share data with specific people, you will create a basic or advanced share. To create a basic share:

1. Using Explorer, browse to the location of the folder you wish to share.

2. Right-click the target folder and select Share With ➤ Specific People.

3. In the File Sharing dialog, shown in Figure 10.6, choose the people or groups with which you wish to share the content and click Add.

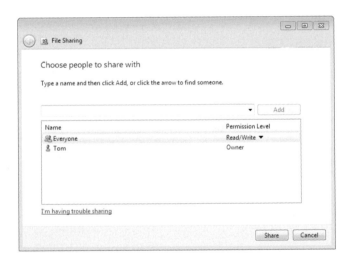

FIGURE 10.6 Using the File Sharing dialog to share a resource

4. After adding the people or groups, click the Permission Level option to choose among the available permissions and then click Share to create the basic share.

When you need to have fine control over the permissions and settings for the share, you will need to use advanced sharing. To enable advanced sharing, do the following:

1. Open Explorer.

2. Click Organize ➢ Folder And Search Options.

3. Select the View tab.

4. Deselect Use Sharing Wizard (Recommended), as shown in Figure 10.7, and click OK.

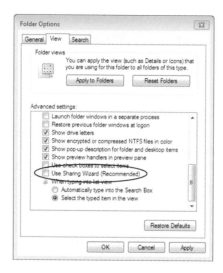

FIGURE 10.7 Turning off the Use Sharing Wizard to enable advanced sharing

Now that advanced sharing is enabled, take the following steps to create an advanced share:

1. Using Explorer, browse to the location of the folder you wish to share.

2. Right-click the target folder and select Share With ➢ Advanced Sharing.

3. On the Sharing tab, click the Advanced Sharing button.

4. In the Advanced Sharing dialog, check Share This Folder and type a name for the share in the Share Name field, as shown in Figure 10.8.

5. If you want to modify the permissions, click the Permissions button and do so; otherwise, click OK to create the advanced share.

> The various permissions available are explained later in this chapter in the section "Understanding NTFS and Share Permissions."

FIGURE 10.8 Sharing a resource with the Advanced Sharing dialog

Mapping Drives

When you have created shares on your network, you may want to map drives to these shares for easier access. Drives can be mapped in the GUI or from the Windows Command Prompt. Using the Command Prompt is useful for logon scripts as you can map drives automatically when users log into the network. Mapping a drive indicates that you are assigning a drive letter to a network location.

To map a drive, you will need to either browse to the location on the network and then map it or know the Universal Naming Convention (UNC) path. The UNC path consists of two components: the computer name and the share name. For example, if a computer named CPU1 shares a folder with the share name of USERSTUFF, the UNC path is \\CPU1\USERSTUFF.

Follow these steps to map a drive letter to a share in the GUI:

1. Browse to the network share location.

2. Right-click the share or a folder in the share and select Map Network Drive.

3. In the Map Network Drive dialog, shown in Figure 10.9, specify the drive letter to use and determine whether you want to reconnect at logon. Additionally, you can provide different credentials for access to the share than those with which you are currently logged on.

4. When you have configured the Map Network Drive settings to your needs, click Finish to map the drive.

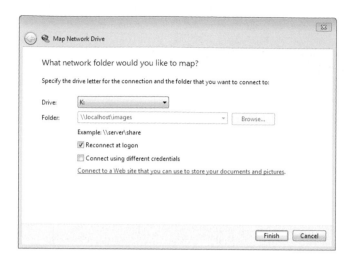

FIGURE 10.9 Mapping a network drive in the GUI

To map this same drive at the Command Prompt, you will need to know the UNC path, which was \\localhost\images in the previous example.

To map the drive at the Command Prompt, use this procedure:

1. Click Start, search for **cmd** in the search field, and press Enter.

2. At the Command Prompt, execute the command **net use k: \\localhost\images**, as shown in Figure 10.10.

FIGURE 10.10 Mapping a drive with the NET USE command

3. Execute the **exit** command to close the Command Prompt.

Regardless of how you map the drive, once the drive mapping is created, you can access it through the Explorer interface as if it were a local drive. Figure 10.11 shows the mapped drive letter K: in the Network Location section of Explorer.

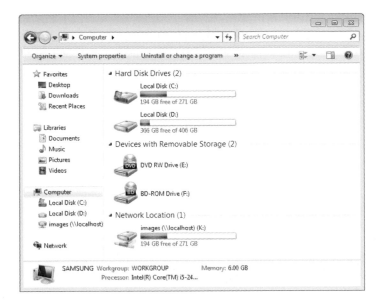

FIGURE 10.11 The mapped drive displayed in Windows Explorer

Understanding NTFS and Share Permissions

While it is important to know how to create shares and map network drives to those shares, it is also important to understand how to use permissions properly. To understand permissions, you must first be familiar with the concepts of *authentication* and *authorization*. Next, you will need to learn about both NTFS filesystem permissions and share permissions. This section covers all of these topics.

Understanding Authentication and Authorization

Authentication should not be confused with authorization. Authentication can be defined as proving a person or object is who or what he or it claims to be. Authorization is defined as granting access to a resource by a person or object. Authorization assumes that the identity has been authenticated. If authentication can be spoofed or impersonated, authorization schemes fail. You can see why authentication is such an integral part of network and information security; when an attacker breaks your authentication system so that he is seen as an authenticated user, the authorization becomes irrelevant. Authentication must be strong if authorization is to serve its purpose.

Windows 7 supports both authentication and authorization. When you define permissions on a folder or share, you are configuring authorization settings.

Many different credential solutions are available for securing your networks. It's important that you select the right solution for your needs. While most web servers use passwords, it is possible to provide authentication for internal users using other means. The following three authentication methods are common:

▶ Something you know—for example, a password or a personal identification number (PIN)

▶ Something you have—for example, a smart card or a key

▶ Something you are—for example, biometrics such as thumb scanners and retina scanners

>
> A smart card is a credit card–sized authentication device that includes identity information on the card in the form of a certificate.

A credential solution should provide a means of user or computer identification that is proportional to your security needs. You do not want to select a credential solution that places unnecessary burdens on the users and results in greater costs (of both time and money) than the value of the information assets you are protecting.

Sometimes, one type of authentication alone is not sufficient. In these cases, multifactor authentication can be used. Multifactor authentication is a form of authentication that uses more than one set of credentials. An example of a multifactor authentication process would be the use of both passwords and thumb scanners. Typically, the user would place her thumb on the thumb scanner and then be prompted for a password or PIN code. The password may be used for network authentication or it may only be used for localized authentication before the thumb data is used for network authentication. However, in most cases the password and thumb data are used to authenticate to the local machine and then the network or just to the network alone. A common example of multifactor authentication would be your ATM card. You have the card, and you know the PIN (something you have and something you know).

DO YOU HAVE CRED?

Remember the word *credentials*? Consider other important "cred" words, like *credit* and *credibility*. Do you see how they are related? They all have to do with having proof of something. When you have good credit, you have proof of your trustworthiness to pay debts. When you have credibility, you have proof that you are authentic, persuasive, and dynamic. When you have

(Continues)

Comparing NTFS and Share Permissions

Share permissions are used to control who can access shared folders and the capabilities they will have in those shared folders when accessing the resource across the network connection. Three share permissions exist and they are defined as follows:

Read   Users with read permission to a share may list and open documents and folders within the share, assuming NTFS permissions do not override the share permissions.

NTFS permissions can override share permissions for increased granularity in permission management.

Change   Users with change permission can list and open documents and folders. They can also modify documents, create new documents, and create new folders. They can also delete documents or folders. All of these actions may be taken as long as NTFS permissions do not override the share permissions.

Full Control   Users with full control can do everything the change permission allows and they can manage permissions. When you have full control of a share, you can modify the permissions on that share. Typically, only administrators are given full control of a share.

Depending on the Windows version you are using and the way the computer is configured, you may see these three permissions represented as Reader (read), Contributor (change), or Co-owner (full control). Under the hood, the permissions are still read, change, and full control. Microsoft changed their names in some interfaces to make them easy to understand for beginning administrators.

NTFS is the NT File System dating back to the first release of Windows NT Server. It is required for permission management on Windows internal drives.

NTFS permissions are defined on the local drive within the computer. The drive must be formatted as NTFS to use these permissions. FAT32 does not support security permissions. NTFS permissions may be explicit or inherited. Explicit permissions are set on an individual folder or file. Inherited permissions are set through the parent object. For example, by default a file inherits the permissions of the folder in which it is created. Subfolders also inherit the permissions of parent folders. This inheritance can be blocked, but it is the default behavior.

NTFS permissions are defined in Table 10.1. They are called standard permissions because they are used for most permissions you will need to configure. In addition to the standard permissions listed in Table 10.1, NTFS supports special permissions. The standard permissions are really a collection of special permissions. You can find the complete listing of special permissions and the standard permissions to which they map at http://technet.microsoft.com/en-us/library/cc732880.aspx.

TABLE 10.1 NTFS standard permissions

Permission Type	Description
Read	Users can read files.
Write	Users can read, modify, and create new files or folders.
Read and Execute	Users can read files and also execute files (such as EXE, BAT, and COM files).
List Folder Contents	Users can view the contents of a folder, but not read the contents of actual files.
Modify	Users can do everything read, write, and read and execute can do, and they can also delete files and folders.
Full Control	Users can do anything, including manage permissions. No previously listed permission allows for the management of permissions.

Always remember that explicit denial wins over granted permissions every time. If you explicitly deny full control, the user will have no permissions on the resource.

▶

It is important that you understand what happens with combined permissions, which are also called effective permissions. For example, you may belong to several groups and, of course, you are a user. Permissions may be assigned to groups and users, so you must determine how the permissions will apply if you access a resource with permissions specified for groups to which you belong and for your user account.

When dealing with only share permissions or only NTFS permissions, the general rule is that the most liberal permission set applies. For example, if you are given read permissions on a share as a user, but you are given change permissions through a group membership, the change permission will apply. If you are given NTFS read permissions as a member of the Accounting group to the C:\Data folder, but NTFS read and execute permissions as a member of the Management group, you will have read and execute permissions. The only exception to this "most liberal" rule is the deny permission. Explicit denial of a permission overrides the granting of that permission through any other group membership or the user account.

When dealing with share and NTFS permissions, the most restrictive applies. For example, if the share allows change permissions, but an NTFS permission on a folder in the share allows only read permissions, the user will have read permissions when accessing that folder through the share. You can think of the share as something like a permission pipe. By this I mean that you can never give the user more permissions than the share provides, just as only so much water can flow through a given width of pipe. If the share provides read permissions and a folder within the share provides modify NTFS permissions, the user will still have only read access when using the resource across the network, because the share is limiting the permissions of the user. In the end, NTFS permissions can further restrict the permissions granted at the share but they can never expand the permissions granted at the share when accessing resources across the network.

USER RIGHTS VS. USER PERMISSIONS

User rights should not be confused with permissions. Permissions are granted on objects to allow the user to access those objects with different levels of capabilities. Rights are not granted on objects, but rather on actions. For example, a user may be given the right to change the system time. Without this right, the user cannot change the time on the system (it will be set automatically in most environments based on a central time server and the time zone in which the user is located). By default, only administrators can change the system time, but users can change the time zone in newer versions of the Windows operating systems. Another example is the right to shut down the system. By default all users can shut down the system if they are logged on locally. These rights are managed in Group Policy using the Computer Configuration ➢ Windows Settings Security Settings ➢ Local Policies ➢ User Rights Assignment node.

Creating Share Permissions

To manage permissions on a share, use the following procedure (assuming advanced sharing is enabled):

1. Open Explorer and navigate to the shared folder location.

2. Right-click the shared folder and select Properties.

3. Select the Sharing tab and click Advanced Sharing.

4. Click the Permissions button.

5. Set the permissions according to your needs, as shown in Figure 10.12.

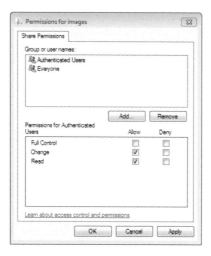

FIGURE 10.12 Setting share permissions

Creating NTFS Permissions

To manage permissions for the NTFS filesystem, use the following procedure:

1. Open Explorer and navigate to the file or folder on which you wish to manage permissions.

2. Right-click the target and select Properties.

3. Select the Security tab and set the NTFS permissions according to your needs, as shown in Figure 10.13.

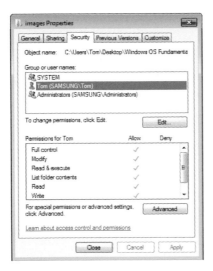

FIGURE 10.13 Setting NTFS permissions

Sharing Printers

Much as you share files and folders, you can share printers on the network. Sharing a printer allows remote users to print to your locally connected printer. Before a printer can be shared, it must be installed and configured on the local machine. You can create printer shares for printers connected directly with USB, parallel, or serial connections, and you can create printer shares for printers mapped to TCP ports on the machine. This section explains how to create and manage printer shares for connected printers.

You'll learn more about printer connections and installing printers in Chapter 11, "Device Management."

Creating Printer Shares

If you have a printer connected to your Windows 7 computer, you can easily share the printer so that other users can print to it. To share a connected printer, take the following steps:

1. Click Start ➢ Devices And Printers.

2. Right-click the target printer and select Printer Properties.

3. Select the Sharing tab.

4. Check Share This Printer and provide a share name, as shown in Figure 10.14.

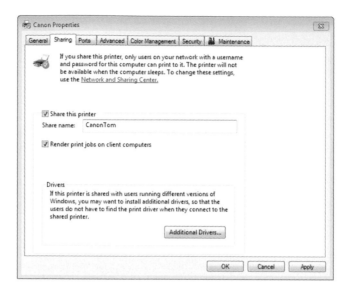

FIGURE 10.14 Sharing a printer on the network

5. Click Render Print Jobs On Client Computers if you want to alleviate some of the processing overhead for the local computer during print operations for remote computers.

6. Click OK to save the changes and share the printer.

Managing Printer Shares

The most important printer share element that you must manage is the share permission configuration. Of course, you will have to manage the print queue as well, but this is addressed in Chapter 11. To manage permissions for printer shares, use the following procedure:

1. Click Start ➤ Devices And Printers.

2. Right-click the target printer and select Printer Properties.

3. Select the Security tab.

4. Configure the permissions according to your needs, as shown in Figure 10.15.

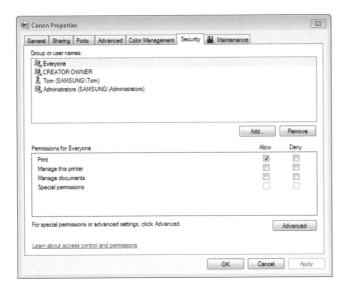

FIGURE 10.15 Configuring printer permissions for a shared printer

The following permissions are available for printer shares:

Print   Users with this permission can print to the printer, but they cannot perform any other management-level actions.

Manage This Printer   Users with this permission can rename, delete, share, and choose preferences for the printer. They can manage printer permissions as well.

Manage Documents   Users with this permission can manage print jobs for the printer. They can pause and restart print jobs, and they can also delete print jobs.

Special Permissions   Users with this permission can change the owner of the printer. The owner can do anything with the printer, and only administrators are typically given this ability.

Providing Printer Drivers

Finally, you may be required to provide printer drivers for operating systems other than the one used to share the printer. For example, if you are running Windows 7 64-bit, you can also provide drivers for Windows 7 32-bit systems. This way, when the 32-bit computers attempt to connect to the shared printer, they will automatically download and install the appropriate drivers for printing.

To add additional printer drivers, perform the following procedure:

1. Click Start ➤ Devices And Printers.

2. Right-click the target printer and select Printer Properties.

3. Select the Sharing tab and click Additional Drivers.

4. Select the alternate driver type to provide (such as Itanium, x64, or x86) and click OK, as shown in Figure 10.16.

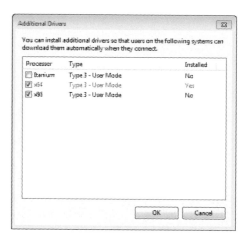

FIGURE 10.16 Providing alternate drivers for shared printers

5. Provide the location for the alternate drive files so they can be installed and click OK.

THE ESSENTIALS AND BEYOND

In this chapter, you learned to create network shares. You began by exploring the important planning aspects of network sharing, including network devices and protocols and the various network types. Then you learned how to join a Windows 7 machine to a workgroup, homegroup, or domain. Next you learned how to create and manage file shares and mapped drives. You saw how to create public shares, basic shares, and advanced shares. Then you explored both NTFS and share permissions and how they are managed. Finally, you discovered the various aspects related to printer sharing.

(Continues)

THE ESSENTIALS AND BEYOND *(Continued)*

ADDITIONAL EXERCISES

▶ Create a folder and share it using advanced sharing.

▶ Enable public sharing and view the available Public folders in your libraries.

▶ Install a printer driver and share the printer on the network.

To compare your answers to the author's, please visit www.sybex.com/go/ osessentials.

REVIEW QUESTIONS

1. What share permission is equal to full control of those listed here?

   A. Reader

   B. Contributor

   C. Co-owner

   D. Modify

2. True or false. Windows 7 computers can be joined to a domain by any authenticated user by default.

3. Of the following items, which one is required to join an existing homegroup?

   A. The IPv4 address of the homegroup server

   B. The IPv6 address of the homegroup server

   C. The homegroup password

   D. The domain administrator's account and password

4. What is the process used to prove a person or object is who or what he or it claims to be?

5. How many bits are used to define an IPv6 address?

   A. 8

   B. 32

   C. 64

   D. 128

6. Define effective permissions.

7. Define a communication channel.

8. What single NTFS permission allows users to read and write data, but not alter permissions or delete files?

   A. Write

   B. Modify

   C. Full Control

   D. Execute

(Continues)

THE ESSENTIALS AND BEYOND *(Continued)*

9. What kind of permission is always assigned to a file through the parent folder in which it is stored?

   A. Explicit
   C. Deny

   B. Inherited
   D. Allow

10. True or false. The change share permission allows users to do anything in the share except manage permissions.

CHAPTER 11

Device Management

Hundreds of different devices may be connected to computers. With the introduction of Universal Serial Bus (USB) several years ago, the number of devices increased dramatically. Today, you can connect scanners, printers, keyboard, mice, gaming controllers, microphones, sound systems, video cameras, and many other devices through USB. This chapter introduces device management through the following topics:

► **Understanding device drivers**

► **Exploring plug-and-play operations**

► **Connecting and managing devices**

► **Printers**

► **System devices**

Understanding Device Drivers

In this first section of the chapter, you will learn about device drivers, beginning with a clear definition of what a device driver is and does. With this understanding, you can better grasp the problems that can be caused by poorly coded device drivers and the reasons why the same hardware with different device drivers can perform very differently. Next, you'll discover how to locate device drivers and then install them. You'll learn about the various driver maintenance options, and although it's not an issue you face as often today as in the past, you'll learn about hardware resources and how resource conflicts can cause problems when your device drivers attempt to communicate with the hardware.

> A device driver is a software module that talks to the device and the operating system.

Defining Device Drivers

Attempting to discover exactly what a device driver is confuses many people. Don't be confused. A device driver is simply a software module or application that knows how to do at least two things: talk to the hardware device and talk to the operating system and applications. If you think of device drivers as software applications that run on your computer, they are much easier to understand.

However, it is important to know that the device driver software runs in a very powerful place within the Windows operating systems. Device drivers run in Kernel mode, and this is also where the operating system itself runs. In other words, the device drivers run at the operating system level, and this means that when they have problems they often crash the entire operating system. Only device drivers retrieved from a trusted source, such as a hardware or software vendor, should be used on Windows servers.

Device drivers are needed for all hardware in the system. Many beginning support professionals do not realize this, simply because Windows operating systems usually come with several device drivers out of the box. The following are just a few of the devices that require—and in most cases already have—device drivers in your Windows computers:

- ▶ Video cards
- ▶ Audio cards
- ▶ Motherboard chipsets
- ▶ Network interface cards (NICs)
- ▶ Storage controllers
- ▶ USB-based devices
- ▶ Printers

Locating and Downloading Drivers

In many scenarios, you will have to use hardware with Windows 7 computers that require drivers that are unavailable by default. For example, you may have an older printer or peripheral device that was originally sold for use on 32-bit Windows XP systems. Such devices will require new drivers for 64-bit versions of Windows 7 because vendors typically shipped only 32-bit drivers when Windows XP was the most common OS. Additionally, Windows 7 uses a new driver model. Device drivers should always be acquired from trusted sources. In most cases, this means getting drivers from one of the following three sources:

- ▶ The device vendor
- ▶ The operating system vendor
- ▶ The computer vendor

If you purchase an aftermarket hardware item, such as an improved NIC or a different storage controller, you will usually have to acquire the drivers from the device vendor. The operating system vendor and the server vendor will rarely have the device drivers you need in such cases. To acquire device drivers from the device vendor, follow these basic steps:

1. Visit the vendor's website.

2. Click the support link.

3. Find the link that suggests you can download software or drivers and click it.

4. Locate your specific device and download the drivers for it.

Thankfully, the vast majority of vendors have implemented their websites in a manner that allows you to follow this sequence each time. Figure 11.1 shows the driver download section of the Intel website.

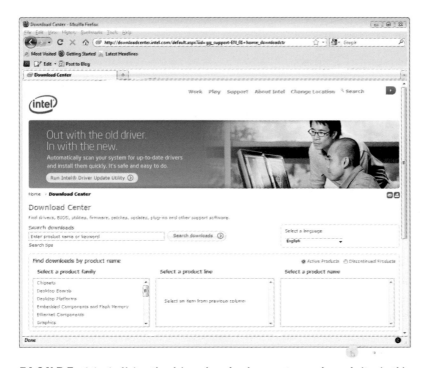

FIGURE 11.1 Using the driver download page at a vendor website, in this case Intel.com

You can also acquire drivers from the operating system vendor or the computer vendor. When the computer is shipped with specific hardware from the vendor, they will usually provide the drivers for download at their website. For example, if you purchase a Dell computer, you can download drivers for all of the hardware included in the purchased computer from the Dell website. As new computers are released, after the initial release of Windows 7, it will become more and more common to have to visit the vendor website to acquire the proper drivers for the hardware. Vendors may also supply the drivers on resource CDs or DVDs that ship with the computers.

When you are installing the Windows operating system on older machines, there is a good chance that the operating system installation DVD will come with the needed drivers for your computer. Additionally, drivers may be made available through Microsoft Update. Always be cautious when installing device driver updates through Microsoft Update (or any other automated update system for that matter). While the drivers are typically tested well, you want to know when drivers are updated on your machines. If you begin having problems, but you were not aware that a new video driver was recently installed automatically, you might miss the fact that the driver could be the cause of the problem.

> **Consider installing device drivers only through manual update processes to increase stability for your machines.**

After downloading the needed device drivers, you can install them in several ways, depending on the way in which a driver is provided. Some drivers are provided in executable containers that perform the installation for you. In such cases, simply launch the installation and follow the prompts to install the driver. For USB devices, it is common to install the driver before connecting the USB device. Read your device documentation to find out whether you should install the driver first or connect the hardware first.

Sometimes drivers are provided in a compressed archive, such as a ZIP file, and you must extract them to a folder before installation. In this case, you will need to extract the files to a folder and then use the Device Manager to install the driver. In the extracted folder, you will find an INF file that provides the details of the driver to the operating system. The process for installing a driver for a newly added device through Device Manager is as follows:

1. Click the Start menu, and then right-click Computer and select Manage.

2. Expand the Diagnostics node in the left pane and click Device Manager.

3. Find the device in the Other Devices node in the Device Manager panel, and then right-click it and select Install Driver.

4. Follow the prompts in the driver installation wizard to locate the driver in the extracted folder and perform the installation.

Installing Third-Party Software

Some hardware may require or benefit from additional software. While a device driver is required for the hardware to work, the additional software may add extra capabilities or features. For example, you can install the device driver for a wireless network adapter and use it with the built-in Windows 7 networking features. Alternatively, you can download custom management software for the wireless adapter and use this software to manage wireless connections. Figure 11.2 shows the built-in wireless network connection manager from Windows 7 with several configured wireless networks.

Figure 11.3 shows an example of a custom third-party network manager used to manage wired and wireless network connections. The Easy Network Manager ships with some Samsung laptops, and it can be downloaded from the Samsung support website if the machine must be reloaded and the Easy Network Manager software is required.

The most important thing to remember about third-party software related to devices is that it is often optional. Laptops and the extra software they come with today make a perfect example. The websites for driver downloads for most laptops list nearly as many software options to download as they do device drivers. However, only a very few of these software applications are required. While such applications may make the devices easier to use (and even this is debatable), they may also degrade the performance of the system.

Extra software that comes with laptops and desktops but is not absolutely required for functionality is often called *bloatware*.

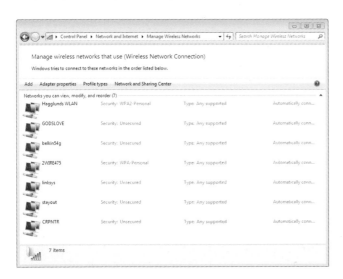

FIGURE 11.2 The built-in wireless network manager in Windows 7

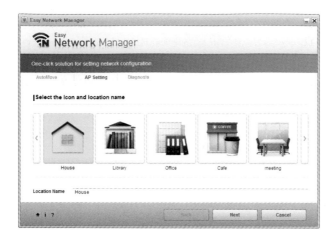

FIGURE 11.3 A custom network manager running on Windows 7

In the end, you may choose to run third-party software in relation to your hardware for any of the following reasons:

▶ To gain extra features

▶ To improve usability

▶ Because the hardware requires it

▶ To improve performance

▶ To increase security

Third-party wireless clients are often used instead of the built-in Windows client to get access to additional security features.

Using the Device Manager

The Device Manager is the traditional Windows interface used to manage devices and device drivers. It was first introduced in Windows 95 and remains with only slight modifications in Windows 7 today.

As time passes, the device drivers for your hardware will likely become outdated. Vendors often release more than 5 to 10 device drivers for a single device in its lifetime. The new device drivers may not be relevant to your installation, as their new features or fixes may not impact you. When evaluating device driver updates, consider the following questions:

▶ Is the update a security update? If it is, you will likely need to plan for the driver update in the near future.

▶ Are you having stability or performance problems with the current driver? If you aren't, and the update is not security related, you may be able to skip the driver update.

▶ Do support contracts depend on updating the driver? While it is not common, some support contracts require that you update device drivers periodically.

If you review these questions and determine that you must update the device driver, you will need to install the new driver. Like new driver installations, an update or upgrade of a driver may come as a self-installing executable or as a compressed archive containing the driver. To update an INF-based device driver (one that comes from the compressed archive), follow these steps:

1. Extract the downloaded driver to a temporary directory, if required.

2. Launch the Device Manager.

3. Locate the target device in the Device Manager panel.

4. Right-click the device and select Update Driver Software.

5. Choose Browse My Computer For Driver Software (see Figure 11.4) and then direct the wizard to the extracted driver location to perform the update.

FIGURE 11.4 Performing a device driver update

> **You can roll back a device driver only when a new version has been installed on the machine.**

After upgrading a device driver, your system may begin to experience problems. In such scenarios, you can roll back the device driver. This action simply means that you are reverting the system to the previous device driver. It is like taking a new car for a test drive and then deciding to go home in your old car. The new car didn't quite work out (because of costs, features, or some other source of discontent). In the same way, you can upgrade a device driver and then later decide it is not working properly, so you can roll back to the previous version of the device driver. If a driver update has not occurred, the option to roll back the driver will not be available. You can roll back a driver to a previous version with the following steps:

1. Launch the Device Manager.

2. Locate the target device in the Device Manager pane.

3. Right-click the device and select Properties.

4. On the Driver tab, if the button is available, choose Roll Back Driver (see Figure 11.5; notice that the button is not available).

FIGURE 11.5 Checking to see if a device driver can be rolled back

In some scenarios, you may think that a device driver is causing problems on your server. If the driver is not essential to all operations (as, for example, the PCI bridge driver or storage controller driver is), you can temporarily disable the driver and device to see if the problem is removed. To disable a driver:

1. Launch the Device Manager.

2. Locate the target device in the Device Manager pane.

3. Right-click the device and select Properties.

4. On the Driver tab, select the Disable button.

The final action you may need to perform on a device driver is simply removing it. To remove a device driver, right-click the device in the Device Manager and select Uninstall.

> Be careful when removing device drivers. If you uninstall an essential driver, the system may stop functioning.

DRIVER SIGNING

In newer versions of Microsoft Windows, including the client and server versions, device drivers may be signed. A signed device driver comes with a digital signature based on a certificate. The vendor acquires a certificate from a trusted third party (such as VeriSign or Thawte) and then signs the driver using that certificate. You can verify the signature to ensure that the device driver you are using really came from the vendor.

When a device driver is signed from the vendor, it will install with no notifications. When a device driver is unsigned or is signed with an untrusted certificate, you will see a notification indicating that. If you see this notification, it does not mean that you cannot use the driver. It simply means that you must ensure that the driver is safe and then force the operating system to install the driver even though it is not properly signed.

One major advantage of driver signing is that it allows nonadministrators to install drivers as long as they are signed. By default, unsigned device drivers can be installed only by an administrator.

Exploring Plug-and-Play Operations

Plug-and-play allows much simpler device management today than we experienced years ago with manual configurations. In this section, you will learn about plug-and-play features and the process used for plug-and-play implementation in Windows 7.

Understanding Plug-and-Play Features

Add-on hardware components must have some method for communicating with the CPU in a computer. Computers use interrupt requests (IRQs) and I/O addresses for these communications.

▶

The IOAPIC receives interrupt requests from devices and sends them to the CPU. The CPU gets the IRQ from the IOAPIC so it can contact the appropriate device.

The IRQ is used to get the attention of the CPU. When a device needs the attention of the CPU, it places voltage on the interrupt wire or connection to the CPU. The interrupt wire connects the CPU to an I/O advanced programmable interrupt controller (IOAPIC), which is the proxy between the add-on devices and the CPU. Every device must have an IRQ number associated with it so that the CPU knows which device is seeking attention. For example, it is not uncommon for a network interface card to work on IRQ 19 and COM port 1 to work on IRQ 4. Table 11.1 lists common IRQ assignments in desktops and servers.

TABLE 11.1 Common IRQ assignments

IRQ	Device
0	System Timer
1	Keyboard
2	A hook into IRQs 8–15 to allow more devices
3	COM 2
4	COM 1
5	LPT 2 or Audio
6	Floppy Disk
7	LPT 1
8	Real-Time Clock
14	Primary Hard Disk Controller
15	Secondary Hard Disk Controller

IRQs provide the communication from the device to the CPU, but the CPU still requires a method for communicating with the devices. For this, the system uses I/O addresses. You can think of an I/O address much like the street address for your home. Just as the mail carrier requires the street address to get mail (messages) to your house, the CPU requires I/O addresses to get messages to a device. The I/O addresses are 32-bit addresses and look like those shown in Figure 11.6. To see the information in Figure 11.6, open Device Manager and click View ➢ Resources By Type.

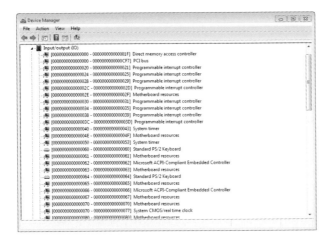

FIGURE 11.6 Viewing I/O addresses in the Device Manager

Plug-and-play (PnP) makes all of this easier. PnP was introduced in the 1990s, and Windows 95 was the first Microsoft OS to fully support it. This technology allows for automatic configuration of hardware resources. In the past, you often defined the IRQ and I/O addresses for devices using jumpers or dual-in-line package (DIP) switches on the physical adapter cards. Today, you simply plug the device in and let the OS do all the work for you.

Thanks to PnP technology, we rarely have to configure IRQs today. The OS configures these settings during startup so that the many devices in the system can work together in harmony. However, you still might install more devices than the system can automatically configure. In such cases, you will need to use the Device Manager to determine which devices are in conflict. Thankfully, this problem is rare and systems usually work without resource conflicts.

Defining the Plug-and-Play Process

During the boot process, the Windows plug-and-play implementation ensures that the hardware resources are allocated as necessary for existing devices. However, plug-and-play is also responsible for detecting and responding to device insertions that occurring while the system is up and running. Plug-and-play detection occurs based on the following process:

1. The bus driver detects a new device on the system bus.

2. The bus driver informs the Plug and Play Manager that something has changed in the device structure.

The Plug and Play Manager is part of the Executive and runs in Kernel mode.

3. The Plug and Play Manager queries the bus driver for a list of devices currently connected to the bus.

4. The Plug and Play Manager compares this current list with its known list to locate new devices.

5. Information about the new device is gathered from the device, such as the device ID.

6. The system looks in the Registry to see if the device has been installed before, and if so, it uses the existing drivers.

7. If the device has not been installed before, the Plug and Play Manager creates a Registry entry for the device and attempts to locate and load the proper drivers.

8. The Plug and Play Manager assigns resources, such as IRQs and I/O addresses, to the device so that it may function.

> The Windows driver store is used to provide drivers for devices. Many times the driver will already exist in the driver store.

Connecting and Managing Devices

As you connect and manage devices, you must consider several factors. First, you must plan for device driver provisioning. This can be done at device connection time or before the device is connected. Second, you must plan for device driver updates and maintenance. These topics are covered in this section.

Initial Device Installation

If you plan to install devices on a Windows 7 computer, you should be a member of the local Administrators group. Only administrators can install device drivers and therefore add new devices that require device driver installation. You have two options for initial device installation:

Install the driver during device installation.   The most common method used is to install the device and then add the device driver. This is true for internal adapters and components as well as external devices that connect through USB, eSATA, FireWire, and other ports. In this case, you connect the device and then install the driver as the operating system prompts you for the driver location.

Prestage the driver before device installation.   The alternative method is to prestage or preinstall the drivers. A prestaged driver is a driver that is installed or injected into the OS before the device is connected. Then, when the device is later connected, the driver is already there and can be loaded automatically by the OS.

To install the driver for a PnP device during device installation, follow this procedure:

1. Connect the new device to the computer.

2. If the device is an internal device, power on the computer.

3. In the Found New Hardware dialog, select one of the following options:

   ▶ Locate And Install Driver Software

   ▶ Ask Me Again Later

   ▶ Don't Show This Message Again For This Device

To prestage a device driver, you will use the PNPUTIL command at the Windows Command Prompt. You will need the INF-based driver to prestage a driver. You cannot prestage a driver using the executable or compressed download that is often provided by the manufacturer. However, these downloads have the INF files and driver files (usually SYS files) in them. Extract them to a temporary location and use them to prestage the driver. To prestage a driver:

1. Click Start and search for CMD.

2. Right-click the CMD program and select Run As Administrator.

3. Execute the following command:

```
pnputil -i -a driverfile.inf
```

Of course, you should change the filename from *driverfile*.inf to the name of your device driver's INF file.

Updating Drivers

Driver management is an important part of system stability. A perfectly stable machine can become an unstable nightmare quickly because of poor device drivers. Video drivers seem to cause the most problems on modern systems, but any driver can certainly be problematic. For this reason, it is a good idea to track drivers in a larger environment, such as a business setting, and update drivers only after thorough testing.

Before updating drivers, be sure that you can answer yes to all of the following questions:

▶ Were the drivers acquired from a known and reputable source?

▶ Are the drivers designed for your hardware?

▶ Does the hardware vendor support the drivers?

▶ Have the drivers been tested in your configuration and verified to be problem-free?

Creating a Driver List

A little-known Command Prompt command can be useful for creating driver lists. The command is DRIVERQUERY. You can use this command with the /V switch for verbose output and the /FO switch to format the output as comma-separated values (.csv). The resulting file can be opened in Microsoft Excel or another spreadsheet application and used to track and analyze installed drivers.

To use this trick, follow these steps:

1. Click Start and search for CMD.

2. Right-click the CMD program and select Run As Administrator; provide credentials if required.

3. Change to your Desktop folder with the cd\users\%*username*%\ desktop command.

4. Execute the following command:

```
driverquery /v /fo csv >drivers.csv
```

5. Open the DRIVERS.CSV file in Excel or another spreadsheet program.

You should see a display similar to Figure 11.7. This file can be used to sort, filter, and track your device drivers.

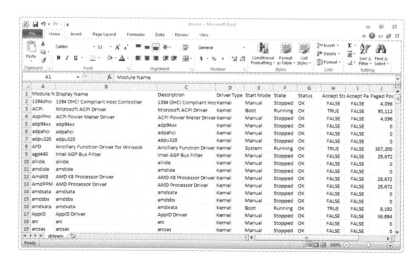

FIGURE 11.7 Tracking drivers in an Excel spreadsheet or CSV file

Printers

One of the most important devices used on modern networks is the printer. Printers may be attached locally or they may be on the network, with printing actually taking place on the server. In this section, you will learn about the differences between local and network printers. You will then learn to connect, disconnect, and manage printers.

Comparing Local and Network Printers

Local printers are connected directly to your machine. In most cases today, the printer will connect using a USB cable; however, older printers use parallel cables, or what are often simply called "printer cables." These older cables connect to line print terminal (LPT) ports on your machine. Because USB ports take up less space on the system board and provide more features, they have all but replaced LPT ports today.

Network printers are those printers that are available on the network. These printers can be made available on the network in one of three primary ways:

Printer Sharing   With printer sharing, the printer is actually connected to another computer as a local printer and is then shared by that computer with the network. This allows the use of Windows permissions to control access to the printer. Printer sharing was covered in Chapter 10, "Network Shares."

Network Printer Devices   Network printer devices are devices that connect printers to the network. The device has an IP address on the network and has LPT ports or USB ports to connect to the printer. Many network printer devices can provide network printing for more than one connected printer. This method is useful when you are sharing printers on the network that do not have internal networking capabilities.

Networked Printers   Networked printers are printers that include Ethernet ports or wireless adapters built into their cases. They can usually be configured for either static or dynamic IP addresses and they often offer permission management as well. In most cases, networked printers can be accessed either through a server that shares the printer or through direct access to the printer.

Connecting and Disconnecting Printers

The first thing you should understand before you connect any printer is the difference between a *print device* and the *printer* in Microsoft's terminology. The print device is the hardware, such as an HP LaserJet printer. The printer, according to Microsoft, is the software: the printer driver and management software. When you install a printer driver, you are installing the printer. This terminology difference is mostly important when you take Microsoft exams or read their documentation.

By default, in Windows, all print jobs go to the print spooler. The print spooler is a folder on the computer where print jobs are stored until they can be printed. Each printer has its own set of jobs retained for it until they may be printed. The print spooler is managed by a service that is displayed as Print Spooler in the Services console.

Assuming you have a print device connected to your computer through a USB port or an LPT printer port, you can use the following steps to install the printer:

1. Click Start ➢ Devices And Printers.

2. Click Add A Printer.

3. In the Add Printer dialog, choose Add A Local Printer.

4. Click the Use An Existing Port radio button and select the appropriate port, as shown in Figure 11.8, and then click Next.

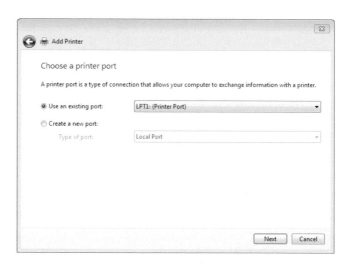

FIGURE 11.8 Selecting the printer port

5. On the Install The Printer Driver screen, choose the manufacturer and printer or click Have Disk and provide the driver from a disk, and then click Next.

6. Provide a name for the printer and then click Next.

> If you encounter "hangs" when printing, they can often be resolved by restarting the Print Spooler service.

7. On the Printer Sharing screen, if you want to share the printer, select the option Share This Printer So That Others On Your Network Can Find And Use It and enter the information for the share. Otherwise, select Do Not Share This Printer, as shown in Figure 11.9, and click Next.

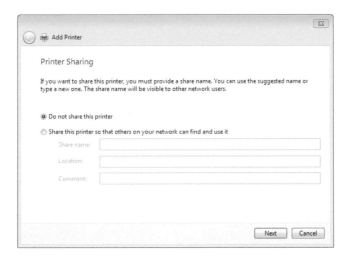

FIGURE 11.9 Selecting not to share the printer with others

8. On the final screen, either select Set As The Default Printer, if you want this new printer to be the default, or leave it deselected if you don't. You can also click Print A Test Page or simply click Finish to complete the installation.

In many cases, vendors provide installation routines for adding their printer drivers. In such cases, you will not have to use the Add Printer wizard, but will instead use the vendor's installation routine. However, in business settings, it is usually more efficient to prestage printer drivers (using the PNPUTIL command discussed earlier in the chapter) so that they will be available as users require them.

Using Print Queues

Each printer on a Windows system has a print queue. The print queue contains the currently printing job and the jobs waiting to print. You can access the print queue using Devices and Printers with the following steps:

1. Click Start ➢ Devices And Printers.

2. Right-click the target printer and select See What's Printing.

3. Manage the print queue in the resulting interface (see Figure 11.10).

FIGURE 11.10 The printer print queue manager in Windows 7

You can pause, restart, or cancel print jobs in the printer queue. You can also open the properties page for a job by right-clicking it and selecting Properties. From here you can schedule the job, set a priority, and even view the layout and paper/quality settings used when the job was created. Figure 11.11 shows the print job Properties page used to schedule the job or change its priority.

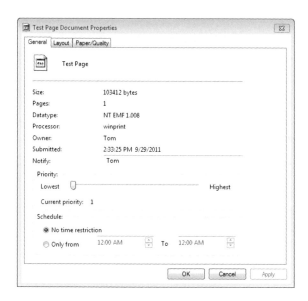

FIGURE 11.11 Viewing the print job Properties

When you increase the priority of a job, you indicate that it should print before other jobs with a lower priority. If someone has submitted a very large job, you can schedule it to run after hours so that it does not interfere with print jobs during the work day.

Printing to a File

More and more organizations are moving to paperless offices. While few truly ever reach "paperless" at this point, many have greatly reduced their paper needs by printing to various file types. Windows 7 includes a new file type and a viewer for reading such files called the XPS document.

You can print to an XPS file from any application by selecting the Microsoft XPS Document Writer as the printer for the print job. Figure 11.12 shows a Microsoft Publisher document with images and text. Figure 11.13 shows this document in the XPS Viewer application that ships with Windows 7 after it is printed as an XPS document.

The XPS acronym stands for XML Paper Specification. It is a Microsoft standard for storing complex documents in XML format.

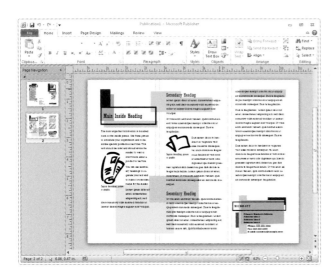

FIGURE 11.12 Viewing a complex document in Microsoft Publisher before printing to an XPS file

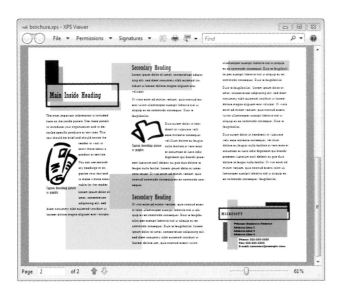

FIGURE 11.13 Viewing the document printed to an XPS file

Internet Printing

The final concept related to printers that you should understand is Internet printing. This technique allows client computers to print to printers using the HTTP protocol. This is the same protocol used to browse web pages, so most firewalls will allow it through. Because of this allowance, users can often print to work printers from their home networks without requiring a VPN connection.

The Internet printing process works as follows:

1. A user connects to the printer server across the Internet based on a URL assigned to the device.

2. The print server requests client authentication, and the client responds and is authenticated. This prevents anonymous users from printing to the printers.

3. The print server provides status information to the client so that only available printers will be used.

4. The user connects to the printer to which he desires to print. If a driver must be installed, the screens will prompt for driver installation.

5. Now that the connection exists, users send print jobs to the printer as if it were a local printer.

For a Windows 7 machine to print to an Internet printer, it must have the Internet Printing Client installed. This client can be installed in the Programs and Features Control Panel applet if required.

System Devices

This final section discusses several device types that are used on modern computers. These include video and audio devices as well as input devices. Finally, you'll learn about system board (motherboard) chipsets and the impact they have on device availability.

Understanding Multimedia Devices

Video and audio devices can be considered from two directions: input and output. Input devices are used to capture media, and output devices are used to play or display media.

The following devices may be used for video input:

▶ Video camera attached through USB or another video input device

▶ Web camera (or web cam), which is often built into the screen area of laptops

▶ Any specialty video capture device

Like any other device, these video input devices will require drivers and may require special software as well. For example, you need drivers just to make cameras work, and then you need software to have practical use of the camera. As an example, Skype can be used with a video camera to implement video calls over the Internet.

The following devices may be used for audio input:

▶ Internal microphones on laptops

▶ Analog microphones connected with one-eighth-inch mini jacks

▶ Digital microphones connected through USB ports

▶ Professional microphones connected through USB-based mixers

Like video input devices, these devices will require drivers and special software. Audio software such as Audacity (shown in Figure 11.14) is used to record and edit audio files.

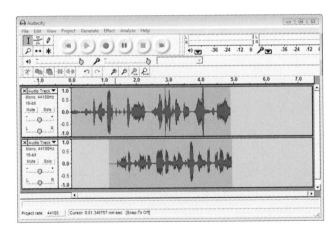

FIGURE 11.14 Audacity, a free audio capture and editing program

Using Input Devices

Modern computer mice use infrared lasers or visible light lasers to capture the movement of the mouse. Regardless of the capture type, wireless mice and keyboards are becoming more and more popular. These wireless devices will use a USB sensor inserted into an available USB port in the computer or connect through internal Bluetooth adapters. As with other devices, the proper device drivers must be acquired and installed. If the hardware is bundled with Windows 7 drivers, you may choose to use the drivers on the accompanying CD or DVD. Even when the hardware comes with drivers, you may choose to visit the vendor website and check for newer drivers.

Exploring System Board Chipsets

Technically, these chips and chipset drivers tell the different parts on the system board how to work together.

The final topic of this chapter is crucial, even though the discussion is brief: chipsets. Computer system boards or motherboards include chipsets that manage access to various devices and ports on the boards. Without the proper chipset drivers installed, you may not have access to all devices. In fact, if the drivers are not installed in the proper order, you may not have access to all devices. For more information on this, see the sidebar "Who's Out of Order?"

Chipset drivers are commonly provided by the following vendors:

- ▶ Intel
- ▶ Nvidia
- ▶ VIA
- ▶ SiS
- ▶ AMD
- ▶ ATI

You will need to acquire a stable version of the chipset drivers and ensure that they are installed on your Windows 7 computers. You should not update chipset drivers as soon as they are released in most cases. Thorough testing should be performed to make sure you do not introduce stability issues or hardware compatibility issues by installing the new version.

Who's Out of Order?

In this chapter, you learned that plug-and-play makes everything easier. Well, this isn't always the case. Computers are becoming so complicated today that you often have to install the hardware drivers in a specific order just to get them all to work together.

(Continues)

WHO'S OUT OF ORDER? *(Continued)*

For example, I acquired an ASUS G73-SW laptop and reloaded it with Windows 7 Ultimate the moment I received it. I used another computer and, from the ASUS support website, I downloaded all of the needed drivers and began installing them one by one. Everything seemed fine until I connected the Ethernet port to a network cable that was connected to my network. The network wasn't working.

When I inspected the Device Manager, it seemed to think that the internal gigabit Ethernet adapter was working fine. When I looked at the adapter in the NCPA.CPL Control Panel applet, it said the cable was unplugged. I connected another laptop to the cable and everything worked fine, so I knew it wasn't the cable. I booted the laptop using the BackTrack live distribution Linux disc and it booted fine with a functioning wired network adapter. The network adapter was clearly working as well.

To make a long story short and to explain more than a day of work in a short sentence: I had to install the device drivers in a specific order for the Ethernet adapter to work. If I'd installed them in the right order, everything would have been fine. But since I didn't, well, it wasn't fine. Of the 14 computers that I owned at this time, this was the only one with this problem. What is the moral of the story? Save yourself some time and call technical support to see if they recommend a specific order for driver installation before you begin your fresh load of the OS.

THE ESSENTIALS AND BEYOND

In this chapter, you learned about device management. You began by learning what a device driver is, where you can get them, and how to install and manage them with the Device Manager. Tasks that can be performed in the Device Manager include installing, updating, rolling back, and deleting devices and device drivers. Next you learned about the benefits of plug-and-play and how it operates in the Windows OS. After this, you learned how to plan initial device installation and driver updates.

Printers were covered next. You learned the difference between local and networked printers and how to manage print queues. You also learned to print to a file and about Internet printing.

(Continues)

THE ESSENTIALS AND BEYOND (Continued)

Finally, you explored more system devices, including video and audio devices and input devices. This chapter ended by discussing chipsets and the importance of these drivers for your systems.

ADDITIONAL EXERCISES

▶ Using any computer model as an example, go to the vendor's website and locate the drivers. Determine for which operating systems the vendor provided device drivers for that computer model.

▶ Use the Device Manager to explore the various devices installed on a computer.

To compare your answers to the author's, please visit www.sybex.com/go/osessentials.

REVIEW QUESTIONS

1. What new file format was introduced as a printer driver in Windows 7 and also included a viewer within the OS?

   A. PDF   **C.** XPS

   B. XLS   **D.** TXT

2. True or false. Installing chipset drivers is optional on modern computers because they are not really used anymore.

3. Which one of the following components that existed in Windows 95 is still in Windows 7 today?

   A. Program Manager   **C.** Action Center

   B. Calendar   **D.** Device Manager

4. Other than the specific hardware device vendor, the Windows 7 Installation DVD, and Microsoft Update, what source do you have for device drivers?

5. Why would you consider running third-party software in relation to a device in addition to the device driver that is required? (Choose all that apply.)

   A. To gain extra features   **C.** Because the hardware requires it

   B. To improve usability   **D.** To reduce drive space consumption

6. Define a device driver.

7. Define the driver store.

(Continues)

THE ESSENTIALS AND BEYOND *(Continued)*

8. What switch is used with the DRIVERQUERY command to indicate that it should format the output as CSV?

   A. /V

   B. /SI

   C. /FO

   D. /CSV

9. You are attempting to revert a device driver to a previous version, but the Roll Back Driver button is disabled. Why is this button disabled?

   A. You are logged on as an administrator.

   B. The device driver is corrupted.

   C. The device driver has never been updated since initial installation.

   D. None of the above

10. True or false. Device drivers run in User mode.

CHAPTER 12

Storage Management

One of the primary reasons for using a computer is the use of applications that generate data, and this data must be placed in storage somewhere. Centralized storage can be used to provide file storage, data storage, and configuration storage for network connected devices on a server. In addition to the centralized storage provided for your networked computers, Windows clients must use storage for the operating system, applications, and services that they run.

In this chapter, you will learn about data storage concepts and the specific storage management features and tools available in Windows, including the following:

▶ **Data storage concepts**

▶ **Understanding RAID**

▶ **Identifying storage technologies**

▶ **Understanding disk types**

▶ **Using online storage**

Data Storage Concepts

You need to understand several technologies in order to plan and implement storage solutions for Windows computers. First, you must be familiar with the physical devices used for storage, primarily hard drives. Second, you should know how data is stored on these devices, which means you need to understand filesystems. Filesystems were covered in Chapter 10, "Network Shares," but additional information is provided in this chapter. Finally, you should understand the technologies, such as Distributed File System (DFS) and network storage mechanisms, that utilize hard drives and filesystems and that your Windows clients may access. The primary focus of this section is on defining these concepts. The later section "Identifying Storage Technologies" will provide more detail on specific hard drive types and network storage types.

Selecting Hard Drives for Your Computers

Nonvolatile storage allows data to be retained when power is removed.

Hard drives (also called hard disks) provide nonvolatile storage of data. *Volatile* storage loses all data when power is removed. *Nonvolatile* storage retains data even if power is removed. Volatile storage includes the following:

System RAM   The system random access memory (RAM) is the memory used by the operating system and internal to your computer.

Video RAM   The memory used for video processing is video RAM. Some computer vendors are now combining system RAM and video RAM together to indicate total RAM. For example, one vendor that sells a computer with 8 GB of system RAM and 1 GB of video RAM states that the computer comes with 9 GB of RAM.

Nonvolatile storage includes the following:

Hard Drives   The internal and external disks with large storage capacity are typically hard drives. Several different speeds and form factors are available for hard drive selection.

Flash Drives   An external drive that is typically a USB drive with small to medium storage capacity is a flash drive. Flash drives, often called cards, also include Secure Digital (SD) cards, Compact Flash (CF) cards, and Micro-SD cards.

NVRAM   The internal storage chips used for system BIOS settings are called nonvolatile RAM (NVRAM). This type of storage is also used in other computing devices like switches and routers.

Traditional hard drives use moving platters for data storage. These platters are simply spinning disks used to store the actual data. Such a device consists of a motor, spindle, platters, read/write heads, and electronics. The motor spins the spindle so that the read/write heads can read and write data from and to the platters. The electronics include a printed circuit board (PCB) and various chips for drive operations. Some drives have all of the electronics integrated, and others rely on controllers to send commands to the drive for normal operations.

SOLID STATE DRIVES

Newer technology, called *solid state drive* (SSD) technology, uses nonmoving storage. SSD is far more expensive than traditional storage hard drives and is not currently used for typical server storage solutions, but it is growing in

(Continues)

SOLID STATE DRIVES *(Continued)*

popularity for client computers that run Windows 7. SSD may be used for the operating system drive, but it is rarely used for data storage because of the high cost per gigabyte of storage. Modern computers often store thousands of gigabytes of data, and cost is a significant factor when you're deciding whether to use SSD technology or traditional storage.

The best hard drive for your needs depends on the answers to these questions:

- ► What storage capacity is required?

- ► What read and write speeds are required?

- ► What hard drive types are supported by the drive system?

- ► How many drive bays or drive connections does the target system provide?

The first step is to clearly define the required storage capacity. When selecting the drive for operating system installation, you can define this requirement based on the operating system vendor's recommendations. When selecting a drive for data storage, you must estimate the amount of data that will be stored on the drive.

Once you've determined the capacity requirements, you must define the drive speed requirements, measured as *revolutions per minute* (RPM). Within each type of hard drive are variable speeds. For example, the *serial advanced technology attachment* (SATA) hard drives commonly come in 4,200 RPM, 5,400 RPM, 7,200 RPM, and 10,000 RPM speeds. The newer SATA drives can even support 15,000 RPM rates. The RPM rate has a direct correlation to the speed at which the drive reads and writes data. During each revolution, only so much data can be read. The higher-RPM drives will read data faster because they read the same amount of data per revolution as the lower-RPM drives, but many more times per minute. Drives with a higher RPM are typically more expensive, so your budget may also help define the speed you select.

All else being equal, a drive with higher RPM ratings will provide faster data access.

Several hard drive types have been developed over the years. The following list describes the newer standards that are still supported today:

Integrated Drive Electronics (IDE)   IDE was the first version of a hard drive technology that later became known as AT attachment. It was very popular in the mid-1990s and is still supported by many production computers. It is often used for optical drive connections, but the newest computers no longer use it for hard drive connections, having moved on to the newer SATA drives in most systems.

ATA   The Advanced Technology Attachment (ATA) technology was later renamed Parallel ATA (PATA) to differentiate it from SATA technologies. Like IDE, ATA drives are falling out of popularity, but may still be seen in some older computers that remain in production.

SATA   Serial advanced technology attachment (SATA) is still widely supported in computers and likely will be for some time. It has speeds that are comparable to SCSI drives, ranging from 1.5 Gbps (SATA 1.0) to 6 Gbps (SATA 3.0). SATA drives are supported in both server and desktop computers, and many SATA RAID controllers are available for RAID implementation. External SATA (eSATA) drives may be connected using external connectors on the computer. SATA has mostly replaced PATA in both clients and servers today.

SCSI   Small Computer System Interface (SCSI) is a peripheral connection technology. It is not used for storage drives alone, but can also be used for scanners and other devices. SCSI drives come in many versions; the Ultra-640 SCSI version can support speeds up to approximately 5 Gbps. SCSI commands are used across TCP/IP connections when iSCSI is used.

Removable Storage   In addition to SATA and SCSI drives, many removable drive form factors are supported. The most common removable drive form factors are *Universal Serial Bus* (USB) and *FireWire* (also called IEEE 1394). *External SATA* (eSATA) is also growing in popularity. For lower-capacity drives, flash-based media is popular. Flash-based media includes USB flash drives, CF, and Secure Digital (SD) storage.

Of course, you can only use drive types that are supported by the target system. The target system may be the actual computer (when selecting internal storage) or a dedicated storage system (when selecting external storage). In either case, you must use the supported drive types. If the storage system supports only SCSI drives, you must select SCSI drives of the size and speed you require.

The final factor is the number of drives the target system supports. Most computers have at least two hard drive bays, and some have six or more. When the computer does not have sufficient internal drive bays, you can select external storage solutions that connect to the computer through USB, eSATA, SCSI, or FireWire connections. In many cases, external storage solutions are preferable to internal storage because the external system can be accessed by more than one computer.

Table 12.1 provides an overview of the speeds available with different external storage solutions.

TABLE 12.1 External storage types and speeds

Storage Type	Speeds
USB	1.5 Mbps (low bandwidth) and 12 Mbps (full bandwidth)
USB 2.0	480 Mbps
USB 3.0	5 Gbps
IEEE 1394 (FireWire)	400 Mbps (FireWire 400), 800 Mbps (FireWire 800), 1.6 Gbps (FireWire S1600), and 3.2 Gbps (FireWire S3200)
eSATA	3 Gbps
iSCSI	Speed controlled by the network speed; currently up to 10 GB Ethernet

Choosing a Filesystem

A filesystem defines the way in which data is placed on a storage medium and the file access methods used. For example, the filesystem defines the minimum data size that must be written to the drive and the method used to index the data on the drive. The minimum data size used for storage is known as the *cluster size* or the *allocation unit size*. The index of the data is the file table, which tracks the files on the drive and the storage locations used for those files.

Windows computers today support two primary filesystems: FAT and NTFS. The File Allocation Table (FAT) filesystem is the older of the two, and the NT File System (referring to the Windows NT operating system for which it was originally created) is the newer. FAT is a simple filesystem, and NTFS is a more complex filesystem offering advanced features, including security. Although FAT is the older filesystem, it is still commonly used on removable drives today. Table 12.2 compares the features of the FAT and NTFS filesystems.

The FAT filesystem has been with us since the 1980s. The NTFS filesystem has existed since the release of Windows NT 3.1 in 1993.

Sparse files are special files that consume no actual drive space when created even though they may be created as large files. This allows the files to be created almost instantly without requiring intensive system resources, such as CPU time. Even as the sparse files fill, they consume only space required and do not consume space for empty or zero data elements within the files.

TABLE 12.2 FAT and NTFS filesystem comparison

FAT (File Allocation Table)	NTFS (NT File System)
Maximum volume size of 2 TB with FAT32 or 4 GB with FAT16	Maximum volume size of 256 TB with a 64 KB cluster size (when using the master boot record partition table, this is limited to 2 TB).
Maximum file size of 4 GB	Maximum file size of approximately 16 TB.
Up to 4.2 million files per volume	Up to 4.3 billion files per volume.
File attributes provide limited security	NTFS permissions provide advanced security.
No sparse file support	Sparse files are supported.
Best performance on smaller drives	Best performance on larger drives.
No inherent support for encryption	Built-in data encryption support, using the Encrypting File System (EFS).

A mount point is an additional feature of NTFS, which was introduced with the release of Windows 2000 Professional and Windows 2000 Server. A *mount point* is a directory or folder on an existing volume that points to another volume on the same physical drive or a separate physical drive. Mount points allow you to add storage to an existing drive letter through the use of a folder on that drive. Applications are unaware that the folder is actually a reference to a completely separate storage volume.

A new version of FAT called Extended FAT (exFAT) is supported in Windows XP and later versions of Windows. Although the *extended FAT* (exFAT) filesystem is sometimes referred to as *FAT64*, that isn't a Microsoft-supported name. exFAT overcomes the 4 GB limit of FAT volumes, but it is intended for removable storage devices.

When selecting a filesystem, be sure to check the software vendor's literature. To perform properly, some applications may require either FAT or NTFS. In some cases, you may have to create a special FAT16 or FAT32 volume on a drive just to support a specific application, although this has become less common today.

Understanding Networked Storage

Modern networks demand more storage space than ever before. You may be required to support storage for thousands of users and hundreds of applications.

In such environments, using the built-in computer storage may be insufficient. Networked storage provides a viable solution. The users can store their data on networked hard drives. In most cases, these hard drives will be managed by network servers, such as Windows Server 2008 R2.

Networked storage systems come in two basic implementations:

► Network-attached storage (NAS)

► Storage area network (SAN)

In spite of their similar names, these two technologies are very different, and you must understand them so you can choose the right technology for a given scenario.

NAS solutions are nothing more than dedicated file servers. You can purchase NAS devices at consumer electronics stores, and you can purchase more advanced NAS devices directly from vendors such as HP and IBM. Advanced NAS devices support internal drive redundancy and special communications protocols; however, they are accessed using communications protocols that run across your existing network. In other words, NAS devices are accessed using standard network communications—in most cases, on the same network as all other network communications. Although NAS devices could be implemented on a dedicated Ethernet network separate from the user access network through the use of multiple network adapters in a server, the performance will still not equal that of a SAN.

A SAN uses block-level access across the network, which means that it reads and writes blocks of data instead of entire files. NAS devices typically read and write entire files. This is a key difference between the two. Special protocols are implemented to provide far better performance than can be provided by a NAS device. Two major SAN solutions are common today:

The Fibre Channel and iSCSI solutions are discussed in more detail later in this chapter in the section titled "Identifying Storage Technologies."

► Fibre Channel

► iSCSI

Using DFS

In addition to storage hardware, such as internal hard drives and networked storage, you need to consider storage-related software when planning your storage solutions. Microsoft provides a storage solution called the *Distributed File System* (DFS), which is used to distribute files across multiple servers or to aggregate files that exist on multiple servers. This allows users to store their data on a network location and potentially have that data automatically replicated to other locations.

DFS can be used to replicate files to multiple locations and to aggregate files from multiple locations into one virtual share.

DFS is available only on Windows Server operating systems, but the DFS shares can be accessed by Windows clients. No special software is required on the Windows clients, as they see the DFS shares as standard network shares.

DFS can distribute files across multiple servers using the File Replication Service (FRS). Users place files into a share, and the FRS automatically copies those files to multiple locations as defined by DFS. This allows files to be distributed to locations that are closer to the users who need the files, as shown in Figure 12.1.

FIGURE 12.1 DFS used to distribute files to multiple locations

DFS can also aggregate files that exist on multiple servers into a single virtual location. For example, notice that Figure 12.2 shows multiple file shares on multiple physical servers. After DFS replication, all of these shares appear as subfolders in the DFS root share on Server1. This DFS-provided aggregation makes file access simpler for the network users.

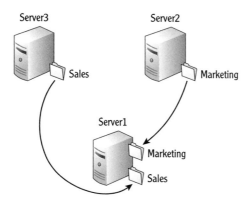

FIGURE 12.2 DFS used to aggregate files from multiple shares into a single virtual location

When DFS is used to aggregate multiple shares into a single virtual location, the files still exist in the individual shares, but they appear to be in a single location to the users. This single location is the DFS root. The access to the actual shares is made transparent to the users. This functionality simplifies access for users and provides simpler administration for applications as well. For example, an application may require access to multiple files. For performance reasons, you may want to place some files on one server and other files on another server. DFS can be used to make those files appear to be in a single location for the application.

Because DFS is a server-only technology, it is not covered in detail here; however, you can learn more about DFS here:

```
http://technet.microsoft.com/en-us/library/cc732863(WS.10).aspx
```

Understanding RAID

Redundant array of independent disks (RAID) is an internal or external storage technology that uses an array of hard disks and may be hardware- or software-based. Hardware-based RAID uses hardware drive controllers that have built-in RAID processing software. Software-based RAID uses standard hard drive controllers and handles the RAID processing as a software layer that is either built into the OS or installed as an extra feature. RAID can be used in either Windows clients or servers.

◄

RAID is sometimes also said to stand for redundant array of inexpensive disks. Regardless of the acronym's meaning, RAID always involves an array of disks.

The phrase *RAID level* is used to define the different implementations of RAID. Many different RAID levels exist, but the most commonly used are listed here:

- ▶ RAID 0
- ▶ RAID 1
- ▶ RAID 5
- ▶ RAID 0+1
- ▶ RAID 1+0 or RAID 10

Figure 12.3 shows the various RAID levels in a graphical representation. RAID 0 is depicted as three physical drives acting as one logical drive. Under the hood, data is *striped* (written) evenly across the three drives. For example, if 99 KB of data is being written to drive D using RAID 0, one third would be written to Drive 1, one third to Drive 2, and the final third to Drive 3. No fault tolerance is provided by RAID 0 alone. RAID 0 is used only to improve read and write performance, and it is typically referred to as a *striped set*.

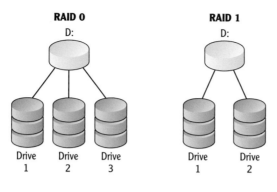

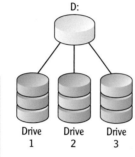

Parity is a mathematically calculated value used to regenerate missing data. Fault-tolerant RAID uses parity bits for recoverability.

FIGURE 12.3   RAID levels 0, 1, and 5

Most controllers require a minimum of two drives to create a RAID 0 array—that is, a striped set without parity. Some will require three drives in the array. The drawbacks of RAID 0 include the fact that one drive failure makes the entire array unavailable and that the large amount of storage represented by the individual physical drives aggregates into one very large, possibly difficult to manage, storage location. The positives include faster data reads and writes because the data is spread across multiple drives that can be simultaneously accessed, as well as complete availability of the drive space from the hard drives included in the array.

Fault tolerance is the ability to handle a failure or a fault and continue operations.

The next level of RAID represented in Figure 12.3 is level 1. At RAID level 1, data is mirrored across two physical drives. If the RAID is implemented through hardware as opposed to software, users and applications see only a single logical drive at the OS level. When RAID is implemented through software, the OS sees the separate drives (in tools like Disk Management). RAID 1 provides fault tolerance by writing all data twice:

▶ The data is written to the "visible" drive, called the *primary drive* in the mirror set.

▶ The data is also written to the "invisible" drive, called the *mirror drive* in the set.

There is no striping of data during writes, but some RAID controllers (hardware drive controllers that support RAID configurations) will read the data from both drives. RAID 1 is used to provide fault tolerance and quick failover. The negatives of RAID 1 include the loss of half of your storage space and the reduced performance of writes. The positive is that RAID 1 provides the highest level of data availability because all the data is completely written to two separate physical devices. RAID 1 is frequently used for the OS drive. This usage provides fault tolerance for the OS.

RAID 5 attempts to balance RAID 0 and 1. RAID 5 arrays stripe data across the drives in the array. However, unlike RAID 0, RAID 5 arrays also provide fault tolerance. They do this through the generation of *parity bits*. For example, assume there are three physical drives that make up the logical drive array. When data is written to the array, half the data will be written to one drive, half the data to another, and then parity bits will be written to the third drive. In most implementations, the parity bits are stored evenly across the drives in the array. Now, if any single physical drive fails, the controller or software can regenerate the data that was stored on the failed drive from the parity stored on the remaining drives. This regeneration generally happens on the fly with no administrative intervention. Of course, should another drive fail at this time, the entire array will be lost.

Because parity bits are used with RAID 5, it requires a minimum of three drives: Two drives store the data and one drive stores the parity bits during each write. Most implementations rotate the parity bits across the drives for each write operation. If a drive fails, it should be replaced as soon as possible so that the RAID system can rebuild, onto the new drive, the data that was lost.

To understand how RAID 5 functions, consider a simple analogy. Imagine you have the numbers 5 and 7 that you want to store. If you store 5 in one notebook and 7 in another, when either notebook is lost, you've lost the ability to recover all of your meaningful data. However, imagine you have a third notebook. In this third notebook, you store the number 12 (5+7). Now, if you lose one of the three notebooks, you will always be able to get your data back. For example, if you lose notebook two, you can subtract 5 (the number in notebook 1) from 12 and recover the number 7 that was in the second notebook. While RAID 5 striping and parity algorithms are more complex than this analogy, it should help you conceptualize how the RAID level functions. It is also important to keep in mind that when you add more drives to your system, you increase the likelihood that one of those drives will fail on any given day and actually increase the need for fault tolerance.

RAID 0+1 combines the stripe sets with mirroring. First, you would configure two stripe sets and then configure those two sets to appear as one drive that is a RAID 1 implementation. For example, you might have three drives in each stripe set, and all six drives will appear as one virtual drive. This gives you a balance between the performance of RAID 0 and the complete fault tolerance of RAID 1.

RAID 0 is a stripe set without parity. RAID 1 is mirroring. RAID 5 is a stripe set with parity.

When using drive arrays, it is more likely that one of the drives will fail simply because you are running multiple drives. Increased heat can also increase the likelihood of failure.

RAID 1+0, also known as RAID 10, is just the opposite of RAID 0+1. In this case, you will actually implement two or three mirror sets and then stripe data across those mirror sets. This provides fault tolerance as the foundation and performance as an added layer.

Understanding the various levels of RAID is important. As you make decisions related to the hardware that you purchase, this knowledge will prove useful. If you determine that you need fault tolerance at the drive level, you will want to purchase a computer that provides this feature through hardware. Although you can implement RAID through software, the performance is not generally as high and it will take away processing power from the computer itself. Although it is rare to use RAID in a client computer, you can do so to optimize performance for disk-intensive applications. Software-based RAID can also be used in small businesses where a user's workstation also plays the role of a file-sharing server. This configuration is common in small businesses with just a few computers.

HARDWARE RAID VS. SOFTWARE RAID

Software-based RAID levels 0, 1, and 5 are supported through the Disk Management snap-in in Windows. When you implement RAID in this way, you are implementing software-based RAID, which means that the RAID operations are controlled through an operating system driver and not through hardware processes. Multiple physical drives are still used, but the actual RAID implementation and management is provided through software. Hardware-based RAID is handled within the RAID controller and is typically configured through a special application provided by the hardware vendor.

Hardware-based RAID is preferred over software-based RAID for performance reasons. When a hardware RAID controller is used, it has a processor that performs the RAID operations. In other words, the computer's CPU is not used to separate the data for striping or to generate the parity bits for RAID calculations, and it is not required to regenerate data in a RAID 5 array when a single drive fails.

Software-based RAID is useful for stripe sets or mirror sets because they are not as CPU-intensive as RAID 5 arrays; however, hardware-based arrays are still preferred even in these scenarios. I typically use software-based RAID for educational purposes and the implementation of lab environments. I use hardware-based RAID for production implementations whenever possible.

Identifying Storage Technologies

At this point, the storage concepts have been addressed and you understand hard drives, filesystems, networked storage, and specialized storage solutions such as DFS and RAID. Now, it's time to explore in greater detail the various networked storage solutions that you may choose to implement.

Earlier in this chapter, NAS and SAN storage solutions were briefly introduced. This section addresses NAS and SAN storage in more detail. First, you will learn about the Network File System (NFS), which is often supported by NAS devices. Then you will learn about the hardware required to implement SAN solutions such as Fibre Channel and iSCSI.

NFS is the filesystem most often used with NAS devices. While many NAS devices support operating as *server message block* (SMB) share servers, they also typically support NFS. NFS was originally developed by Sun Microsystems and is an open standard defined in RFCs today. RFC 1090 defines the NFS version 2 standard, RFC 1813 defines the NFS version 3 standard, and RFC 3010 defines the NFS version 4 standard.

NFS runs across TCP and UDP (Used Datagram Protocol), meaning that it is an OSI Model Layer 5 and upward technology that relies on the IP infrastructure for communications. This is a main difference between NAS and SAN solutions. Most SAN solutions use specialized adapter cards to communicate with the SAN. NAS typically uses the same network adapter to communicate with the NFS server as the one used to communicate with all other network services. The result is typically poorer performance than SANs. However, NFS does allow remote directories to be mounted to local directories and appear as if they are part of the local filesystem on a machine. This is similar to the way SMB works for Windows shares, with the exception of data-writing granularity. NFS supports granular data writes at the block level, whereas SMB supports only complete file writes to the server.

Fibre Channel is a SAN technology that uses special adapters known as *host bus adapters* (HBAs). HBAs are basically network adapters that are specially designed to communicate with the Fibre Channel SAN. Fibre Channel offers high-speed communications with the SAN and true block-level access so that drives can be written to and read from as if they were internal drives. In fact, Windows servers use special drivers for Fibre Channel SAN access that make the SAN appear to be normal local storage in applications and file management software. Windows clients can also directly access a SAN, but this is less common.

SMB is the protocol used for Microsoft computers to provide and access shared folders on the network.

In larger implementations, Fibre Channel switches are used to build a more complex SAN infrastructure. The switches provide access to the storage so that the clients (the servers accessing the SAN) do not have to be aware of the actual drives that are being accessed.

iSCSI is an implementation of the SCSI storage system across the internetwork. iSCSI uses TCP/IP protocols, including TCP and UDP, to access the SAN. In the best-performing implementations, special iSCSI network adapters are installed in the computers so that the iSCSI communications are offloaded from the system CPU and memory. This allows for high-speed iSCSI communications. In most cases, a dedicated TCP/IP network is created for iSCSI communications between the computers and the iSCSI SAN.

Understanding Disk Types

The Windows operating systems, including both servers and clients, support three disk types for hard drive access. The first two types define the way in which a standard internal hard drive is used. The third type defines a file that is mounted as a hard drive. In addition to the three hard drive types, Windows operating systems can use optical media, which you also need to understand.

Basic and Dynamic Disks

When you initialize a new hard drive in a Windows operating system, the disk type for the hard drive needs to be specified before logical partitions or volumes can be created and formatted for use. Windows operating systems support either the basic or the dynamic disk type. Depending on the features you require, you can choose how to configure your disks within the Disk Management utility.

Basic disks provide the basic features and functions required for typical storage tasks. For this reason, they are the most common disk type used. A basic disk contains partitions, which may include up to four primary partitions or three primary partitions and one extended partition. An extended partition can be divided into additional logical disk drives. When the partitions or logical drives are formatted with a filesystem, such as FAT or NTFS, they are called *volumes*. When formatted with NTFS, volumes on basic disks can be expanded to include space from other partitions or logical disks on the same physical disk.

Some tasks can be performed on a basic disk that cannot be performed on a dynamic disk:

> ▶ Creating and deleting primary or extended partitions

> ▶ Creating and deleting logical drives

Basic disks support the most commonly used features of Windows computers when software-based RAID is not required.

- ▶ Formatting partitions
- ▶ Marking partitions as active

Dynamic disks, which were a new feature in Windows 2000, provide several features not available in basic disks. The most important feature that dynamic disks support is software-based RAID. If you want to implement RAID arrays using software, the disks used in the array must be dynamic disks.

The following tasks can be performed only on dynamic disks:

- ▶ Creating RAID volumes
- ▶ Creating spanned volumes (non-RAID arrays that use space from multiple disks)
- ▶ Extending spanned volumes
- ▶ Repairing RAID 1 and RAID 5 arrays
- ▶ Breaking a mirror array
- ▶ Reactivating missing or offline disks in arrays

Regardless of the disk-level management features you want to implement, the Disk Management utility is used to perform the tasks. To access Disk Management, click Start, right-click Computer, select Manage, and then expand the Storage node. Figure 12.4 shows the Disk Management tool.

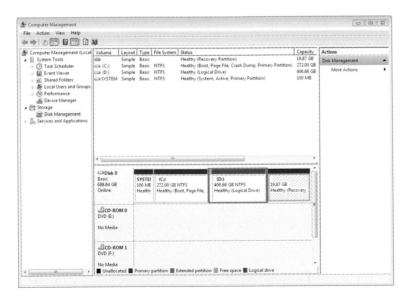

FIGURE 12.4 The Disk Management utility with a basic disk

WHAT IS A GUID PARTITION TABLE?

Microsoft introduced support for a new partition table type in Windows XP and later versions. This is called the Globally Unique Identifier (GUID) Partition Table (GPT). The GPT provides a more flexible tool for partitioning disks than the MBR. MBR disks are limited to four partition table entries, and GPT partitions are not constrained to such a low number. Instead, Windows systems allow for up to 128 partitions on a GPT disk. To learn more about the GPT partitioning system in Windows, visit `http://msdn.microsoft.com/en-us/windows/hardware/gg463525`.

Virtual Hard Disks

Virtual hard disk (VHD) files have been used with virtualization systems such as VMware and Hyper-V for several years. VHD files are data files on a physical hard disk that are used as hard drives within virtual machines. VMware can import VHD files and convert them to its native virtual disk format, and Hyper-V can use them without conversion. Windows 7 and Windows Server 2008 R2 introduced the ability to mount a VHD file as a hard drive within the operating system as if it were a physical drive. You can even boot an operating system, such as Windows Server 2008 R2 or Windows 7, from a VHD file that is stored on the local disk. Additionally, the Disk Management tool can now be used to create a VHD file, using these steps:

1. Launch the Disk Management utility by clicking Start, right-clicking Computer, and selecting Manage. Then expand the Storage node.

2. Right-click the Disk Management node and select Create VHD.

3. In the Create And Attach Virtual Hard Disk window, choose the location for the VHD file and the size of the drive.

4. Choose whether the drive should immediately consume the required space (Fixed) or consume space only as data is placed into the VHD file (Dynamically Expanding), as shown in Figure 12.5.

5. Click OK when finished.

FIGURE 12.5 Creating a new VHD
file in Disk Management

When the system finishes creating the VHD file, it will be mounted automatically. You can then initialize the disk and create a volume on it for data storage. Because the drive is really a VHD file, you can easily dismount it (right-click the disk and select Detach VHD). One huge benefit of using VHD files to store data content is that once they are dismounted, they can be copied to another server and then mounted for use on the new server.

Optical Media

In addition to the hard drive storage technologies discussed in this chapter, Windows computers support optical media. Of course, the computer must provide the drive bay space for the optical drive. Today, you can use CD-ROM, DVD, and Blu-Ray drives in Windows computers. In fact, Blu-Ray writers are becoming increasingly popular as backup devices for Windows servers. With 50 GB of storage available on dual-layer Blu-Ray discs, they are useful as a backup solution. A newer Blu-Ray specification (Blu-Ray Disk XL) provides up to 128 GB of storage.

Using Online Storage

The final storage type that must be considered is online storage. Storing data online or in the cloud allows you to dismiss concerns over the exact physical storage methods and focus only on the amount of storage needed, the access methods required, and the data backup assurances of the storage providers. When selecting cloud storage providers for a business storage solution, it is important to choose a vendor with a data backup guarantee. You certainly do not want to store data in the cloud only to have it disappear without the ability to recover it. The primary focus of this section is on Microsoft online storage solutions; however, third-party solutions are also briefly considered.

Microsoft Online Storage Solutions

Microsoft provides online storage as part of Windows Live. The service is called SkyDrive (indicative of the fact that it is a storage "drive" in the cloud). SkyDrive promises enhanced storage and management features, including the following:

5 GB of Storage You can store documents, images, and other files in SkyDrive and consume up to 5 GB of space.

Organization The data can be organized into top-level folders and subfolders that you create and name.

Security You can set permissions for each folder, determining whether only you can access the data or you want to share it with your Windows Live network of friends.

Flexibility You can upload files in sizes as large as 100 MB and then copy, move, delete, rename, and caption the files after uploading them.

Display If the files are graphics files (JPEG, GIF, BMP, PNG, or TIF), you can view them as thumbnails. Users can also view them as a slide show.

Sharing You can share links directly to your SkyDrive folders so that others can access the data. You can also synchronize the data to your local Windows 7 machine so that it is automatically updated wherever you make changes.

Figure 12.6 shows the Windows Live SkyDrive interface.

OneNote to SkyDrive is a feature that allows you to synchronize your OneNote notebooks with SkyDrive. In fact, you can create Word documents, Excel workbooks, PowerPoint presentations, and OneNote notebooks all within SkyDrive directly. This is done using the Office WebApp feature, similar to the one in Microsoft SharePoint Server 2010.

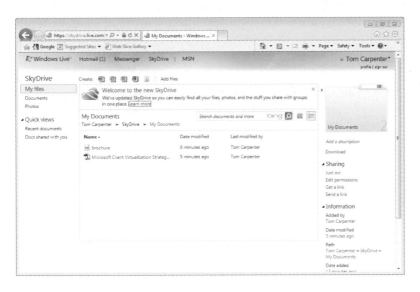

FIGURE 12.6 The Windows Live SkyDrive interface showing documents available

Windows Live Mesh 2011 is a solution that, when installed on a Windows computer, can synchronize local files with Windows Live. It lets you do the following:

▶ Sync folders onto SkyDrive

▶ Sync program settings so that they duplicate on all computers, including the synchronization of Internet Explorer favorites

▶ Sync data between computers using Windows Live as the intermediary

▶ Connect to your PC from a remote location

Third-Party Online Storage Solutions

The most popular third-party online storage solutions include Dropbox and Google Docs. Dropbox provides 2 GB of free storage and paid subscriptions with up to 100 GB of storage. An application is provided on the local machine so that you can literally drag-and-drop files to the Dropbox and they will be uploaded for you automatically. Additionally, Dropbox keeps a one-month history of all changes, allowing you to recover previous versions of your documents.

Google Docs provides the ability to create spreadsheets, word processor documents, and presentations online. Google Docs provides 1 GB of storage, half of that provided by Dropbox and only 20 percent of that provided by SkyDrive; however, it also integrates well into Gmail and other Google services.

THE ESSENTIALS AND BEYOND

Windows computers support many storage solutions. Storage may be implemented as internal, external, and networked storage. Internal storage is usually implemented with hard drives. Hard drives come in many sizes and form factors, and you should choose based on storage requirements and performance requirements. Networked storage includes both network attached storage (NAS) and storage area networks (SANs). The FAT filesystem does not offer the security enhancements offered by the NTFS filesystem. When implementing internal storage, you must choose between basic and dynamic disks. In most cases, basic disks are used unless software-based RAID is required.

RAID provides fault tolerance or improved performance, and it can be implemented in several levels. RAID level 0 provides improved performance using at least two drives as a stripe set. RAID level 1 provides fault tolerance using two drives as a mirror set. RAID level 5 provides improved performance and fault tolerance using at least three drives in a stripe set with parity.

ADDITIONAL EXERCISES

▶ Research the different speeds available in SATA storage solutions.

▶ Browse the features of a vendor's SAN solutions.

▶ View the filesystem used for a drive on Windows 7.

▶ Create and mount a VHD file in Windows 7.

To compare your answers to the author's, please visit www.sybex.com/go/osessentials.

REVIEW QUESTIONS

1. What filesystem supports the use of EFS?

   A. FAT   **C.** exFAT

   B. FAT32   **D.** NTFS

2. True or false. exFAT is primarily used for removable media.

(Continues)

THE ESSENTIALS AND BEYOND (Continued)

3. What kind of storage solution provides block-level access across the network in every implementation?

    A. NAS   **C.** SATA

    B. SAN   **D.** SCSI

4. What level of RAID provides mirroring on the drives?

5. Why is software-based RAID inferior to hardware-based RAID?

    A. Because software-based RAID does not support the same RAID levels

    B. Because software-based RAID requires the computer's CPU for RAID processing

    C. Because software-based RAID has a dedicated hardware CPU for RAID processing

    D. Because hardware-based RAID is less expensive

6. What type of disk must be used in order to implement software-based RAID in a Windows operating system?

7. What Microsoft services can be used to aggregate multiple server shares into one virtual location for user access?

8. What is the maximum file size on FAT filesystem drives?

    A. 4 TB   **C.** 4 KB

    B. 4 MB   **D.** 4 GB

9. What is the adapter called that provides access to a Fibre Channel SAN?

    A. NIC   **C.** SCSI

    B. HBA   **D.** NAS

10. True or false. You can create a primary partition on a dynamic disk.

CHAPTER 13

Windows Troubleshooting

Troubleshooting skills are essential for computer administrators and even self-sufficient users of modern computers. Resolving problems in operating systems depends on an understanding of troubleshooting processes and tools. Users often measure their satisfaction with the services support professionals provide based on the time it takes to fix their problems.

The master troubleshooter has an understanding of the tools and techniques available. Effective administrators understand the two primary topics of this chapter: troubleshooting processes and troubleshooting tools. These two important topics are covered throughout the following sections:

▶ **Troubleshooting processes**

▶ **Using Disk Defragmenter**

▶ **Performing a disk cleanup**

▶ **Scheduling tasks**

▶ **Accessing additional troubleshooting tools**

Troubleshooting Processes

Troubleshooting processes and procedures are used to resolve problems as quickly as possible. Many IT professionals develop their own troubleshooting processes over time, and established troubleshooting processes are often defined by hardware and software vendors. You can group troubleshooting processes, procedures, and best practices together as a *methodology*. A troubleshooting methodology defines the processes used to troubleshoot a problem. It also defines the procedures to perform at each step in the process. Finally, it will recommend best practices for documentation and procedural actions, such as the best environment in which to perform hardware maintenance or the proper way to install or remove hardware.

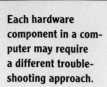

Each hardware component in a computer may require a different troubleshooting approach.

Troubleshooting may require a systematic approach or a specific approach. A systematic approach considers the entire system and is sometimes called *systems thinking*. A specific approach is used for each troubleshooting category. For example, when troubleshooting network adapter problems, you can follow a specific process, which may look something like this:

1. Verify that the network adapter is physically installed properly.

2. Verify that the operating system has detected the network adapter.

3. Verify that the driver has been installed appropriately.

4. Verify that the network protocols, such as TCP/IP, are configured properly.

Notice that each step is working up in the order required for the adapter to work. It must first be installed. Then the operating system must detect it. Next, the driver must be properly installed and configured. Finally, the network protocols must be correctly configured. This is a *bottom-up* approach to a specific problem. Alternatively, you could start at the top (with the network protocols) and work down to the bottom (the physical installation of the adapter). Either way, this is a specific process for a categorical problem: a nonfunctioning network adapter.

To help you fully understand troubleshooting methodologies, several are explained in this section:

▶ REACT

▶ OSI model

▶ Hardware/software model

▶ Symptom, diagnosis, and solution

▶ Systems thinking

REACT

REACT is the troubleshooting methodology used at SysEdCo, the training and consulting firm that I founded in Ohio. It is presented here as an example of a methodology you may develop for yourself after working in the IT industry for some time.

How I Developed REACT

Early in my IT career, I worked as a help desk analyst and a telephone troubleshooter. I found that I would frequently forget some important step in the troubleshooting process that would cost me minutes or even hours of time—not to mention the added stress. For this reason, I developed an acronym to remind me of the stages I should go through when troubleshooting a problem. This way, I can work through the acronym until I reach a solution. I always reach a solution by the end of the acronym. The reality is that sometimes the solution is a complete reload of a device's firmware and settings and sometimes it is a complete reload of a client computer's operating system; more often than not, however, a simpler solution is found.

The acronym REACT stands for the five stages of troubleshooting:

► Research

► Engage

► Adjust

► Configure

► Take note

The methodology is represented in Figure 13.1 with the common tasks performed in each stage. I'll cover each one briefly in the following sections so that you can understand how they fit together and why I go through these stages.

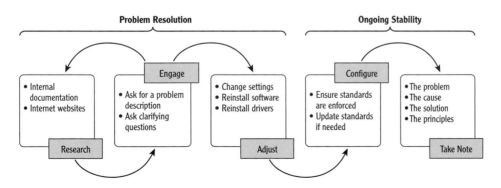

FIGURE 13.1 The REACT methodology

Research

Here's an anecdote. It was probably in 1997 that I was trying to resolve a problem with a Microsoft Access 95 database. Every time the user tried to open the database, she received an error that read, "A device attached to the system is not functioning." Now, I don't know about you, but when I see an error about a device, the first thing I think of is hardware. I spent more than two hours trying to verify that all the hardware was functioning properly, and of course, it was. By this time, the end of the day had arrived and I went home tormented by my failure to resolve the problem (hopefully I'm the only one who suffers like this when I can't fix a computer problem).

The next day, I decided to do some research, so I opened the MSDN CD (that's right, it used to fit on one CD and have plenty of space left over). I searched for the error message and found that the error could be generated if VBRUN300.DLL was corrupt. (If you haven't been around long, VBRUN300.DLL was used by all Visual Basic 3.0 applications.) The only problem for me was that Microsoft Access and this database did not rely on Visual Basic 3.0's runtime for anything; however, my mind was racing. The jungle of my mind was suddenly clear and I realized the implications: If the corruption of VBRUN300.DLL could cause the error, maybe any corrupt DLL could cause the error. I reinstalled Microsoft Access and the error went away.

You are probably wondering what the moral is of this intriguing story. The moral is that I could have saved the first two hours of work with a few minutes of research. My new standard became: Research at least 15 minutes before moving to the adjust stage with any new problem that requires troubleshooting. Not all problems require troubleshooting, and the confusion that usually comes into play is the result of a misunderstanding of what troubleshooting really is. Here is my favorite definition:

> *Troubleshooting is the process of discovering the unknown cause*
> *and solution for a known problem.*

You see, if I know the solution to a problem, I am repairing and not troubleshooting. In other words, I will start with research only when it is a real troubleshooting scenario according to this definition. In the end, by researching for just 15 minutes, I often find that the cause and solution are learned without spending any time adjusting various settings and parameters to resolve the issue. For example, if a server is displaying a specific error message, I will search for this error message at Google to see what I can discover. I may also search the vendor's website. If I don't find the cause or solution, I will usually get direction so that I can focus on the right area as I move to the engage or adjust stage.

▶ Today, a wealth of troubleshooting information is provided at the Microsoft TechNet site as well as the MSDN site on the Internet for free.

During the research stage, you will use both internal documentation and Internet websites. Your internal documentation will become more and more valuable as you use this methodology because the last stage is all about documenting what you've learned. Several websites are useful when troubleshooting Windows servers, including the following:

TechNet   The Microsoft TechNet site is located at `technet.microsoft.com`. Here you can find a wealth of technical knowledge related to Microsoft products.

MSDN   The MSDN site is located at `msdn.microsoft.com` and includes specific information for programmers as well as useful troubleshooting information.

EventID.Net   The site at `www.eventid.net` is useful for tracking down the causes of event log entries.

The EventID.Net website provides a search engine for locating event ID information. Entries from other administrators who have analyzed the same event IDs are often valuable.

Engage

While you may be eager to move from researching to adjusting, you should engage users if they are involved in the problem. You should ask for a problem description and then ask clarifying questions to better understand the situation.

Ask a clarifying question like, "Do you know if anything has changed about your system in the past few days?" Notice I didn't say, "Did you change anything?" The latter question will usually cause people to become defensive and fail to get you any valuable information. The users do not usually have any knowledge of what caused the problem, but when they do, it can save you hours or even days of trouble. Always engage the user. Other questions that might be beneficial include these:

User interaction is important in the troubleshooting process when analyzing user-related problems.

> ▶ When did the problem start happening?

> ▶ Is this the first time this problem has occurred or did it happen in the past as well?

> ▶ Are you aware of any others experiencing similar difficulties?

> ▶ When was the last time it worked?

> ▶ Is it turned on? (Seriously.)

You may find that you loop back-and-forth between the research and engage stages a few times before moving on to the adjust stage. This is represented in Figure 13.1 with the left-pointing arrow above the stages. For example, you may discover new information while engaging the user that causes you to perform more research on the Internet.

The amount spent in the research and engage stages will vary depending on the complexity of the problem.

Adjust

Interestingly, we've just now arrived where I see many techs, server administrators, or network administrators beginning. Don't feel bad—I've done it many times myself. This is the stage where either you begin trying different things to see if you can track down the cause of your problem, or you make the changes you discovered should be made in the research and engage stages. You might try updating the software on a computer or installing new device drivers. You could also change settings or disable features to see if the problem goes away. The point is that this is where you begin the "technical" side of troubleshooting.

Once you've completed these first three stages, you've always come to a solution. Again, this solution is sometimes reinstalling the application or operating system, but things are working again. You may have your solution after the research stage, or you may have it after the engage stage. Whether you make it all the way to the adjust stage or you solve the problem earlier in the process, you are now ready to move to what I call the ongoing stability stages: configure and take note.

Configure

This is the first of the two ongoing stability stages. In the configure stage, you ensure that the systems and devices are configured and are operating according to your standards before leaving the physical area (or remote management tool). This allows you to maintain a standardized environment, and a standardized environment is usually more stable. Of course, with a reinstallation, you will need to reinstall according to the original specifications for the installation and then apply any configuration changes that have been approved or processed since that time.

In some cases, you may discover that your configuration standards are insufficient and changes must be made to them. The configuration manager should be notified so that he can make the appropriate changes. In such scenarios, you may be required to revisit the problem system at a later time after the configuration standards have been updated to ensure the new standards are properly enforced on the machine.

> ▶
>
> **Standardized environments are easier to manage and support. They are easier to troubleshoot because they provide a consistent set of configurations.**

Take Note

This final stage completes the process and ensures that you get the greatest benefit out of this methodology going forward—this is the second ongoing stability stage. By documenting your findings—the stage I call "take note"—you provide a searchable resource for future troubleshooting. For example, situations like the one I described earlier, where the device error was generated, should be documented, and I suggest documenting the following at a minimum:

Although it takes time to document a problem and solution, this action can save much more time in the future when you need the information again.

▶ The problem with any error messages if they existed

▶ The cause concisely explained

▶ The solution with any necessary step-by-steps

▶ Any principles learned, such as a DLL being referenced as a device by the operating system

If your organization does not provide a centralized trouble ticket–tracking system or help desk solution, I encourage you to consider creating your own database. You can use any desktop database application like Microsoft Access or FileMaker. Just be sure you can document the needed information and query it easily.

Remember, REACT is a custom troubleshooting methodology used at my training and consulting firm, SysEdCo; however, you can feel free to implement it or use concepts from it in your career as a technology professional. It is presented here as an example of an in-house-developed troubleshooting system or methodology.

OSI Model

The Open System Interconnect (OSI) model can also be used for troubleshooting purposes when you experience networking problems. The OSI model provides a seven-layer architecture for network modeling and analysis:

▶ Layer 7: Application

▶ Layer 6: Presentation

▶ Layer 5: Session

▶ Layer 4: Transport

▶ Layer 3: Network

▶ Layer 2: Data Link

▶ Layer 1: Physical

For a detailed explanation of the OSI model, see *Microsoft Windows Networking Essentials* by Darril Gibson (Sybex, 2011).

The concept here is to walk up or down the OSI model, analyzing the system at each layer. This allows you to break the problem into logical sections and then verify that the system is operating properly in each of these sections (OSI layers). You may choose only to analyze Layers 1 through 3, or you may choose to evaluate all seven layers (or even eight layers if you're considering the user layer, which is sometimes called Layer 8).

Layer 1

Layer 1 is the Physical layer, which would mean evaluation of the computer network adapters, client devices, or infrastructure devices to ensure that they are working properly at the hardware level. For example, is the radio in a wireless adapter still functioning appropriately? With client devices, this can be tested quickly by removing the wireless LAN client device (assuming it's a USB, CardBus, or another kind of removable device) and installing it in another computer that is using exactly the same model device and is working. If the new computer stops working, too, the wireless LAN device is most likely at fault, at either the hardware or the software level (firmware). If it is an access point (AP) and you have a spare, you could load the identical configuration on the spare and place it in the same location to see if the problem persists. If the problem does not persist, again, the radio—or some other hardware/firmware issue—may be failing.

An additional key is to evaluate the hardware used by Layer 1 (sometimes called Layer 0). On the wired network, you can evaluate patch panels, connectors, and cabling at this point.

> ▶
>
> **Although a network cable can last for many years, it can also fail after a short period of use. Always verify that the network cable is operational.**

Layer 2

The second layer you will usually evaluate is Layer 2. This is where the network switches live. Make sure the switch ports are still working properly, that VLANs are configured appropriately, and that port security settings are set accurately on your switches. Switches evaluate incoming frames and forward them based on information in the frame, so be sure that your switching rules or filter are set up appropriately. Of course, the problem can be at the cable and connector level, but you will have checked that already at Layer 1. Within the computer, ensure that the network adapter is installed and configured with the appropriate drivers. The adapter provides the Layer 2 address (known as a media access control [MAC] address) for the network.

Layer 3

If you've evaluated the radios, cabling, and connectors at Layer 1, and you've checked the switches and network adapters at Layer 2, and you still haven't found a solution, you might have to move on to Layer 3. Here you'll need to check the IP routing tables to ensure proper configuration. Make sure any filters applied are accurate. Using common operating system tools like IPConfig, PING, and ARP, you can ensure that you can route data from one location on the network to another and that networking is functioning at Layer 3—the Network layer of the OSI model.

IPConfig is used to view the IP configuration on the computer. It is also used to request a new IP address when DHCP is used; however, DHCP is rarely used to acquire an IP version 4 address for a server. To use IPConfig to view all available IP addressing information, execute the following command at a Windows Command Prompt:

```
ipconfig /all
```

Listing 13.1 shows a portion of the command's output, listing the basic IP configuration settings on the computer and the specific settings for the Ethernet adapter.

Listing 13.1: The `ipconfig all` output

```
Windows IP Configuration

    Host Name . . . . . . . . . . . . : CPU1
    Primary Dns Suffix  . . . . . . . : training.local
    Node Type . . . . . . . . . . . . : Hybrid
    IP Routing Enabled. . . . . . . . : No
    WINS Proxy Enabled. . . . . . . . : No
    DNS Suffix Search List. . . . . . : training.local

Ethernet adapter Local Area Connection:

    Connection-specific DNS Suffix  . :
    Description . . . . . . . . . . . : Intel(R) PRO/1000 MT
                                        Network Connection
    Physical Address. . . . . . . . . : 00-0C-29-AF-52-45
    DHCP Enabled. . . . . . . . . . . : No
    Autoconfiguration Enabled . . . . : Yes
    Link-local IPv6 Address . . . . . : fe80::a8e8:8c7c:efb5:
                                        c175%11(Preferred)
    IPv4 Address. . . . . . . . . . . : 192.168.10.80(Preferred)
    Subnet Mask . . . . . . . . . . . : 255.255.255.0
    Default Gateway . . . . . . . . . : 192.168.10.1
    DHCPv6 IAID . . . . . . . . . . . : 234884137
    DHCPv6 Client DUID. . . . . . . . : 00-01-00-01-15-0C-16-82-
                                        00-0C-29-80-BC-23
    DNS Servers . . . . . . . . . . . : ::1
                                        127.0.0.1
    NetBIOS over Tcpip. . . . . . . . : Enabled
```

The PING command is used to test connectivity to a remote node on the network. It is useful when you are testing different scenarios. For example, if a network service on a server is not responding, you may want to ping the server to see if it is still up and running even though the service has failed. The PING command is used as follows:

```
ping ip_address | host_name
```

For example, to ping the IP address of 192.168.10.1, you should execute the following command:

```
ping 192.168.10.1
```

The output of this command is shown in Listing 13.2. Notice that the results are successful in this case.

Listing 13.2: The ping 192.168.10.1 output

```
Pinging 192.168.10.1 with 32 bytes of data:
Reply from 192.168.10.1: bytes=32 time<1ms TTL=64
Reply from 192.168.10.1: bytes=32 time<1ms TTL=64
Reply from 192.168.10.1: bytes=32 time<1ms TTL=64
Reply from 192.168.10.1: bytes=32 time<1ms TTL=64

Ping statistics for 192.168.10.1:
    Packets: Sent = 4, Received = 4, Lost = 0 (0% loss),
Approximate round trip times in milli-seconds:
    Minimum = 0ms, Maximum = 0ms, Average = 0ms
```

When the ping fails, you will see output similar to that in Listing 13.3. This time the IP address of 192.168.10.113 is tested and is unresponsive.

Listing 13.3: The ping 192.168.10.113 output

```
Pinging 192.168.10.113 with 32 bytes of data:
Reply from 192.168.10.80: Destination host unreachable.
Reply from 192.168.10.80: Destination host unreachable.
Reply from 192.168.10.80: Destination host unreachable.
Reply from 192.168.10.80: Destination host unreachable.
```

By default, the PING command sends four ping requests. You can adjust this default with the -N switch. For example, the command

```
ping 192.168.10.1-n 25
```

would send 25 ping requests to the target IP address. Figure 13.2 show the command-line switch options available for customization of the PING command. When troubleshooting IPv6 problems with the PING command, you can use the -6 option to force IPv6 testing.

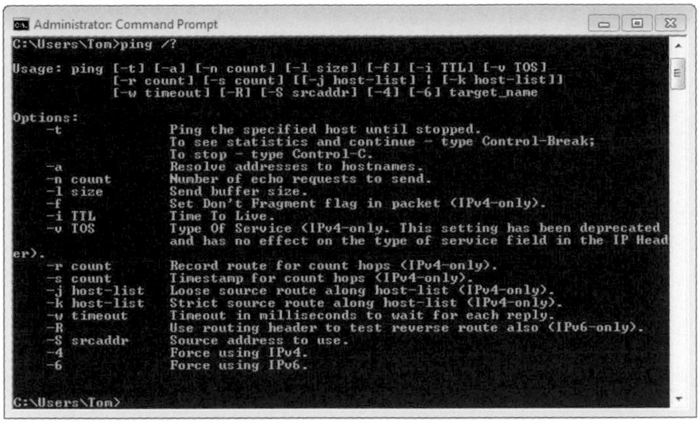

FIGURE 13.2 Viewing the help for the PING command

The ARP command is used to view the Address Resolution Protocol (ARP) cache on the local machine. ARP resolves IPv4 addresses (Layer 3 addresses) to MAC addresses (Layer 2 addresses). IP addresses are used to communicate across the routed network; MAC addresses are used on the local network links. If you are unable to communicate with a device on the local network segment (usually within the same IP network address), you can use the ARP command to view the local cache and verify that the proper MAC address is listed for the target machine. For example, Listing 13.4 shows the output of the ARP -A command on a Windows machine.

Listing 13.4: The output of the ARP -A command

```
Interface: 192.168.10.80 --- 0xb
  Internet Address      Physical Address      Type
  192.168.10.1          00-24-b2-5a-2d-76     dynamic
  192.168.10.252        00-0d-0b-95-8b-b1     dynamic
  192.168.10.255        ff-ff-ff-ff-ff-ff     static
  224.0.0.22            01-00-5e-00-00-16     static
  224.0.0.252           01-00-5e-00-00-fc     static
```

Upper Layers

Finally, if you've tested the first three layers and can't find a problem there, the network infrastructure is probably working fine. It's time to move to the upper layers. Look at the configuration settings in your computer applications and services. Be sure that the authentication mechanisms are installed and configured correctly. Try using different tools and software that provide the same basic functionality. Do they work? If so, there may be a compatibility problem between the specific application you're using and the hardware on which it is operating.

As you can see, the OSI model of troubleshooting can help you both focus and move through a sequence of testing procedures until you find the true source of the networking problem. I've only touched on the concept here, but you can take it further by learning more about what happens at each layer and the tools that can be used to test at that layer. For example, you can use a spectrum analyzer to test and troubleshoot the physical layer of a wireless network and a protocol analyzer to inspect the Data-Link layer of wired and wireless networks.

The Hardware/Software Model

The hardware/software model is a troubleshooting methodology that is used in an attempt to narrow the problem to either hardware or software. There are certain problems that are commonly caused by hardware and there are others that tend to be software problems. Many administrators will attempt to troubleshoot software first and then hardware. Others will do the opposite. In most cases, the situation will help you to determine which should be your first point of attack. If everything is working in a system except one application, that is often a good sign that the software is the problem. If multiple applications that use the same hardware are experiencing the same problem, that is often a good sign that the hardware is the problem. These are not absolute rules, but they are good general guidelines.

Hardware Problems

When troubleshooting computers, you'll find that specific hardware problems tend to generate common symptoms. Although I cannot provide you with an exact list of symptoms mapped to every problem, the list in Table 13.1 is a good place to start.

TABLE 13.1 Common hardware problems and symptoms

Hardware Problem	Symptoms
Memory failure	Random application crashes, random operating system crashes, and system lockups
Insufficient processing capabilities	Poor performance, inability to launch applications, and temporary system lockups
Disk failure	Corrupted data, inability to boot, and system crashes
Network adapter failure	Intermittent loss of connectivity and complete loss of connectivity

Hardware Problem	Symptoms
Video adapter failure	Corrupted display and system crashes
System board failure	Any of the previously listed symptoms

Software Problems

Software problems are related to the software running on the computer and can cause many symptoms similar to hardware failures. Table 13.2 lists common software problems and their symptoms.

TABLE 13.2 Common software problems and symptoms

Software Problem	Symptom
Corrupted files	System crashes, inability to boot, and application crashes
Poorly written drivers	System crashes and nonfunctioning hardware
Unsupported bit-level software	On 64-bit operating systems, error messages indicating that 16-bit software is not supported and on 32-bit operating systems, error messages indicating that 64-bit software is not supported
Improperly configured software	Application crashes, error messages, and lack of functionality
Poorly written software	Corrupted data, application crashes, and error messages

Symptom, Diagnosis, and Solution

Because certain symptoms usually surface with specific problems, many issues can be resolved in a similar way to human health issues. Look at the symptom, identify the most likely cause (diagnosis), and then treat it (solution). Repeat this process until the problem is resolved.

Symptom Defining the symptoms means gathering information about the problem. What is happening? Where is it happening? What technology is involved? Which users, if any, are involved? Has it always been this way? Answering questions like these will help you determine the various details about the problem. Good questions are at the core of effective problem definition.

Diagnosis   Based on the information gathered from your symptoms analysis, what is the most likely cause or what are the most likely causes? You can treat one or all, but you will most likely learn more by treating one cause at a time. In others, try one solution based on your diagnosis first and evaluate the results. This gives you expert knowledge over time, or what some call "intuition."

Solution   The solution is the potential fix for the problem. You may try replacing a hardware adapter because you determine that, based on the symptoms, the most likely cause is a failed card. After replacing the card you note that you are experiencing the same problem. Next you may decide to try using the adapter in another machine that is currently using the same adapter model and is working. When you do this, the adapter works in the other computer. Next you may attempt to reload the drivers in the malfunctioning computer, but this doesn't help either. In the end, you discover that the expansion port is experiencing intermittent failures in the malfunctioning computer. You send it to the vendor for repairs.

This illustration demonstrates what the diagnosis and solution process looks like. This process is what I call the adjust stage in my REACT methodology. You make changes and try different tactics until something solves the problem. You document the solution for future reference, but you also mentally document it. This is called "experience," and as you get more and more of it you eventually approach the level of expertise that helps you solve problems more quickly. For this reason, I look at problems as stepping stones to a better future, because the solving of this network or computer problem today will only make me better able to solve similar and different problems tomorrow.

Systems Thinking

Systems thinking is the process of analyzing all interdependent components that comprise a system. In other words, it is the opposite of being narrow-minded in the troubleshooting process. I've seen administrators blame everything from network connectivity to application errors on an operating system or a particular brand of PC instead of looking for the actual problem. While some operating systems and some PC brands may seem more prone to problems than others, the reality is that there are probably thousands of individuals out there who have had the opposite experience as you. In other words, if you like the computers from company A because they are very stable and you don't like the computers from company B because of your experience with them, there are probably thousands out there who feels exactly the opposite because of their experiences.

The point is simple: Rather than focusing on a vendor that you do not like, you must focus on the actual problem and seek a solution. When you do this, you're less likely to just reinstall every time a problem comes up. You want to ask questions like these:

▶ What are the systems or devices between this device and the network or device with which it is attempting to communicate?

▶ What other devices are attempting to communicate with the same system at this time?

▶ What has changed in the environment within which the system operates?

▶ Has the system been physically moved recently?

Asking these kinds of questions causes you to evaluate factors that are more related to the actual system you have in place and less related to the vendors that have provided the components. Indeed, if a vendor has provided you with bad components over a period of time, you will probably discontinue partnering with that vendor; however, blaming the problem on a single vendor every time does not help you solve the problems you are facing right now. For that, you need systems thinking and a good methodology.

Whether you adopt one or more of these methodologies, pursue another methodology, or create one of your own, you should consider how you troubleshoot problems and then be sure it is an efficient and effective process.

ITIL AND TROUBLESHOOTING

The Information Technology Infrastructure Library (ITIL) is a set of documents that define best practices for technology management. ITIL was initially created by the UK Office of Government Commerce, but has found widespread acceptance in IT departments around the world.

The ITIL includes seven publications describing best practices:

▶ Service Support

▶ Service Delivery

▶ Infrastructure Management

▶ Security Management

▶ The Business Perspective

▶ Application Management

▶ Software Asset Management

(Continues)

ITIL AND TROUBLESHOOTING *(Continued)*

Within Service Support are the concepts of incident and problem management. According to ITIL, an incident is an event that is not part of standard operations and that may cause an interruption or a reduction in the quality of a service. The problem is the underlying cause of the incident. The suggestion is that you first resolve the incident (get things back up and running) and then discover the root cause so that it can be prevented in the future. For more information on ITIL, see www.itil-officialsite.com.

Using Disk Defragmenter

Hard disks can become *fragmented* over time. This simply means that files are not stored in contiguous blocks of space; instead, parts of them are stored all over the drive. When this happens, it takes much longer to access files because the drive head has to move around to different places to pull the data into memory. Windows 7 ships with a defragmentation utility you can work with via both GUI and Command Prompt. This section explains how to use it and also introduces a freeware defragmentation utility that provides extra features.

Working with the Defragmenter GUI

The GUI tool for defragmenting your hard drives is located in the System Tools group on the Start menu. The tool, shown in Figure 13.3, is simple to use. You click the drive you want to defragment and then click the Defragment Disk button.

In addition to defragmenting the disk using the default settings, you can perform the following related tasks in the GUI Disk Defragmenter:

Configure A Scheduled Defragmentation   The default schedule is configured to defragment the disk once each week on Wednesday at 2 a.m.; however, you can change this to a more frequent or less frequent schedule.

Analyze A Disk   This process inspects a selected disk and reports on the level of fragmentation on the disk. It will make recommendations as to whether or not you should defragment the disk.

Using the *DEFRAG* Command Prompt Tool

Windows 7 also provides a Command Prompt tool for defragmenting disks. It is aptly named DEFRAG. The syntax for the DEFRAG command is shown in Figure 13.4.

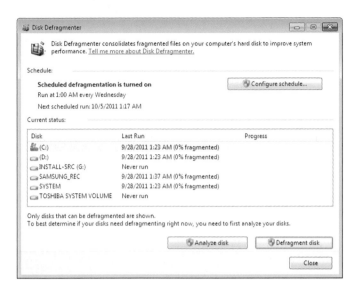

FIGURE 13.3 Using the GUI Disk Defragmenter

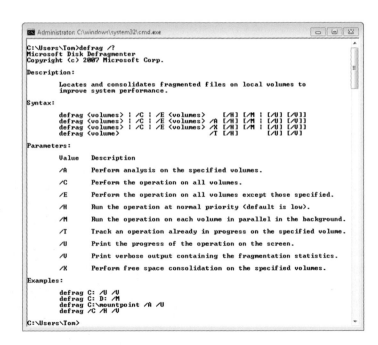

FIGURE 13.4 Viewing the DEFRAG command syntax

Using the Command Prompt DEFRAG command, you can defragment multiple disks at the same time. You can also perform free space consolidation, which is not an option in the GUI Disk Defragmenter. Because DEFRAG is a standard

Command Prompt utility, you can schedule it in a batch file to perform more complex defragmenting processes.

Using Defraggler

Sometimes the built-in utilities are sufficient, but other times you want a little more power. The free disk defragmenter called Defraggler is an excellent alternative to the built-in tools. It provides the following features:

▶ Fast analysis of fragmentation on volumes

▶ The ability to defragment selected files instead of only entire volumes

▶ A free version for personal use

▶ A command-line version with more power than the DEFRAG command

Figure 13.5 shows the Defraggler interface. It is available for download from www.piriform.com/defraggler.

When downloading freeware for business use, always read the license agreements carefully. Tools are often free only for personal use.

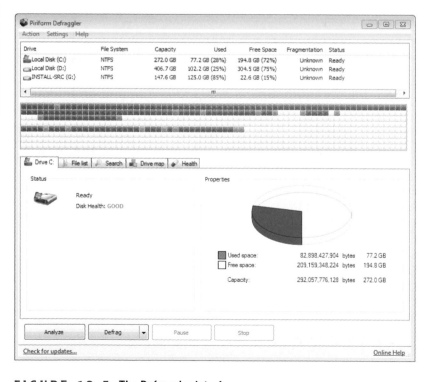

FIGURE 13.5 The Defraggler interface

Performing a Disk Cleanup

After a computer has been in use for a long period of time, files of many different types begin to accumulate. Some of these files contain important data. Others are temporary files that provide no lasting value. The Disk Cleanup tool is used to delete these useless files, as you will learn in this section. Additionally, you will learn to search for large files that may be consuming space.

Using the Disk Cleanup Tool

Like the Disk Defragmenter, the Disk Cleanup utility is in the System Tools group, within Accessories, on the Start menu. When you launch it, you will see a screen like the one in Figure 13.6. Select a drive and click OK to begin using the tool.

FIGURE 13.6 The Disk
Cleanup utility

The Disk Cleanup utility will then scan the computer for files that it could potentially delete for you. When the scan is complete, you will see the screen shown in Figure 13.7. The Disk Cleanup tab allows you to select the following categories of files for deletion:

- ▶ Downloaded Program Files

- ▶ Temporary Internet Files

- ▶ Offline Webpages

- ▶ Recycle Bin

- ▶ Service Pack Backup Files

- ▶ Setup Log Files

- ▶ System Error Memory Dump Files

- ▶ Temporary Files

- ▶ Thumbnails

▶ Per User Archived Windows Error Reports

▶ Per User Queued Windows Error Reports

▶ System Queued Windows Error Reports

FIGURE 13.7 The Disk Cleanup
tab in the Disk Cleanup utility

If you select all the available file types on the Disk Cleanup tab for deletion, it is not uncommon for the total amount of disk space saved to reach more than 1 GB. On the More Options tab, you can select to free more space by removing programs that are no longer in use but are still installed. You can also delete all but the most recent restore point on the More Options tab.

Searching for Large Files

Another useful trick for freeing up drive space is to locate and remove very large files that may not be required. You can do so easily from the Explorer search field. Open Explorer and navigate to the root of the drive on which you wish to search for large files. Next, in the Search field enter **size:** and select from the pop-up box the size you want to search for. Figure 13.8 shows the optional search sizes available.

FIGURE 13.8 The Explorer interface used to locate large files

Scheduling Tasks

One of the important administrative benefits of the Windows OS is the ability to schedule tasks. You can schedule tasks in Windows using the GUI Task Scheduler interface or with the Command Prompt using SCHTASKS.EXE or the traditional AT command.

The Task Scheduler provides a GUI with the ability to schedule tasks using a wizard. The Task Scheduler is located in the System Tools group on the Start menu. Figure 13.9 shows the Task Scheduler interface.

FIGURE 13.9 The Task Scheduler graphical interface

Using this tool, you can do any of the following:

- ▶ Create a scheduled task for the computer
- ▶ Display running tasks on the computer
- ▶ Import scheduled tasks that have been exported from other computers
- ▶ Connect to another computer as an administrator and manage scheduled tasks
- ▶ Configure the task service (the AT Service) so that it runs with the permissions required for your tasks

The Command Prompt version of the tools can be used to perform all the same functions.

Tasks can run on a schedule, or they can run based on triggers. Available triggers include the following:

- ▶ System startup
- ▶ User logon
- ▶ System is idle
- ▶ An event log entry is created
- ▶ Workstation is locked
- ▶ Workstation is unlocked

This flexibility allows you to create very useful tasks. For example, you can create a task that runs every time an event log entry is created. The event log entry may be created based on an application error. The task could send you an email with information about the error. This option provides exceptional flexibility for administrators today.

Accessing Additional Troubleshooting Tools

You should be aware of three additional tools that are helpful in the troubleshooting process: the Event Viewer, the Task Manager, and the Resource Monitor.

Using Event Viewer

The Event Viewer is used to inspect the event logs on a Windows computer. Windows Vista and Server 2008 added important features to the Event Viewer, which allowed it to support central logging. You can access the Event Viewer in the Administrative Tools group of the Start menu, or you can click Start, search for Event Viewer, and press Enter. Figure 13.10 shows the Event Viewer interface on Windows 7.

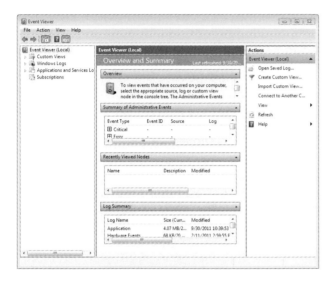

FIGURE 13.10 The Event Viewer application on Windows 7

Four entry levels may be shown in an event log:

Critical   A failure has occurred, and the application or components could not automatically recover.

Warning   An issue has occurred that may impact a service or component and may require action by the administrator to prevent more severe problems.

Error   A problem has occurred, and it may impact functionality within the triggering service or component.

Information   A change has occurred in a service or component, which was not an error but was logged for documentation purposes.

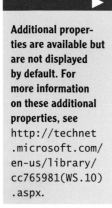

Additional properties are available but are not displayed by default. For more information on these additional properties, see http://technet .microsoft.com/ en-us/library/ cc765981(WS.10) .aspx.

An event log entry includes several information elements that are useful for troubleshooting problems. The information elements are called *properties*, and each event log entry has one or more of these properties. The properties include:

► Source

► Event ID

► Level

► User

► Operational Code

► Log

► Task category

► Keywords

► Computer

► Date and Time

The Event Viewer supports filtering logs so that you can see only the information you desire. For example, you may want to view only log entries with a level of critical, warning, or error. The vast majority of log entries are informational. By filtering to only the three levels mentioned, you enable a view with less information that is easier to browse through and locate potential problems. Figure 13.11 shows the Filter Current Log dialog with filtering configured. You can access this dialog by right-clicking a log and selecting Filter Current Log.

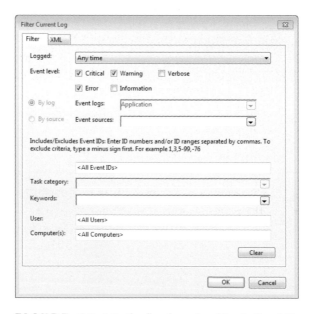

FIGURE 13.11 Configuring a log filter in Event Viewer

Be aware of the four primary event logs and the information they contain:

Application   The Application log includes events generated by applications or services running on the computer. This is where you might find errors generated by services like Internet Information Services and applications like Microsoft Office.

Security   The Security log includes events generated based on audited security events. Failed logon attempts, failed file access, successful logon attempts, and successful file access are all representative of what you might find in the Security log. The actual events generated for this log will depend on the auditing configuration on your computer.

Setup   The Setup log contains events generated by installation programs. Most modern installation programs use the Microsoft Software Installer (MSI) format and will add entries to this log.

System   The System log includes events generated by the Windows operating system components. For example, a failed driver would cause a log entry to be added to this log.

In most cases, you'll use the Event Viewer when a problem occurs and you are performing research to locate the cause of the problem. You may locate a suspect entry in the log and want to learn more about it. You can search for the Event ID value at EventID.net and find useful information.

In other scenarios, you want to centralize the log files. Windows Vista and later versions support this option through event subscriptions. One computer acts as the subscriber to the other computers and pulls the events into its local log databases. For you to use event subscriptions, the Windows Remote Management (WinRM) service must be enabled and configured on each computer. You do not usually subscribe to all events on a remote computer, only to important events that you wish to centralize. For a more detailed explanation of the steps required to enable event subscriptions, see

```
http://technet.microsoft.com/en-us/library/cc749183%28WS.10%29.aspx
```

Task Manager

When it comes to troubleshooting, the Task Manager is one of the most frequently used applications in Windows. It lists the running processes on your system and allows you perform several actions against these processes, including the following:

- ▶ Raising the priority
- ▶ Lowering the priority

▶ Killing the task

▶ Viewing information about the processes

To launch the Task Manager, follow these steps:

1. Right-click the taskbar (the area where your application buttons are displayed).

2. Select Start Task Manager.

Figure 13.12 shows the Task Manager running with the Processes tab selected. The Processes tab is the primary tab used for the actions listed. For example, this is the tab you would use to view information about processes running on your computer.

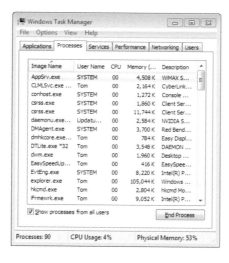

FIGURE 13.12 The Task Manager with the Processes tab selected

If you want a process to get more processor time, you can raise its priority. Six priorities are supported; from low to high they are Low, Below Normal, Normal, Above Normal, High, and Realtime. By default most processes run at the Normal priority. To change that, you can right-click a process in the Task Manager and select the priority you desire.

Sometimes an application or service will lock up and become unresponsive. In such scenarios, you may have to kill the process associated with the application or service so that you can restart it. When you kill a process, you force its removal from memory on the system. You can right-click a process and select End Process to kill it.

> ▶
>
> **You can also press Ctrl+Shift+Esc as a shortcut key to launch the Task Manager.**

> ▶
>
> **You can also use the** TASKKILL **command at the Command Prompt to kill a task.**

In many cases, you want to view information about the processes. The Task Manager displays the process name (it calls this the image name), the Process ID (PID), the username under which the process runs, the CPU time percentage consumed, the memory used for the private working set, and a description. While these are the default displayed columns, you can add several other columns to the display using the View Select Columns menu option. Figure 13.13 shows the Select Process Page Columns dialog.

FIGURE 13.13 Adding new columns to the Process tab in Task Manager

The Processes tab is the tab most commonly used by administrators in the Task Manager for managing processes. However, the other tabs are also useful. The Application tab lists the current user applications running on the computer. The Services tab lists the background services running. Depending on the version of Windows you are running, you may have a Networking tab that provides performance information related to the network adapters in your system. You may also have a Users tab, which shows the users currently logged into the system.

All Windows operating systems include a Performance tab in the Task Manager. This tab shows the current CPU usage and the recent history of CPU usage for each processor in the computer. It also shows memory consumption and provides a button that links to the Resource Monitor, discussed next.

Resource Monitor

The Resource Monitor was added in Windows Vista and is also found in Windows 7. In both systems, you access the Resource Monitor from within the Task Manager or by running RESMON on the Start menu. The Resource Monitor is like the Task

Manager all grown up. It is more powerful and provides more valuable information than the Task Manager ever has.

To launch the Resource Monitor and view the information it provides, follow this procedure:

1. Press the Windows key on your keyboard (if you do not have a keyboard with the Windows key, press Ctrl+Esc to get the same results).

2. You will default to the Search field on the Start menu. Enter the following command:

```
perfmon /res
```

3. Press Enter.

At this point, you should see a screen similar to the one in Figure 13.14. As you can see, the Resource Monitor shows information related to four areas of the system: the CPU, disk, network, and memory.

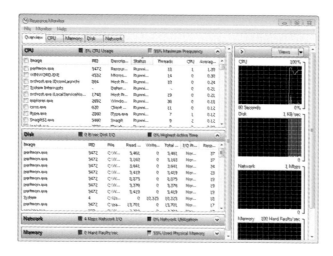

FIGURE 13.14 Viewing the Resource Monitor on Windows 7

To see another interesting feature of the Resource Monitor, execute the following command:

```
perfmon /report
```

You'll see a screen indicating that the performance analysis will run for approximately 60 seconds. When the analysis is complete, you will see a report like the one in Figure 13.15. The Resource Monitor is one of the components of the Reliability and Performance Monitor on Windows Server 2008 and Vista or the Performance

Monitor on Windows Server 2008 R2 and Windows 7. Now you know how to access
it directly.

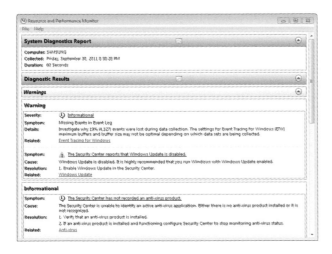

FIGURE 13.15 Viewing the Resource Monitor report

You can also view the reliability report for a Windows Vista, Windows 7, or
Windows Server 2008 and 2008 R2 machine with the following command:

```
perfmon /rel
```

This is most useful since the reliability report was obvious and easy to find in
Windows Vista, but it's a bit more buried in Windows 7 and Windows Server 2008
R2. The reliability report shows the history of updates, errors, and alerts on the
system. For example, if a new driver was installed recently, it will be logged in the
reliability report. If an application or service crashes, that will be logged in the
report as well. This information is very important to the troubleshooting process.
It is also available by searching for Reliability Monitor on the Start menu.

You will find the reliability report helpful when troubleshooting intermittent problems on a computer.

THE ESSENTIALS AND BEYOND

Troubleshooting requires technical skills and an understanding of processes and procedures. Processes and procedures are often documented as troubleshooting methodologies.
You may develop your own methodology over time or use existing methodologies that
have been proven and tested by other organizations. The ITIL provides documents that
include troubleshooting best practices. Windows Server provides several tools that can
be used for troubleshooting, including the Task Manager, Performance Monitor, Resource
Monitor, and Event Viewer.

(Continues)

THE ESSENTIALS AND BEYOND *(Continued)*

ADDITIONAL EXERCISES

▶ Using the Event Viewer, filter the Application log to show only Critical and Error level events.

▶ Launch the Notepad application and then use the Task Manager to kill its process.

▶ Use the PING command to test connectivity to www.sysedco.com.

To compare your answers to the author's, please visit www.sybex.com/go/osessentials.

REVIEW QUESTIONS

1. What is the shortcut key used to open the Task Manager?

    A. Ctrl+Esc   **C.** Ctrl+Shift+Esc

    B. Ctrl+T   **D.** Alt+T

2. True or false. The ITIL defines an incident and a problem differently.

3. You experience the following symptoms: corrupted display and system crashes. Which one of the following hardware items has most likely failed?

    A. Disk   **C.** Memory

    B. CPU   **D.** Display adapter

4. Name an OSI model layer that may be used in the troubleshooting process for network problems.

5. What event log severity level includes entries always indicating an unrecoverable problem?

    A. Error   **C.** Critical

    B. Warning   **D.** Information

6. Define ITIL.

7. Define Event Viewer.

8. What can be used to limit the event log entries displayed in the Event Viewer?

    A. Performance counters   **C.** Event filtering

    B. Event subscriptions   **D.** Task Manager

9. Which one of the following is used to kill tasks running on a Windows machine?

    A. Task Manager   **C.** Event Viewer

    B. Performance Monitor   **D.** ARP

10. True or false. Networking problems are always constrained to the local computer.

CHAPTER 14

Backup and Recovery

Data backup is one of the most important processes performed in modern businesses. The information in our organizations is valuable and it must be secured, managed, and backed up to ensure its availability. In this chapter, you'll learn how to plan for backups and restorations for your Windows computers. You'll learn how to use recoverability features that are built into the OS and how to go about selecting third-party backup tools. The following topics are addressed:

► **Planning for backups**

► **Testing recovery processes**

► **Working with System Restore**

► **Selecting third-party backup software**

► **Using recovery boot options**

Planning for Backups

> **Information can be defined as meaningful data. Data, without context, is just a bunch of 1s and 0s in a computer system.**

Most people reading this book will work in a department or group called Information Systems (IS) or Information Technology (IT), or they are preparing for a career in the field of IT. IT is the collection of technologies and resources used to manage information. Organizations place great value on their information, as they should, and they expect the IS or IT group to manage this information well. It is essential that those of us who work in IT remember that the "I" stands for *information* and our primary responsibility is the collection, retention, distribution, protection, and destruction of that information.

Consider an organization that manufactures and sells the components used to make fishing lures. These components are used by many different fabricators and distributors that sell the lures. What happens if a competing company steals the customer database of the top fishing lure company in the world? The result could be catastrophic, but the event could be prevented or mitigated with the proper information protection mechanisms.

Of less impact, what if the customer service professionals cannot access the data (information distribution) when they need it to answer a customer's question? The customer may be patient, or she may choose a different provider. Effective IT solutions allow for the five key responsibilities of information management to be accomplished. Consider the following brief descriptions:

Information Collection   Users create large numbers of documents and files. This information must be collected by the organization. In most cases, it will be stored in network shares but the information may also be stored locally on client computers. The industry trend is certainly toward centralization of document storage.

Information Retention   A good information storage system also provides effective storage and backup mechanisms. It's not enough to store the information for live retrieval; it must also be backed up for recoverability in the event of a system failure.

Information Distribution   The right people need the right information at the right time, and information distribution solutions allow for this. Windows includes features like Offline Files to allow users to access data when they need it and where they need it.

Information Protection   Of course, every user should not have access to all information in most organizations. Security solutions from authentication to storage encryption should be used to protect valuable data.

Information Destruction   Sometimes information needs to be destroyed. Your IT solutions should account for this and ensure that a nonrecoverable method is used to destroy the data when it is required.

These five facets of information management must be included in any IT plan, and Windows backup and recovery features can be part of the plan; however, it cannot provide all of the best solutions alone. Windows clients integrate with Windows Server Active Directory domains, for example, to provide stronger authentication and centralized storage. This section focuses on understanding the tools and methods available for backup and recovery in Windows 7 systems.

Comparing Backup Methods and Tools

The primary backup methods available for Windows 7 clients fall into three categories:

> ► Local backups stored on removable media and local drives

▶ Online backups stored with Internet-based backup services or on the local network

▶ Automated backups, which include system recovery options that create automatic backups for disaster recovery

Windows 7 includes several tools to help with your backups. These backup tools include the following:

Backup and Restore   Backup and Restore is a utility used to create backups of many types in Windows 7. It can be used to back up the entire computer or just the files and folders you select. It is also used to create system images and to restore from backups. You will use Backup and Restore throughout this chapter for various backup purposes.

System Images   System images are created with the Backup and Restore utility. A system image is a complete copy of the drives Windows requires to run, including the boot drive (which includes the Windows directory) and the system drive (which is used to boot the computer). System images use the virtual hard disk (VHD) format used by Hyper-V and Windows Virtual PC. You can create a system image just after installation of the computer and important applications and then easily revert to that state at any time in the future. You will learn to create a system image later in this section.

System Restore   System Restore is a component of System Protection. When major changes are made to the computer, such as installing software or device drivers, a restore point may be created automatically. If you want to ensure that a system restore point is created, you can manually create one before making the change. At a later time, you can revert to the state of the system when the restore point was created. This feature can also be used to maintain multiple versions of documents locally so that you can revert to previous versions. You will learn more about System Restore operations in "Working with System Restore" later in this chapter.

Recovery Boot Options   Several recovery boot options are available to allow for system recovery in disaster scenarios. You can use Last Known Good to load the device driver set that was last known to work, or you can use various Safe Mode options to start a Windows computer that will not otherwise start. You can also boot into a special Windows recovery mode using the installation DVD to restore from a backup or a system image. You'll see how to implement these approaches in "Using Recovery Boot Options" later in this chapter.

File-Based Backups   The final backup type is a manual file-based backup. In this case, you copy the data you wish to back up to a removable drive or writable

◀

The terminology for the boot drive and system drive has always been confusing to Microsoft professionals. Remember, it is the opposite of what you would expect. See more at http://support .microsoft.com/ kb/314470.

media. This method does not rely on special tools for backup or recovery, but it also does not back up system configuration settings. You can use any tools you prefer to perform file-based backups. The internal Explorer interface can be used to copy files as well as Command Prompt command and batch files. You can also acquire third-party file management tools if you desire.

If you choose to create a system image, it includes the following:

- ▶ Everything needed for Windows to run

- ▶ System settings, personal files, and programs

- ▶ Storage as a VHD file that can be used in Windows Virtual PC for quick access to the image

The system image does not allow:

- ▶ Scheduled backups made within the GUI

- ▶ Restoration of individual files, unless you attach the image as a drive in Disk Management

Although you cannot schedule a system image in the GUI, you can schedule it using the WBADMIN **Command Prompt utility.**

You can also create a system repair disk using the Backup and Restore utility, which allows you to

- ▶ Boot the computer if it becomes unbootable

- ▶ Restore the computer from a system image backup

The system repair disk is a bootable CD or DVD disc with Windows Preinstallation Environment (WinPE) installed. One disk is needed for 32-bit systems, and another for 64-bit systems. The disk also has the necessary Serial Advanced Technology Attachment (SATA) drivers for the laptop on which it was created. For this reason, you may need a recovery disk for each model of laptop you use in your organization.

The Backup and Restore utility is easy to use. To create a system image, be sure to have the storage media ready and perform the following procedure:

1. Log on to the system as an administrator.

2. Click Start ➢ Maintenance ➢ Backup And Restore.

3. In the left pane, select Create A System Image, as shown in Figure 14.1.

4. Choose the destination for the system image (a hard disk, one or more DVDs, or a network location) and click Next.

5. Choose any additional drives you want to include in the system image backup and then click Next.

6. On the Confirm Your Backup Settings screen, shown in Figure 14.2, verify that the proper drives are listed for backup and click Start Backup.

7. A screen will appear, telling you that Windows Is Saving The Backup. Depending on the size of the backup, this process can take a few minutes or more than an hour. You can click Stop Backup at any time to cancel the backup, as shown in Figure 14.3.

FIGURE 14.1 Using Backup and Restore to create a system image

FIGURE 14.2 Confirming your backup settings in the Create A System Image wizard

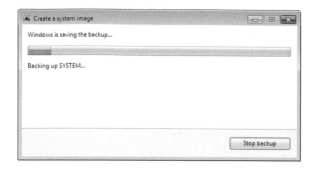

FIGURE 14.3 The system image creation process running

8. When the backup completes, you may be asked to create a System Repair Disk. If you have a CD-ROM burner, you should do this, but you need only one repair disk for 32-bit systems and one for 64-bit systems. You do not need a unique disk for each computer.

9. Click Close when you see the screen that indicates the system image has been created.

To use the system image you've created to restore the machine in cases where the system will still boot, follow these steps:

1. Log on to the system as an administrator.

2. Click Start ➤ Maintenance ➤ Backup And Restore.

3. In the Back Up Or Restore Your Files section, select Recover System Settings On Your Computer.

4. Choose Advanced Recovery Methods.

5. Select Use A System Image You Created Earlier To Recover Your Computer.

6. If you want to back up the most recent files to an external drive before reloading the image, click Back Up Now. Otherwise, click Skip on the screen shown in Figure 14.4.

7. Click Restart to boot into the recovery mode and restore the system image.

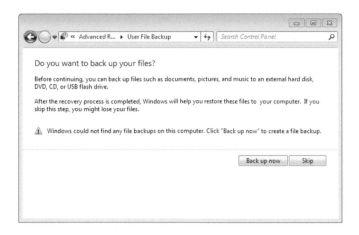

FIGURE 14.4 Determining whether to back up recent files before recovering a system image

8. After the system restarts and the System Recovery Options screen is displayed, select a keyboard input method and click Next.

9. On the Select A System Image Backup Screen, choose the latest or a specific image to use and click Next.

10. Select Format And Repartition Disks if you want to make the system match the drive layout of the image. Otherwise, click Next.

11. Click Finish to begin the system image restore. You can also click Cancel at this point to restart the system without restoring the image.

When the image restoration is complete, you can restart the computer, and everything should appear exactly as it did at the time of image creation.

You can mount a system image VHD file as a drive in the Disk Management utility. With this capability, you can browse the system image and restore selected files if you need to. For example, if you accidentally delete a single file and the only place it is backed up is in the system image, rather than completely reloading the image you can mount it with Disk Management and then copy the file out of the image onto your OS drive. In addition, you can mount a VHD file from the Command Prompt. To learn more, see `http://technet.microsoft.com/en-us/library/cc708295(WS.10).aspx`.

Figure 14.5 shows the system image backup directory with the OS drive VHD file selected. You can install an excellent free add-on utility called VHD Attach so that you can right-click a VHD file and select Attach or Detach to quickly mount it as a drive letter. You can obtain this tool from `www.jmedved.com/vhdattach`.

If you cannot choose the option Format And Repartition Disks, try booting from the system recovery disk to load the image instead.

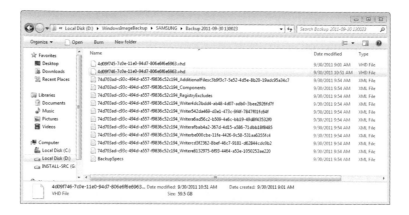

FIGURE 14.5 Viewing the system image backup directory

Understanding Backup Options

The Windows 7 Backup and Restore utility can use several different backup targets, including these:

Internal Hard Drives   Inexpensive storage with large amounts of space and very fast. However, an internal hard drive is not separate from the computer, and installation requires technical knowledge.

External Hard Drives   Inexpensive, fast, and easy to connect; also separate from the computer so that the data can be stored in remote locations.

Network Locations   Convenient and easy to use; may be slow; supported only in Windows 7 Pro, Enterprise, and Ultimate; user must have Full Control on the destination share.

USB Flash Drives   Easy to install and faster than most tape drives, but not as fast as internal hard drives; stored separately from the computer.

Writeable CDs and DVDs   Inexpensive media; stored separately; may be slow when compared to internal hard drives, network hard drives, or USB drives; may need several discs for the backup.

The Backup and Restore utility has the following limitations:

► Volumes formatted as anything other than NTFS, FAT, or UDF cannot be used.

► The drive being backed up cannot be the target.

- ▶ The Windows volume cannot be the target.

- ▶ A recovery partition cannot be the target.

- ▶ A locked BitLocker partition cannot be the target.

- ▶ Tape drives are not supported.

The Backup Planning Process

The backup planning process includes the following steps:

1. Define the business requirements.

2. Select the data to be backed up.

3. Choose the backup tools.

4. Determine the backup strategies.

5. Test and revise.

The planning process begins by defining business requirements. The technical items you are defining are the recovery point objective (RPO), recovery time objective (RTO), and recovery level objective (RLO). The RPO is the maximum time period between the last backup and a potential failure point. Stated differently, it is a measurement of how much data or work effort you can accept losing. The RTO is the maximum time that the recovery process can take. Another way of stating this is to say that it is the maximum amount of downtime you can tolerate. Finally, the RLO is the granularity with which you must be able to recover data. For example, do you require only a system image or must you be able to recover individual files?

Unless you understand the business requirements, you cannot create a proper backup plan.

The next step is the selection of data to be backed up. This will be defined in part by the business requirements. The RTO may dictate that you have a system image (which can be reloaded faster than a complete reinstall of the OS and applications) and create backups of data files because it requires a short recovery time. In this step, you will also define specific data files that should be backed up on a regular basis, such as application configuration files and locally stored data.

Step 3 is easy after you have completed steps 1 and 2. You will select the tools that allow you to accomplish your business requirements for the data that must be backed up. For example, if you require a system image, you can use the internal Backup and Restore utility or purchase a third-party tool for image creation.

Now that the tools are defined, you can determine the backup strategies. This step involves defining when backups should take place, where they should be stored, and how long they will be retained.

Finally, you should test and revise the plan. Perform backups and then restores to verify that the process is working. This is an essential part of the backup planning process. In fact, the next section is dedicated to this step alone.

Testing Recovery Processes

After a backup plan is created, it should be implemented in a lab environment and tested to ensure that it works properly and meets the business requirements. The only way to do this is to perform a recovery and verify that it works. Three tasks should be performed related to testing the recovery process. First, the recovery process should be documented. Second, periodic tests should be performed to ensure that the backups are still working properly. Third, the recovery process should be updated as new software and processes are introduced into the organization. This section briefly describes all three tasks.

Documenting the Recovery Process

The first step should be to document the recovery process. This means that you should create a detailed step-by-step instruction set for recovering in different scenarios. The following scenarios should be documented at a minimum:

▶ Recovering a single file or set of files

▶ Recovering to a point in time using System Restore

▶ Recovering with an image without hard drive failure

▶ Recovering with an image when a hard drive fails

Even though you may be familiar with the processes, document them in great detail. When you have to recover data or an entire system, you are likely to be under stress. In such conditions, you are more likely to forget some important step. Create the documentation and then use it during a recovery to avoid such omissions.

Performing Periodic Tests

You should verify that the recovery process has not changed when major changes are made to your systems. These major changes include

▶ Hardware upgrades

► Service pack applications

► OS upgrades

► Application upgrades

When any of these changes occur, they may also change the recovery process. Additionally, you should test the backup files periodically to ensure that they actually contain backup data. It is possible that something could fail in the backup process and new backups are no longer being created. Testing the backup location ensures that the backups are working properly.

Updating the Recovery Process

Finally, you should update the documentation for the recovery process any time the periodic tests indicate changes in the process. In most cases, this requires adding, removing, or changing a few steps, but it should be done just the same. Again, these documents will be your lifeline during a recovery procedure.

Working with System Restore

The System Restore feature allows you to revert your computer to a configuration status at a past point in time. System Restore monitors installations of software and device drivers and creates restore points, allowing you to return to the state before the software or device driver was installed. In this section, you will learn about the features of System Restore and then learn to create and use restore points.

Understanding System Restore

By default, System Restore is enabled on the system drive. If you want to use it on other drives, such as data storage locations, you must enable it. As shown in Figure 14.6, you can enable it for both system settings and previous versions of files or only for the restoration of previous versions of files. You can also indicate the maximum space it can use. To configure System Restore (called System Protection in the GUI interface, although Microsoft refers to it as System Restore in online documentation) for a specific drive:

1. Click Start, and then right-click Computer and select Properties.

2. Click the System Protection link in the left panel.

3. On the System Protection tab of the System Properties dialog, select the drive you want to configure and then click the Configure button.

4. Select the desired Restore Settings and Disk Space Usage and then click OK, as shown in Figure 14.6.

FIGURE 14.6 Configuring System Restore for a nonsystem drive

System Restore creates restore points automatically based on the following triggers by default:

▶ System restore points are created automatically once each day.

▶ Application installation restore points are made before an application supporting restore points is installed.

▶ Restore points are created when you initiate a system restoration for the machine.

▶ When an unsigned driver is installed, a restore point is created.

In addition to these automatic restore points, you can create manual restore points as you desire. Creating a manual restore point is described later in the section "Creating Restore Points."

The following information is included in restore points:

▶ System files

▶ Registry settings

- ▶ Executable files

- ▶ Script files

- ▶ Batch files

- ▶ Shadow copies of user data files (copies of files retained on the system for recoverability purposes)

To use System Restore, you must have the drive formatted as NTFS. In addition, it must be at least a 1 GB drive with 300 MB of free space. As disk space gets lower on a system, older snapshots or restore points will automatically be deleted to make room for new live data. You can also manually delete existing restore points or delete them using the Disk Cleanup utility.

WINDOWS RECOVERY ENVIRONMENT

System Restore is just one part of an entire collection of solutions called WinRE, the Windows Recovery Environment. WinRE includes the ability to revert to a restore point created by System Restore, but it can also be used for recovery to a system image. Additionally, it provides startup repair to fix boot configuration problems, Windows Memory Diagnostics to check physical memory for errors, and a Command Prompt interface with administrative capabilities for working with your drives and volumes with the DISKPART command. You can access the WinRE through the system repair disk or by using the operating system installation DVD. Using the installation DVD, you select Repair My Computer instead of installing Windows 7.

Creating Restore Points

You can manually create a restore point using these steps:

1. Click Start, and then right-click Computer and select Properties.

2. Click the System Protection link in the left panel.

3. Select the drive for which you wish to create a restore point and then click Create.

You can also clean up older restore points that you no longer need by selecting the drive you want to clean up and then clicking Configure. Next, click Continue, but be aware that all restore points except the most recent will be deleted.

Reverting to a Restore Point

Reverting to a restore point is as simple as manually creating one. Follow this procedure to revert to a restore point:

1. Click Start and then right-click Computer and select Properties.

2. Click the System Protection link in the left panel.

3. Click the System Restore button.

4. If you want the most recent restore point to be used, click Next. Otherwise, click Choose A Different Restore Point and click Next.

5. Select the restore point to which you wish to recover based on date and time or name and click Scan For Affected Programs. After viewing the report, as shown in Figure 14.7, click Close.

6. If you are satisfied with the scan report and still want to revert to the selected restore point, click Next.

7. In the Confirm Your Restore Point screen, click Finish to begin the restore process.

> ▶
>
> **It is always best to scan for affected programs to make sure you want to revert to the restore point and that it won't harm important programs.**

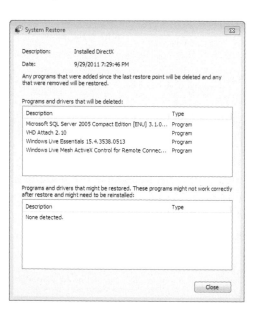

FIGURE 14.7 Viewing the Scan For Affected Programs report before reverting to a restore point

Selecting Third-Party Backup Software

Many organizations select third-party backup solutions instead of using the internal software provided by Windows. The motivation for this is often the simple fact that they run multiple versions of Windows and possibly other operating systems, and they want a solution that works the same on all of them. Many software vendors create backup solutions that work very much the same on Mac OS X, Linux, or Windows. In this section, you'll learn about important considerations and options when selecting third-party backup software.

Determining Backup Needs

The process of determining the backup needs is the same for third-party software as it is for internal software. You must still define the business requirements and the data that is to be backed up. Third-party software, however, may provide benefits such as the following:

► The ability to restore files to a different OS than the one from which they were backed up

► The ability to compress backups for space savings

► The ability to back up to additional devices such as tape drives and Internet locations

► The ability to customize the backup process with more powerful scheduling or scripting options

Customization and scheduling are less of an advantage for third-party backup solutions today, thanks to the improved Task Scheduler in Windows.

The most important thing when selecting third-party backup software for a business or large organization is the assurance of support. Few people use open-source backup software, because it may no longer be supported shortly after implementation. This is not true for all open-source applications, but you must be careful when selecting open-source solutions to ensure that they have a large enough following to keep development processing going.

The following applications are third-party backup solutions that are either open source or free:

DeltaCopy: www.aboutmyip.com/AboutMyXApp/DeltaCopy.jsp
Amanda: www.zmanda.com
Bacula: www.bacula.org
EaseUSTodo Backup: www.todo-backup.com
Cobian Backup: www.educ.umu.se/~cobian/cobianbackup.htm

Figure 14.8 shows the Bacula web management interface for this open-source backup solution. The backup solutions listed here have all existed for several years and are likely to continue being supported on some level for several more.

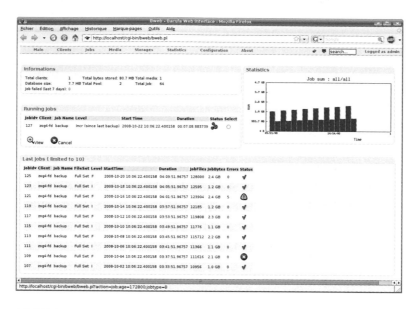

FIGURE 14.8 The Bacula web management interface

Evaluating and Selecting Solutions

When evaluating and selecting third-party backup solutions, you must consider several important factors, including these:

Features   The backup solution should offer the features you require. Third-party backup solutions come in many implementations. Some work as a server-based solution, in which all clients back up to the server. Others work as a client-based solution, where the users must provide the media as a backup destination with each backup. It is important to ensure that you select a solution meeting your needs and the capabilities of the users.

Compatibility   The solution must also be compatible with the operating systems and applications that you run. If you run multiple versions of Windows, it should be compatible with all of the versions you run, if possible.

System Requirements   The hardware must be able to keep up with the software as well. Make sure you check the CPU, memory, storage, and network requirements before purchasing a backup solution.

Support   Support is vital to businesses and organizations. Verify with the vendor that you have support, the type of support (online chat only, forums support only, telephone support, onsite support, or maybe all of these methods), the length of the support contract, and the cost to renew it, if required.

Cost　Finally, you should ensure that the solution is within your budget. Few organizations have the luxury of simply purchasing whatever they want without consideration for price. You must ensure that the cost is in line with the benefits. You should also verify the licensing terms. Software licensing terms can be rather confusing, so don't be embarrassed to ask detailed questions about them.

Using Recovery Boot Options

The final topic we need to consider related to backup and restoration in a disaster scenario is the use of the recovery boot options. In many cases, your system will not boot at all and you must use a system repair disk or the Windows 7 installation media just to boot into the Windows Recovery Environment. In other cases, you can use the advanced boot menu to access special boot-time options. This section addresses these options.

Understanding the Boot Menu

The advanced boot menu, or Advanced Boot Options screen, as shown in Figure 14.9, is used to boot the Windows system using different configuration, recovery, and analysis options. Access this menu by pressing F8 at just the right time when the system starts. In most cases, it is easiest to access this menu by pressing F8 every second or so after powering on the machine until you see the screen in Figure 14.9. If you try to "wait for the right time," you will usually miss it.

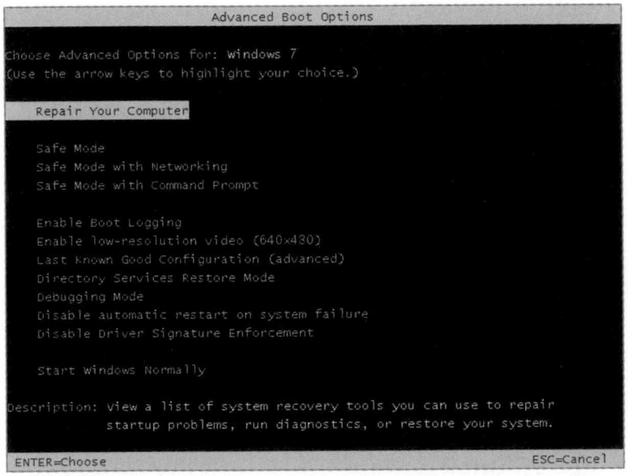

```
                       Advanced Boot Options

Choose Advanced Options for: Windows 7
(Use the arrow keys to highlight your choice.)

   Repair Your Computer

   Safe Mode
   Safe Mode with Networking
   Safe Mode with Command Prompt

   Enable Boot Logging
   Enable low-resolution video (640x480)
   Last Known Good Configuration (advanced)
   Directory Services Restore Mode
   Debugging Mode
   Disable automatic restart on system failure
   Disable Driver Signature Enforcement

   Start Windows Normally

Description: View a list of system recovery tools you can use to repair
            startup problems, run diagnostics, or restore your system.

ENTER=Choose                                          ESC=Cancel
```

FIGURE 14.9 The Advanced Boot Options screen

It is important to understand the different options available on the Advanced Boot Options screen. Last Known Good and Safe Mode options will be covered individually in later sections. The following descriptions explain the other boot options:

Enable Boot Logging   Creates `ntbtlog.txt`, which lists all drivers that load during startup, including the last file to load before a failure. A useful option when the system will start booting but cannot complete the process all the way through to the Desktop. The log file is located in the Windows directory.

Enable Low-Resolution Video (640×480)   Sets the display resolution to 640×480. This option is useful if you have to temporarily start up the system without the normal advanced device drivers for modern graphics cards. It may get you into the system so that you can repair or reinstall corrupted video drivers.

Directory Services Restore Mode   Evidence of the very close ties between Windows 7 and Windows Server 2008 R2, this option is displayed on clients, but works only on Windows servers. It is used on Windows servers to attempt a domain database repair or recovery.

Debugging Mode   Enables the Windows kernel debugger. This provides detailed output of kernel operations and may be required by Microsoft in some support scenarios.

Disable Automatic Restart On System Failure   Prevent Windows from automatically rebooting after a crash. This is useful if the system is crashing on startup and you have insufficient time to read the Blue Screen or other errors before it restarts.

Disable Driver Signature Enforcement   Allows drivers to be installed whether or not they are signed. May be required to install some third-party drivers.

Start Windows Normally   Boots Windows normally with no special boot-time options.

Booting to the Last Known Good Configuration

The Last Known Good Configuration is an important boot option to understand. This option allows you to boot the computer with the hardware configuration that last allowed the system to start up and get all the way to the Desktop. For example, if you install a new video driver and then reboot the computer and start experiencing failures, you can boot with the Last Known Good Configuration option and access the system with the old drivers.

If you boot a system after installing new hardware drivers and you notice that it is not acting normally before you log on, do not log on. Shut the computer down at the logon screen and then start it with the Last Known Good Configuration. If you log on, the current configuration becomes the Last Known Good Configuration, because Windows assumes it is working properly or you wouldn't have been able to get to the Desktop.

Using Safe Mode Options

Finally, you have three Safe Mode options in Windows 7. Safe Mode is a special boot option that loads only the core drivers and services. You use Safe Mode when you cannot boot the system any other way. It is often used after installing a new device or driver that is preventing the system from booting normally. However, it can also be used for troubleshooting scenarios when you think a driver or application may have become corrupted.

The three Safe Mode options work as follows:

Safe Mode   Boot the system with a minimal set of drivers and services. No networking will be available. Use this mode any time you are trying to reinstall network drivers or network software.

Safe Mode With Networking   Boot the system in the same safe mode, but add network drivers only. This is useful when you need to access the network for other drivers or software.

Safe Mode With Command Prompt   Boot the system in the same safe mode, but do not load Explorer as the shell interface. All actions are taken through the Windows Command Prompt. This is useful if you suspect Explorer is corrupted.

THE ESSENTIALS AND BEYOND

In this chapter, you learned how to plan for backups and implement them using Windows tools. You started by learning about the backup methods available in Windows and the tools used to perform backup and recovery operations. Then you explored the importance of testing recovery processes rather than simply trusting that they will work.

Next, you learned how to use the System Restore feature. You saw how to create restore points and revert to restore points. Then, you learned how to plan for and select third-party backup tools. Finally, you explored the recovery boot options available with Windows 7.

(Continues)

THE ESSENTIALS AND BEYOND *(Continued)*

ADDITIONAL EXERCISES

► Create a system image using Backup and Restore.

► Mount a system image VHD file as a drive using Disk Management.

To compare your answers to the author's, please visit www.sybex.com/go/osessentials.

REVIEW QUESTIONS

1. Which one of the following is a valid destination when backing up a hard drive in Backup and Restore on Windows 7?

   A. Tape drive   **C.** DropBox

   B. SkyDrive   **D.** Network

2. True or false. A system image can include more than one drive or volume.

3. What can you do to recover a single file from a system image?

   A. Open it in Explorer and copy the file.

   B. Open it at the Command Prompt and copy the file.

   C. Attach it in Disk Management and use it as a drive.

   D. None of the above

4. What Windows 7 boot option allows you to see a list of the drivers that loaded including the last file to load before a crash?

5. What is defined as the maximum time that a data restore process can take?

   A. RLO   **C.** RPO

   B. RTO   **D.** None of the above

6. Define a restore point.

7. Define an RPO.

8. Define an RLO.

9. In what format are system images stored when created with the Backup and Restore utility in Windows 7?

   A. WIM   **C.** VHD

   B. VHF   **D.** ZIP

10. True or false. You can back up to the network using Backup and Restore.

CHAPTER 15

Windows Update

In this final chapter, you will learn about the processes required to maintain your Windows computers. Both client and server technologies are addressed. No software solution can be used for a long period of time without eventually requiring patches or replacement. The software will prove to have vulnerabilities, or you may encounter stability problems. You may need to add new features. For these and many other reasons, you must know how to update your computer. The following topics explain the update process:

▶ **Understanding hotfixes and service packs**

▶ **Planning for Windows Update and Microsoft Update**

Understanding Hotfixes and Service Packs

Patch management is the process used to maintain the security and stability of a system through updates that repair vulnerabilities and bugs. New security vulnerabilities are discovered daily in the thousands of applications available today. They may also be discovered in the operating system itself. It is important that you understand the concepts surrounding patch management and the types of patches available. This section provides an overview of these concepts.

Microsoft's Recommended Update Life Cycle

Microsoft recommends that updates be applied using strategic life cycle management. Rather than just applying any and all updates, you will investigate the updates and apply those that are needed. The update or upgrade life cycle Microsoft recommends for their SharePoint 2010 products has five stages, as shown in Figure 15.1, and can prove valuable when considering updates or patches to any other system:

Learn In this phase, you will discover the requirements and prerequisites for an update or set of updates. You will also choose an update strategy. You can choose to do an update directly, by downloading it from Microsoft and installing it, or deploy the update automatically, using Windows Server Update

Services (WSUS). Regardless of the deployment method, the focus of this stage is on understanding the update and the implications to your system.

Prepare   During the Prepare phase, you will document the environment, including the network configuration and installed applications. This information may—and should—already be documented. If you lack rigorous documentation, you can create it using tools like Microsoft Assessment and Planning Toolkit, which is a free download from Microsoft Download. Your focus here is on the ability to recover should the update cause problems.

Test   In this phase, you will test the update or updates in a lab environment. Your test lab may consist of just a few Windows 7 computers loaded with various applications that are common in your environment. It may also include a Windows server to simulate the production systems. In this environment, you will first install the update to verify that it works well in a safe setting.

Implement   The Implement phase involves performing the update on your production environment. The update strategy that was developed during the Prepare phase and tested during the Test phase will now be used to implement the update.

Validate   During the Validate phase, you will monitor the computers closely and verify that no disruptive problems are occurring. Ensure that all business processes can still function and that users are satisfied with the deployed update.

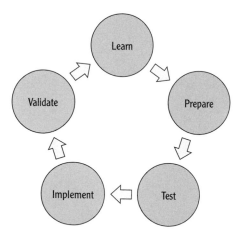

FIGURE 15.1 The Microsoft update life cycle

In most cases, this rigorous update staging process is used only for larger updates like service packs and upgrades to entirely new applications or operating systems. However, on a much smaller scale, we must still think this process through, even for a single update that fixes a single problem. In Figure 15.1, you will notice that this is a recurring cycle. You don't get to do this once and be done. Instead, you will be updating the system as long as you use it.

Hotfixes, Service Packs, and Update Terminology

Microsoft uses several terms to define their update processes and components for Windows and other products. They specifically define the following terms:

Critical-on-Demand (COD)   A critical-on-demand hotfix is requested by a customer who experiences significant loss or degradation of business services.

Critical Update   A critical update is a broadly released fix for a specific problem that addresses a critical, non-security-related bug.

Cumulative Update (CU)   A CU is a roll-up update that contains all previous critical on-demand hotfixes to date. Additionally, a CU contains fixes for issues that meet the hotfix acceptance criteria. These criteria may include the availability of a workaround, the effect on the customer, the reproducibility of the problem, the complexity of the code that must be changed, or other reasons.

Feature Pack   A feature pack is new product functionality that is first distributed outside the context of a product release and that is typically included in the next full product release.

General Distribution Release (GDR)   A GDR fixes an issue that has broad customer impact or that has security implications. A GDR is determined and issued only by Microsoft. Microsoft tries to release as few GDRs as possible.

Guidance   Guidance includes scripts, sample code, and technical documentation that are all designed to help you deploy and use a product or a technology.

Hotfix   A hotfix is a single, cumulative package that includes one or more files that are used to address a problem in a product and are cumulative at the binary and file level (meaning that the hotfix includes repairs to all files and all locations within those files when a repair is required). A hotfix addresses a specific customer situation and may not be distributed outside the customer's organization.

On-Demand (OD)   An on-demand hotfix must meet certain criteria. The customer's business must be functioning with little or no impediment of services. These criteria include a lack of an effective workaround, a critical business effect, or other reasons.

Security Update   A security update is a widely released fix for a product-specific, security-related vulnerability. Security vulnerabilities are rated based on their severity. The severity rating is indicated in the Microsoft security bulletin as critical, important, moderate, or low.

Service Pack   A service pack is a tested, cumulative set of all hotfixes, security updates, critical updates, and updates. Service packs may also contain additional fixes for problems that have been found internally since the release of the product and a limited number of customer-requested design changes or features.

Software Update   A software update is any update, update rollup, service pack, feature pack, critical update, security update, or hotfix that is used to improve or to fix a software product that is released by Microsoft.

Update   An update is a widely released fix for a specific problem. An update addresses a noncritical, non-security-related bug.

Update Rollup   An update rollup is a tested, cumulative set of hotfixes, security updates, critical updates, and updates that are packaged together for easy deployment. A rollup generally targets a specific area, such as security, or a component of a product, such as Internet Information Services (IIS).

Upgrade   An upgrade is a software package that replaces an installed version of a product with a newer version of the same product. The upgrade process typically leaves existing customer data and preferences intact while replacing the existing software with the newer version.

Planning for Windows Update and Microsoft Update

A system or application can be unstable without generating an error. For example, the system may simply stop responding.

Windows must be maintained just like any other operating system. Software must be updated for several reasons, including security, stability, and error resolution. If a security vulnerability is discovered in an operating system, device driver, or application, that vulnerability must be corrected through a software update or patch. Software is typically installed as compiled executables. As such, most commercial software can't be edited or fixed by users or other programmers while maintaining the support of the vendor. The software vendor must provide a new executable, or an update program must be used to modify the existing executable at a binary level. The same types of updates should be used to resolve stability issues and errors.

Windows 7 can be updated through individual updates or through service packs that combine a compilation of changes. An update may fix a single problem or a small number of problems. A service pack typically includes all patches up to the time of the service pack release and may also include new updates or even new product features.

As you plan your patch management for Windows computers, remember to include all applicable software components—including applications such as Microsoft Office, IIS, SharePoint Designer 2010, and any number of third-party products. There are three basic options for patch management:

Manual Patches Manual patches can be applied to the Windows operating system or to other software on the machine, such as Microsoft products like SharePoint, IIS, and SQL Server (all of which are used frequently on desktops by software developers). This method may be useful if you do not use Windows Server Update Services and you need to apply a small number of updates in order to resolve a security or stability problem. In a small environment, manual updates may be an option. In large-scale deployments with dozens or thousands of computers, manual patching is simply not feasible because of the administrative interaction required to perform all the other tasks involved in maintaining any given deployment. However, it is important to know that some patches must be applied manually. For example, SharePoint servers require the administrator to apply the patches manually, although they can be installed automatically. It is really a difference between getting the patch onto the computer and installing the patch into the configured system.

◄

Many server software applications support installing updates or patches that are not applied until the administrator manually applies them.

Windows Update The next viable approach to system updates is through the use of Windows Update. Through Windows Update, you can manually or automatically check for updates. You also can specify whether the updates should be installed automatically once downloaded. This is a feasible process for medium-sized deployments, but it will probably not serve large-scale deployments well. Windows Update defaults to receiving updates only for the Windows operating system components and will not typically cover any non-Microsoft software that may be installed. In the section "Updating with Windows Update," you will learn how to run Windows Update and enable updates for additional Microsoft products as well.

Windows Server Update Services Windows Server Update Services (WSUS) is used to centrally manage updates and specify the ones you want to deploy to client computers. WSUS supports clients ranging from Windows 2000 Professional to Windows Server 2008 R2. You may install all updates or choose only those you want to install. Figure 15.2 shows the deployment architecture for WSUS. In the section "Using Windows Server Update Service," you will learn how to enable WSUS on a Windows Server 2008 R2 server machine. WSUS is an excellent solution for large-scale deployments and can even be used in small deployments with just a few servers and clients.

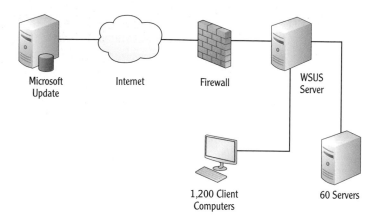

FIGURE 15.2 WSUS implementation architecture

Updating with Windows Update

Windows Update can be used to update Windows server and client computer systems. If you want to receive updates for more than just Windows, you can enable Microsoft Update, which will provide updates for Microsoft Office and many other Microsoft products. To enable Microsoft Update:

1. Open the Start menu and select All Programs ➢ Windows Update.

2. In the Windows Update screen (Figure 15.3), click the Find Out More link in the Get Updates For Other Microsoft Products pane.

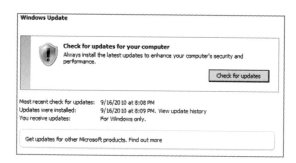

FIGURE 15.3 Enabling Microsoft Update

3. When the new Microsoft Update web page opens, click the More Supported link to see the supported products.

4. In the new browser window, read through the list of products that receive updates from Windows Update and then close that window to return to the Microsoft Update window.

5. In the Microsoft Update window shown in Figure 15.4, check the "I agree to the Terms of Use for Microsoft Update" check box and click Next.

FIGURE 15.4 The Microsoft Update opening screen

6. Select Use Recommended Settings, as shown in Figure 15.5, and click Install. If a screen appears asking you to allow the program to make changes to the computer, click Yes.

FIGURE 15.5 Choosing how Windows can install updates

7. The Windows Update screen will reappear and the check for updates will begin automatically. You may close all windows, because Windows Update is now configured to download updates automatically.

In some cases, you will want to disable automatic updates and configure Windows Update so that it never checks for updates. You would do this if you want to check for updates manually. For example, some organizations assign this responsibility to an administrator, who is required to check for updates at a specific time each week or at some predefined interval and apply the ones that are important. This is often performed in environments that require high levels of uptime and therefore need the newest stability and security patches but where the organization does not want to implement WSUS.

To configure Windows Update for manual updates, you must set it to Never Check For Updates. To do this and then check for updates manually, follow these steps:

1. Click Start and select All Programs ➢ Windows Update.

2. From the options list on the left in Figure 15.6, select Change Settings.

> If you check for Windows updates manually, it should be a scheduled task performed on a regular basis to ensure that no important updates are missed.

FIGURE 15.6 The Windows Update screen

3. From the Important Updates drop-down list shown in Figure 15.7, choose Never Check For Updates (Not Recommended), and then click OK.

4. Click the Check For Updates button and wait patiently while the system looks for available updates.

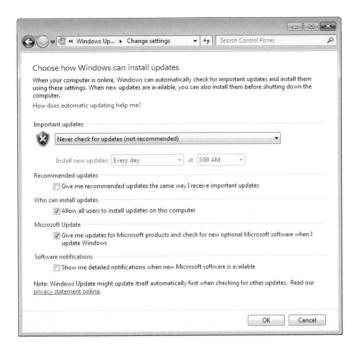

FIGURE 15.7 Adjusting Windows Update settings

5. On the results screen, click the Important Updates link.

6. Choose the updates you want to install from the listed updates and then click OK.

7. Click Install Updates to install the selected updates.

A free add-on to Windows 7 called the Windows Update PowerShell Module is available for download in the TechNet Script Center located at technet .microsoft.com/en-US/scriptcenter. Search the site for **windows update powershell module** to locate it. Instructions are provided at the site for installing the module.

After installing the module, you can open a Windows PowerShell prompt and use the Import-Module PSWindowsUpdate command to import the module. Then you can use the following cmdlets provided for Windows Update administration:

▶ Add-WUOfflineSync

▶ Get-WUHistory

▶ Get-WUInstall

▶ Get-WUInstall_OldMode

- ▶ Get-WUInstallerStatus
- ▶ Get-WUList
- ▶ Get-WURebootStatus
- ▶ Get-WUServiceManager
- ▶ Get-WUUninstall
- ▶ Remove-WUOfflineSync

When you use the Get-WUList cmdlet to view the available updates, it will always display all language packs available as well. It is uncommon to install additional language packs for average users after the initial installation of the OS. To prevent these language packs from being displayed, take advantage of PowerShell's piping architecture with a command like the following:

```
Get-WUList | Where-Object {$_.Title -notlike "*Language Pack*"} |
Select-Object LastDeploymentChangetime, KBArticleID, Title
```

In the preceding command, which should be entered as one command line in PowerShell, the Where-Object cmdlet is used to filter out any results that include the phrase *Language Pack*. The Select-Object cmdlet is used to display only the three most relevant columns for output. This example shows the power of PowerShell: It takes the output from the Get-WUList cmdlet and passes it through two additional cmdlets before providing the ultimate output.

Using Windows Server Update Service

Windows Server Update Service (WSUS) is a service that runs on a set of Windows servers and acts as an infrastructure that provides an internal source of updates to the other servers and clients on your Microsoft network. The benefits of WSUS over manual patches or direct use of Windows Update are twofold:

- ▶ You have the power to choose the updates globally. For larger networks you will not have to select from a list of updates again and again on dozens or hundreds of computers.

- ▶ Your Internet bandwidth is more efficiently used. The updates are downloaded once to the internal server. All internal machines then download the updates from that internal server, which reduces the required Internet bandwidth. You can even schedule the WSUS server to download all the updates in the middle of the night when fewer employees are accessing the Internet in most organizations.

Figure 15.1 showed the deployment model for a typical WSUS deployment. The WSUS server sits between the internal servers and clients and acts as the update server to those internal clients. The WSUS server becomes a client of the Microsoft Update servers. All updates are downloaded to the WSUS server; the clients and other servers download and apply the updates from the WSUS server. Because the WSUS server acts as an intermediary, you have the opportunity to choose the updates you want to deploy before they are applied.

To use WSUS on a Windows Server installation, you must add the WSUS role. Early versions of Windows Server require that you download and install WSUS. Windows Server 2008 R2 has the WSUS server role on the distribution DVD, so you can add it like any other server role. To install the WSUS server role on Windows Server 2008 R2:

1. Open the Start menu, and select Administrative Tools ➢ Server Manager.

2. In the left page, expand the Roles node; then right-click Roles and select Add Roles.

3. If the Before You Begin screen appears, click Next.

4. Select the Windows Server Update Services role, as shown in Figure 15.8, and click Next.

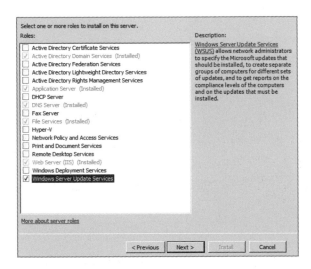

FIGURE 15.8 Selecting the Windows Server Update Services server role

5. On the Introduction to Windows Server Update Services screen, read the information and then click Next.

6. On the Confirm Installation Selections screen, click Install.
   If a newer version is available online, the process will download that version and install it on your Windows Server 2008 R2 machine.

7. The WSUS installation screen appears. Click Next.

8. Accept the terms of the license agreement, and click Next.

9. If any missing-component notifications appear, as in Figure 15.9, document the component names so you can download them and install them later; then click Next.

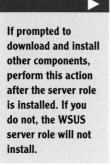

If prompted to download and install other components, perform this action after the server role is installed. If you do not, the WSUS server role will not install.

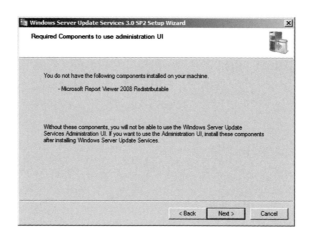

FIGURE 15.9 Viewing the list of required components for WSUS

10. Specify the location for local update storage, and click Next.

11. Accept the defaults on the Database Options screen, which indicates that you are using Windows Internal Database, and click Next.

12. On the Web Site Selection screen (Figure 15.10), choose Create A Windows Server Update Services 3.0 SP2 Web Site, and click Next.

13. On the Ready To Install screen, click Next. The installation will begin.

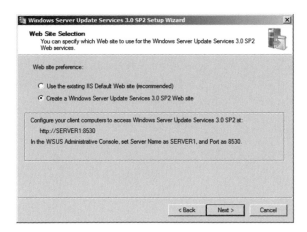

FIGURE 15.10 Choose the option Create A
Windows Server Update Services 3.0 SP2 Web Site.

After performing the steps in this procedure, you will need to configure WSUS
according to your needs. Complete configuration is beyond the scope of this book;
however, you will need to use the WSUS Configuration Wizard to configure the
following items:

▶ Participation in the Microsoft Update Improvement Program.

▶ The upstream server, which indicates whether updates are received
  from Microsoft Update or another internal WSUS server. (A layered
  hierarchy of WSUS servers is often used in large organizations to better control update management and optimize the delivery of updates
  to various network segments and locations.)

▶ Whether a proxy server is required for Internet access.

▶ The languages for which you want to download updates (you can
  greatly reduce downloads by selecting only needed languages).

▶ The products for which you want to receive updates.

▶ The types of updates to receive, such as Security, Tools, or Critical.

▶ The synchronization schedule, which determines when the WSUS
  server will acquire updates from the Microsoft Update server on
  the Web.

Figure 15.11 shows the Choose Products screen of the Windows Server Update Services Configuration Wizard with the Office and SQL Server selections in view.

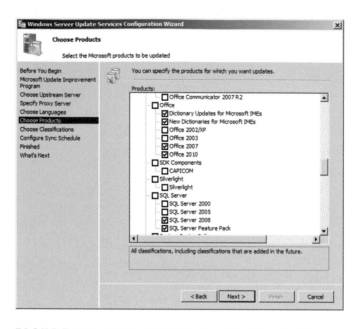

FIGURE 15.11 The WSUS Configuration Wizard's Choose Products screen

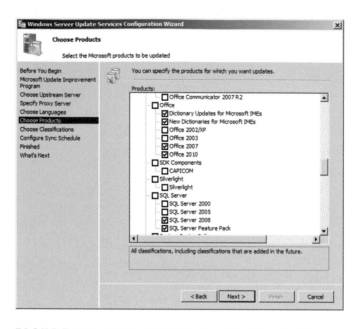

For more information on updating individual Microsoft products, search for *product_name patch management*, where *product_name* is the name of the product, such as Windows 7.

Although WSUS and the other update methods discussed in this section can be used for Windows 7, Windows Server, SQL Server, IIS, Exchange Server, SharePoint, and many other programs, special consideration must be made for each product. One often overlooked factor in performing updates is the impact the update will have on custom code. For example, if your organization has implemented custom code on top of the existing default code in a SharePoint Server 2010 deployment, an update could cause the custom code to fail. You can usually avoid this by encouraging programmers to follow Microsoft's best practices when writing code and by testing the updates in lab environments before applying updates to an active production server.

A SMALL BUSINESS CHOOSES AN UPDATE SOLUTION

Widgets America, a small business, wanted to implement SharePoint Server 2010, which requires a SQL Server installation. They did not have a SQL server in their environment, so the SharePoint Server 2010 project demanded more than simply installing a web server application (which is what SharePoint

(Continues)

A Small Business Chooses an Update Solution *(Continued)*

Server itself actually is). The project entailed a SQL Server deployment, an IIS server deployment, and a SharePoint services deployment.

The company had been performing all updates manually. This was not a huge problem for this small business; however, they were about to install three additional servers. Two servers would run both SharePoint and IIS, and the third server would be a dedicated SQL Server for the backend database. The business already had four other servers, and they also had more than 40 client computers. During the project planning process, the administrator realized it was time to move beyond manual updates.

The good news for Widgets America was that WSUS is not processor- or memory-intensive. With some analysis, it became clear that one of the servers running SharePoint and IIS would be underutilized. WSUS was installed on this server and scheduled to download updates between 1 a.m. and 5 a.m. This small business did not have a second or third shift, so the heaviest Internet downloads could happen in the middle of the night when no other users needed Internet access.

In the end, Widgets America was able to implement an automated update solution with absolutely no extra cost to the project. The administrator set up the WSUS service on the server so no consulting fees were required. Even small businesses can benefit from and easily implement WSUS in their environments.

THE ESSENTIALS AND BEYOND

In this chapter, you learned about the importance of updates. You learned about the different terms Microsoft uses for the update concepts and components, and the update cycle of Learn, Prepare, Test, Implement, and Validate. Then you explored using Windows Update and Microsoft Update. Finally, you learned about installing and configuring Windows Server Update Services (WSUS), the preferred network update method.

ADDITIONAL EXERCISES

▶ Install the Windows Update PowerShell module.

▶ Use the Windows Update PowerShell module to check for updates. Then, use the Get -WUList cmdlet to view all available uninstalled updates.

(Continues)

THE ESSENTIALS AND BEYOND *(Continued)*

To compare your answers to the author's, please visit www.sybex.com/go/
osessentials.

REVIEW QUESTIONS

1. What is the name of the PowerShell module used with the `Import-Module`
   command to add Windows Update support to PowerShell after the proper module
   is downloaded and installed?

   A. `PSWindowsUpdate`   **C.** `WindowsUpdate`

   B. `PSMicrosoftUpdate`   **D.** `MicrosoftUpdate`

2. True or false. You cannot disable automatic updates any longer in Windows 7.

3. Which one of the following is a benefit of using WSUS instead of Windows Update
   directly?

   A. The number of required internal servers is reduced.

   B. Internet bandwidth use is reduced.

   C. The amount of time spent installing Windows 7 is reduced.

   D. None of the above.

4. What is the second stage in the Microsoft recommended update life cycle?

5. What can you use to indicate that the WSUS server will require a proxy server
   for Internet access?

   A. Internet Options   **C.** Network and Sharing Center

   B. WSUS Configuration Wizard   **D.** None of the above

6. Define WSUS.

7. Define a security update.

8. How do you execute Windows Update on Windows 7?

   A. Start ➢ All Programs ➢ Windows Update

   B. Start ➢ All Programs ➢ Accessories ➢ Windows Update

   C. Start ➢ All Programs ➢ Maintenance ➢ Windows Update

   D. None of the above

9. What is the third stage of the Microsoft recommended update life cycle?

   A. Prepare   **C.** Implement

   B. Learn   **D.** Test

10. True or false. Microsoft Update provides updates for Microsoft Office as well as
    Windows 7.

Answers to Review Questions

Chapter 1

1. **C** The Disk Operating System (DOS) preceded Windows. It was the boot engine under Windows 3.1 and Windows 95. OS/2 is an OS managed by IBM. Mac OS X is the Apple OS. Linux is an open-source OS based on or similar to Unix.

2. **True** DOS supported batch files, and in fact, many modern batch files look and behave identically to the way they would have in DOS.

3. **D** The Control Panel was included in Windows 3.1 with 11 applets out of the box. Windows 7 still uses the Control Panel. The Program Manager and Calendar were in Windows 3.1 but are no longer in Windows 7. The Action Center is new in Windows 7 and was not in Windows 3.1.

4. **Kernel mode** User mode is where applications and environmental subsystems run. Kernel mode includes the executive, device drivers, kernel, HAL, and windows and graphics management.

5. **A** The POWERCFG.EXE command can be used to generate a report on power issues. The other commands exist, but are not new in Windows 7.

6. A new text-mode interface to the Windows operating system based on .NET and providing more powerful scripting and remote administration capabilities.

7. An instance of application code including the resources it requires for operations.

8. **D** The %WinDir%\SysWOW64 folder contains 32-bit versions of applications on 64-bit editions of Windows.

9. **A** The CMD command is used to launch the Windows Command Prompt. COMMAND .COM is the older 16-bit command interpreter from Windows 3.1 and DOS.

10. **True** To customize the system icons on the desktop, right-click the Desktop and select Personalize; then choose Change Desktop Icons on the Personalization screen. From here, you can add the Control Panel icon to the desktop.

Chapter 2

1.   **C** The Windows Anytime Upgrade is used in such scenarios. You can use it to upgrade from one edition to a higher-level edition in the same bit level (for example, 64-bit).

2.   **False** While it is often recommended that you have at least 2 GHz of processing power, the minimum requirement is actually only 1 GHz.

3.   **B** When you execute the diskpart command you are placed into the diskpart shell. From here, you can execute additional commands that prepare the USB flash drive for bootable use.

4.   **Hyper-V** Hyper-V was first introduced with Windows Server 2008, and it is still the virtualization solution available in Windows Server 2008 R2.

5.   **C** Remote Desktop Services (RDS) requires a licensing server and valid licenses for continued use. Remote Desktop does not.

6.   When you are dealing with software applications or operating systems, requirements are the list of hardware or software components required to use the software or operating system.

7.   An application compatibility fix for Windows 7 computers.

8.   **B** The Lite Touch Installation (LTI) requires that a technician begin the installation, but the rest is automated using scripts.

9.   **B** The Application Compatibility Manager (ACM) is used to create the DCPs, configure the ACT infrastructure, and work with the inventory database.

10. **True** The Standard User Analyzer (SUA) tool can locate compatibility problems so they can be repaired using shims.

Chapter 3

1.   **D** Anything above 1600×1200 resolution requires 256 MB of graphics memory for Aero functions to work.

2.   **False** Aero Peek allows you to see the Desktop without closing other windows.

3.   **D** The Public profile is the only all-user profile that applies to user-specific profiles that already exist as well as to new profiles. The Default profile applies only when creating a new user-specific profile.

4.   **Jump lists** Jump lists are used to show recently opened documents and applications on the Start menu. Recently opened documents are also shown on the pinned taskbar icons for applications.

5.   **D** The Recycle Bin is used to recover previously deleted files.

6.   A link to a file, folder, or other item that is placed on the Desktop or Start menu.

7.   A special application that resides on the Windows Desktop.

8.   **B** Assuming Windows 7 is installed to the C drive, the default location is C:\Users\ UserName\AppData\Roaming\Microsoft\Windows\Start Menu. However, you may have to enable the viewing of protected system files to see it.

9.   **A** Basic themes do not use Aero features and will increase performance.

10. **True** When optimized for best appearance, all features are enabled. When optimized for best performance, all features are disabled.

Chapter 4

1.   **C** Windows Media Player is used more often in business settings. Windows Media Center is mostly used in home entertainment centers.

2.   **False** The file must be saved as RTF, Office Open XML, or OpenDocument format to save the special formatting.

3.   **A** By default, Windows applications insert a 0d 0a code into a file anytime the Enter key is stored in a text file. Other systems may use 0d or 0a alone.

4.   **ANSI** The default coding is ANSI, but it can also encode in Unicode, Unicode Big-Endian, and UTF-8.

5.   **A** The Set command shows environment or system variables.

6.   An application used to view and configure settings mostly related to system startup in Windows.

7.   An application used to create text files with enhanced formatting and possible images in Windows.

8.   **B** In the Manage Add-ons dialog, you can manage search providers, toolbars, and extensions and accelerators.

9.   **D** Accelerators are used to perform common tasks quickly, and they avoid departing from the current page.

10. **False** Internet Explorer 8.0 comes with Windows 7; however, Internet Explorer 9.0 is available as a free download.

Chapter 5

1.   **D** You can access the Network Connections interface very quickly by searching for NCPA.CPL in the Start menu search field. This is the filename used to launch the Network Connections applet.

2. **True** The original Control Panel, in Windows 3.*x*, used only CPL files. Today, the Control Panel uses CPL files, EXE files, and even web pages.

3. **D** The Set Program Access And Computer Defaults interface allows you to use any of three configuration sets to automatically configure the application defaults for file associations and protocol associations. One of these configuration sets is the Microsoft Windows set.

4. **Event Viewer** The Event Viewer is used to view logs for the OS and applications on a Windows system.

5. A Windows accessibility component that allows the user to selectively magnify areas of the screen for easier visualization.

6. A Windows accessibility component that provides a visual cue for the hearing impaired any time a system sound is played.

7. A Windows OS interface that provides access to administration, configuration, and information tools for support professionals and users.

8. **D** The Get-Command -Module AppLocker command is the most likely method to use. You could also simply execute Get-Module AppLocker and it would list the cmdlets as well; however, the Get-Module cmdlet does not support a -commands parameter.

9. **B** The PowerCfg command, with the -export parameter, is used to export a power plan to a file.

10. **True** Simply drag the Control Panel item to the Desktop and release it to create a shortcut.

Chapter 6

1. **B** The -commandtype parameter is used to limit the returned command types. The -module parameter is used to limit the returned commands to those within a specified module, such as the AppLocker module.

2. **False** Custom consoles may be created; several snap-ins are included for this purpose.

3. **D** The only one of the listed items that is a valid cmdlet is the Get-Process cmdlet. Tasklist is a Command Prompt command used for similar purposes.

4. **MMC** The Microsoft Management Console (MMC) is a special console interface designed to standardize administration tool interfaces. Custom consoles may be created to allow for the needs of different types of administrators and support professionals.

5. **B** The shortcut key is Ctrl+M, but you can also click File and select Add/Remote Snap-in.

6. A component that may be added to a custom MMC console and that may be used to manage the local computer or a remote computer.

7. A Windows feature that allows support professionals to connect to and potentially interact with the Windows Desktop across the network. Remote Assistance requires an invitation from the user.

8. **D** The Sync Center is the primary tool used to view the status for offline files synchronization processes.

9. **A, D** Windows PowerShell uses verb/object combinations. Both Get-Process and Invoke-Command are PowerShell cmdlets.

10. **True** The winrm quickconfig command is used to automatically configure the WinRM service and enable permissions for remote administration.

Chapter 7

1. **C** You can set a recovery action for the first failure, second failure, and then subsequent failures for a total of three.

2. **True** Microsoft Enterprise Desktop Virtualization (Med-V) is essentially a collection of tools that allows support professionals to configure, deploy, and manage Windows Virtual PC virtual machines and the applications they provide.

3. **D** This Group Policy setting will completely disable the Programs and Features applet. Only enable the Hide "Programs and Features" Page setting if you truly want the entire applet to be disabled.

4. **Started, Stopped, or Paused** A service can be started, stopped, or paused. This status is shown in the service's Properties dialog and also in the Status column of the Services management console.

5. **D** The 32-bit editions of Windows 7 can run only 32-bit and 16-bit applications. The 64-bit editions of Windows 7 can run only 64-bit and 32-bit applications.

6. Virtual Desktop Infrastructure (VDI) is a general term used for solutions like Remote Desktop Services with Hyper-V or Citrix that provide virtual desktops or virtual applications running on remote servers.

7. A network or local user account that is used by a service to receive permissions for access to the local machine or network resources.

8. **C** The Start-Service cmdlet is used to start a service. PowerShell cmdlets start with a verb such as start, get, set, or stop.

9. **B** The net stop command is used to stop a service. For example, to stop the print spooler service, you execute the net stop spooler command.

10. **False** AppLocker works only with Windows 7 Enterprise and Ultimate editions.

Chapter 8

1. **B** The new version is released on the second Tuesday of the month, which is also known as Patch Tuesday among the Microsoft user community.

2. **False** Red is the color used for explicitly blocked applications or publishers. Unknown applications have a yellow banner.

3. **D** A backdoor is an application that either provides re-entry to the computer at a later time or allows the attacker to access the local network through the user's computer.

4. **In the Notification Area of the taskbar** The notifications or alerts will show up in the Notification Area, and message balloons may also be displayed.

5. **D** A phishing attack is used to manipulate people into providing information or taking actions that would compromise security. They are frequently made through email.

6. A process used to organize or categorize data for better decision making and management related to that data.

7. A computer program with the ability to regenerate itself by attaching to other applications or documents and with a mission or purpose to perform some action on the machine.

8. **C** The Malicious Software Removal Tool runs once each month in the background. You can run it on demand by downloading it from the Microsoft Download Center.

9. **C** A Trojan, named after the Trojan Horse of Homer's *Iliad*, is an application that appears to be for some useful function but actually installs malicious software on the machine.

10. **True** Forefront Threat Management Gateway can scan data packets as they come into your network or as they traverse the network looking for various types of malware.

Chapter 9

1. **A** Of the listed items, only the unencrypted 100 MB system volume is required. All other items are optional.

2. **True** Using the ATTRIB +H command in relation to the library settings file, you can hide individual default libraries from the Explorer view.

3. **D** Only NTFS provides permission management. If you must manage permissions at the file or folder level, you must use NTFS as the filesystem.

4. **32 GB** Though the filesystem could potentially support larger volume sizes, Microsoft limits it to 32 GB for performance reasons.

5. **C** The Compact Disc Filesystem (CDFS) is used to access CDs in Windows operating systems. The UDFS filesystem is used to access DVDs.

6.   An internal collection of servers used to provide certificates for authentication and encryption on the network is a public key infrastructure (PKI).

7.   The file or database stored on an NTFS volume to track the other files and folders stored on the volume is the Master File Table (MFT).

8.   **A** Library setting files are stored in the `%userprofile%\Appdata\roaming\Microsoft\Windows\Libraries` location as XML files.

9.   **A** The standard `ATTRIB` command is used. By setting the hidden attribute to true on a library settings file, you effectively hide the library from the Explorer view.

10. **True** An individual Group Policy setting must be configured for each library link, but they can be removed from the Start menu if you desire.

Chapter 10

1.   **C** Modify is not a share permission. Read, contributor, and co-owner are all possible share permissions depending on the system used. Co-owner is equal to full control.

2.   **True** This is true because any user can join the computer to the domain; however, an administrator must have already created the computer account in the domain before the user joins the computer to the domain.

3.   **C** Homegroups do not require servers, and they are not part of a domain. The only item required to join the homegroup is the homegroup password, which can be viewed in the Control Panel on any existing homegroup member machine.

4.   **Authentication** Authentication verifies identity; authorization verifies permissions and rights.

5.   **D** IP version 6 addresses use 128 bits to define the address. IP version 4 addresses use 32 bits.

6.   The permissions resulting after combining permissions from the user account and any groups to which the user belongs.

7.   The connection between two computers on a network, which may consist of multiple intermediary links and devices.

8.   **A** The write permission allows users to read, modify, and create new files or folders. It does not allow them to alter permissions or delete files.

9.   **B** Inherited permissions come through the parent container. They may also be passed along the entire chain through several directories or folders.

10. **True** The primary difference between change and full control permissions is that full control allows the users to manage permissions and change does not.

Chapter 11

1.   **C** The XPS document format was included with the Windows 7 operating system in two ways: a printer driver to create XPS documents and the XPS viewer to read them.

2.   **False** Chipset drivers are required to gain access to many hardware components. They should be installed and updated with careful testing.

3.   **D** The Device Manager was first introduced in Windows 95. It looks slightly different in Windows 7, but it is basically the same tool.

4.   **The computer vendor** Computer vendors typically provide downloads for device drivers related to any hardware components that originally shipped with the computer.

5.   **A, B, C** You may choose to run third-party software in addition to the device drivers to gain extra features, improve usability, improve performance, or increase security, or simply because the hardware requires it to be useful.

6.   A software module that communicates with the device and the operating system.

7.   The location for device drivers in the Windows OS. This location is searched for device drivers when new devices are installed.

8.   **C** The /FO switch is used with the CSV parameter. The command looks like this:

    ```
    driverquery /fo csv
    ```

9.   **C** The Roll Back Driver button will be disabled for any device that still uses the first driver version that it used after installation.

10. **False** Hardware device drivers run in Kernel mode. This is one of the major reasons that you must be careful about the sources you use for device drivers.

Chapter 12

1.   **D** Only NTFS supports the Encrypting File System (EFS), which allows for the encryption of data during storage.

2.   **True** Microsoft developed exFAT so that removable media could be formatted and used by multiple systems and so that large volumes could be created.

3.   **B** A storage area network (SAN) provides block-level access using either Fibre Channel or iSCSI. Network attached storage (NAS) may provide block-level access, but it often provides file-level access only.

4.   **RAID 1** RAID 1 is mirroring. Mirroring creates a duplicate copy of all data on the mirror drive while using the primary drive as the active drive.

5.   **B** Software-based RAID relies on the computer's CPU to perform RAID processing. For this reason, software-based RAID does not perform as well as hardware-based RAID in most implementations.

6.   A dynamic disk.

7.   The Distributed Filesystem (DFS).

8.   **D** FAT volumes support a maximum file size of 4 GB. The NTFS filesystem can support files that are multiple terabytes in size.

9.   **B** Both Fibre Channel and iSCSI can use host bus adapters (HBAs) to connect to the SAN. An HBA is a special kind of adapter that does far more than a standard network interface card (NIC).

10.   **False** You can create primary and extended partitions only on basic disks. Dynamic disks contain volumes.

Chapter 13

1.   **C** You can press Ctrl+Shift+Esc to open the Task Manager. This is much faster than the other methods available for accessing it.

2.   **True** According to the ITIL, an incident is an event that is not part of standard operations and that may cause an interruption or a reduction in the quality of a service. The problem is the underlying cause of the incident.

3.   **D** Because display corruption is occurring, this is most likely the display adapter. It could also be the system board, which was not mentioned as an optional answer.

4.   **Physical, Data-Link, Network, Transport, Session, Presentation, Application** While the chapter focused on the lower three layers primarily, any layer can be used in the troubleshooting process.

5.   **C** The Critical level indicates that a failure has occurred and the application or components could not automatically recover.

6.   The Information Technology Infrastructure Library (ITIL) is a set of documents that define best practices for technology management.

7.   An application used to view, search, filter, and manage event logs in Windows operating systems.

8.   **C** Event filtering is used to limit the event log entries to those that come from a specific source, have a specific level of severity, or were created within a specified date range, among other things.

9.   **A** The Task Manager can be used to kill running tasks. You can also use the TASKKILL command from the Command Prompt.

10.   **False** Networking problems can occur anywhere in the chain, from the computer to the network resource it is attempting to access. Switches may fail, routers may fail, and the network cabling may fail.

Chapter 14

1.   **D** Of the listed locations, only the network is a default supported destination in Backup and Restore.

2.   **True** The system image will include the system and boot drive. If they are the same drive, it will include only one drive. If they are separate drives, it will include both. Additionally, it may include another drive for BitLocker usage.

3.   **C** You can recover individual files from a system image, but you must first mount the VHD in the image that included the files.

4.   **Enable Boot Logging** The Enable Boot Logging option will create NTBTLOG.TXT, which lists all drivers that load during startup, including the last file to load before a failure. It is a useful option when the system will start booting but cannot complete the process all the way through to the Desktop. The log file is located in the Windows directory.

5.   **B** The RTO or recovery time objective specifies the maximum time that a data restore process can take. It is based on the maximum amount of acceptable downtime.

6.   A collection of configuration settings and filesystem states used to recover a Windows 7 computer to a historical point in time.

7.   The maximum time period between the last backup and a potential failure point is the recovery point objective (RPO).

8.   The granularity with which you must be able to restore data is the recovery level objective (RLO).

9.   **C** The system images are stored as virtual hard disks (VHDs). This allows you to boot from them and mount them as drives for file access within the Windows 7 and Server 2008 R2 systems.

10. **True** Backup and Restore supports several backup destinations, including network locations.

Chapter 15

1.   **A** The name of the module to import is PSWindowsUpdate. Using the freely downloadable module, you can list available updates, view the update history, check the reboot status, install an update, or uninstall an update.

2.   **False** You can disable automatic updates, but it is not recommended.

3.   **B** When you use WSUS, it downloads the updates from the Internet and then distributes them to the other computers on your internal network. Because of this behavior, Internet bandwidth use is reduced.

4. **Prepare** The five stages are Learn, Prepare, Test, Implement, and Validate, in that order.

5. **B** The WSUS Configuration Wizard can be used to specify that a proxy server is required and to define the proxy server address.

6. Windows Server Update Services (WSUS) is a server role in Windows Server 2008 and R2 that downloads updates from Microsoft's website and makes them available to internal systems on a network.

7. A security update is a widely released fix for a product-specific, security-related vulnerability.

8. **A** Windows Update is in the root of the All Programs folder. It remains named Windows Update even after enabling Microsoft Update.

9. **D** The five stages are Learn, Prepare, Test, Implement, and Validate in that order, so the third stage is Test.

10. **True** When you enable Microsoft Update, you will receive updates for Windows 7 and also for Microsoft Office.

Microsoft's Certification Program

Since the inception of its certification program, Microsoft has certified more than 2 million people. As the computer network industry continues to increase in both size and complexity, this number is sure to grow—and the need for *proven* ability will also grow. Certifications help companies verify the skills of prospective employees and contractors.

Microsoft started with the Microsoft Certified Professional (MCP) program, which validated individuals' knowledge and expertise on a wide variety of products. They have expanded these certifications into several categories:

Microsoft Technology Associate (MTA)　The MTA certifications are entry-level certifications that are available only at academic institutions. They validate an individual's knowledge and basic understanding of key technology concepts. The three IT professional series certifications are Networking Fundamentals, Security Fundamentals, and Windows Server Administration Fundamentals. There are also several developer certifications. You must take and pass one exam to earn each MTA certification.

Microsoft Certified Technology Specialist (MCTS)　The MCTS is the next level of certification. For people who are not in an academic institution, these certifications can be the first certifications they earn. The MCTS certification program targets specific technologies instead of specific job roles. You must take and pass one to three exams to earn an MCTS certification in different technologies.

Microsoft Certified IT Professional (MCITP)　The MCITP certification is a Professional Series certification that tests network and system administrators on job roles rather than only on a specific technology. The MCITP certification program generally consists of one to three exams in addition to obtaining an MCTS-level certification.

Microsoft Certified Professional Developer (MCPD)　The MCPD certification is a Professional Series certification for application developers. Similar to the MCITP, the MCPD is focused on a job role rather than on a single technology.

The MCPD certification program generally consists of one to three exams in addition to obtaining an MCTS-level certification.

Microsoft Certified Master (MCM)   The MCM program is for experienced IT professionals who want to deepen and broaden their technical expertise on specific Microsoft server products. It includes three weeks of highly intensive classroom training, three computer-based tests, and one lab-based exam for each of the MCM certifications. There are five separate MCM certifications.

Microsoft Certified Architect (MCA)   The MCA is Microsoft's premier certification series. Obtaining the MCA requires a minimum of 10 years of experience and passing a review board consisting of peer architects.

Certification Objectives Map

Table B.1 provides objective mappings for the Microsoft Technology Associate (MTA) Windows Operating System Fundamentals Exam (98-349). It identifies the chapters where the 98-349 exam objectives are covered.

TABLE B.1 Exam 98-349 Objectives Map

Objective	Chapter
1. Understanding Operating System Configurations	
1.1 Configure Control Panel options.	
This objective may include but is not limited to: configuring administrative tools, configuring accessibility options	5
1.2 Configure desktop settings.	
This objective may include but is not limited to: configuring gadgets, profiles, display settings, shortcuts, and Aero configurations and capabilities	3
1.3 Understand native applications and tools.	
This objective may include but is not limited to: understanding Windows Internet Explorer, the snipping tool, Windows Media Player, Windows Media Center, and MSCONFIG	4
1.4 Understand mobility.	
This objective may include but is not limited to: understanding Sync Center, Windows Mobility Center, and Remote Desktop	6

Objective	Chapter
1.5 Understand remote management and assistance.	
This objective may include but is not limited to: understanding MMC and Windows PowerShell	6
2. Installing and Upgrading Client Systems	
2.1 Identify Windows operating system editions.	
This objective may include but is not limited to: identifying system requirements, using PC Upgrade Advisor	2
2.2 Identify upgrade paths.	
This objective may include but is not limited to: identifying upgrade paths from Windows XP, Windows Vista, and other operating systems; identifying application compatibility	2
2.3 Understand installation types.	
This objective may include but is not limited to: understanding removable media installations (DVD, ZTI, LTI, and USB), cloud and network installations, and product identification keys	2
2.4 Understand virtualized clients.	
This objective may include but is not limited to: understanding Windows XP Mode, Remote Desktop, and Remote Desktop Services	2
3. Managing Applications	
3.1 Understand application installations.	
This objective may include but is not limited to: understanding local vs. network applications, Group Policy, and application removal	7
3.2 Understand user account control (UAC).	
This objective may include but is not limited to: understanding standard user vs. administrative user, understanding types of UAC prompts and levels	8
3.3 Remove malicious software.	
This objective may include but is not limited to: understanding Windows Defender, Action Center, the Malicious Software Removal tool, Windows Registry, and Microsoft Forefront Endpoint Protection	8

(Continues)

TABLE B.1 *(Continued)*

Objective	Chapter
3.4 Understand services.	
This objective may include but is not limited to: understanding service startup types, service accounts, and service dependencies	7
3.5 Understand application virtualization.	
This objective may include but is not limited to: understanding Med-V and VDI	7
4. Managing Files and Folders	
4.1 Understand file systems.	
This objective may include but is not limited to: understanding FAT, FAT32, NTFS, and 32-bit vs. 64-bit	9
4.2 Understand file and print sharing.	
This objective may include but is not limited to: understanding NTFS and share permissions, HomeGroup, print drivers, and effective permissions; creating public, basic, and advanced shares; mapping drives	10
4.3 Understand encryption.	
This objective may include but is not limited to: understanding BitLocker, encrypting file systems (EFS), and compression	9
4.4 Understand libraries.	
This objective may include but is not limited to: understanding offline files, adding multiple local locations to a library, adding networked locations	9
5. Managing Devices	
5.1 Connect devices.	
This objective may include but is not limited to: connecting plug-and-play devices, connecting and disconnecting printers, installing third-party software for devices	11

Objective	Chapter
5.2 Understand storage.	
This objective may include but is not limited to: understanding disk types (NTFS, FAT, etc.), security (encryption), storage device types (eSATA, USB, USB 2.0, IEEE 1394, iSCSI), storage drive types (basic, primary, extended, logical, dynamic disk, VHDs), and cloud storage (Windows Live SkyDrive, OneNote to SkyDrive, Live mesh)	12
5.3 Understand printing devices.	
This objective may include but is not limited to: understanding local printers, network printers, print queues, print-to-file, and Internet printing	11
5.4 Understand system devices.	
This objective may include but is not limited to: understanding video, audio, and infrared input devices, understanding Device Manager	11
6. Understanding Operating System Maintenance	
6.1 Understand backup and recovery methods.	
This objective may include but is not limited to: understanding local, online, and automated backup methods; understanding backup options; understanding System Restore, recovery boot options such as Last Known Good, and various Safe Mode options	14
6.2 Understand maintenance tools.	
This objective may include but is not limited to: understanding Disk Defragmenter, Disk Cleanup, Task Scheduler, Action Center, and System Information	4, 8, 13
6.3 Understand updates.	
This objective may include but is not limited to: understanding Windows updates, Microsoft updates, and hotfixes	15

INDEX

Note to the Reader: Throughout this index boldfaced page numbers indicate primary discussions of a topic. *Italicized* page numbers indicate illustrations.